THRIFTY YEARS

The Life of Hendrik Meijer

by Hank Meijer

WILLIAM B. EERDMANS PUBLISHING COMPANY
GRAND RAPIDS, MICHIGAN

Copyright © 1984 by Wm. B. Eerdmans Publishing Company
255 Jefferson Ave. S.E., Grand Rapids, Mich. 49503

Reprinted 1995

Library of Congress Cataloging in Publication Data

Meijer, Hendrik G.
  Thrifty years.

Includes index.
    1. Meijer, Hendrik, 1883–1964. 2. Merchants—
    Michigan—Biography.
    3. Meijer Thrifty Acres (Stores)
I. Title.
HF5469.23.U64M456   1984   381'.45'000924 [B] 84-21137

ISBN 0-8028-0038-6

For my mother and father

Contents

Again and again the spirit of enterprise has passed by richer and older regions to settle upon some desolate rim of the world, such as the bleak coast of the Baltic and the dunes and marshes of Holland. It seems to prefer virgin soil to that which has been heavily encumbered by vested interests and prejudices.

—MIRIAM BEARD,
A History of Business

Preface

Hendrik Meijer was my grandfather. When he died in 1964 I was twelve years old, so my memories of him are limited. He cut my hair every other Sunday while I sat on a stool in his kitchen. Sometimes he played a black, potato-shaped musical instrument called an ocarina.

My grandmother, Gezina Mantel Meijer, survived her husband by fourteen years. Not long before she died, in 1978, she brought forth from a closet two shoeboxes filled with letters and postcards. Most of this correspondence dates from the years between 1907, when my grandfather—then only recently engaged to my grandmother—left the Netherlands for America, and 1912, when my grandmother joined him here. For five years they corresponded nearly as frequently as transatlantic postal service permitted. The first three chapters of this book rely heavily on those letters, which were translated from the Dutch by Regina Wybenga of Grand Rapids, Michigan. The letters were written in conversational low Dutch. Where contemporary idioms make sense, I have tried to use them.

The second half of the book chronicles the origins and growth of a family business. Original materials have also been useful here. My aunt, Johanna Meijer Magoon, entered the University of Michigan in the fall of 1935, a year after Hendrik Meijer opened his grocery store in Greenville, Michigan. In its first year, Johanna had been the little store's de facto manager, as well as bookkeeper of the family dairy business. Her departure stimulated a second period of correspondence, this time between Greenville and Ann Arbor. Overlapping the dates of these letters are diaries that my father, Fred Meijer, kept as a teenager. My grandparents, particularly Hendrik, wrote to Johanna regularly with news of the store, while Fred recorded the family's entrepreneurial experiences day by day.

Also indispensable to my research were interviews with family members and friends and associates of Hendrik Meijer. In a series of interviews over several years, Fred Meijer patiently contributed essential recollections. Others who shared their observations and memories included Lena Meijer, Gezina Meijer, Marie Snuiverink Robinson, Harvey Lemmen, Earl

Holton, Leo Schwarz, Fred Welling, Jack Koetje, Art Snell, Ben Muller, Tom Reges, Leonard Kurtz, Verner Kilgren, Bob Vander Ark, George Zane, Elmer Briggs, Maury De Fouw, Pam Kleibusch, John Veldman, Ernie Pettinga, Roman Feldpausch, Robert Fenn, Curt Kornblau, Al Meijer, Charlie Johnson, Jack Ward, Glenn Lehr, Barbara Hansen, Thorwald McFarland, Vic Spaniolo, Darrell Steinke, Nina Babcock, Dennis Guernsey, Hank Doornbos, Jerry Laug, Ali and Willy Mantel, Jo and Jan Scholten, Willem Scholten, Ike Schepers, Roland Van Valkenberg, Fred Ver Schure, Len Ver Schure, Fred Veltman, Jeanette Oudman, Ada Ver Hulst, and Jack Nuiver.

The *Greenville Daily News* was a valuable source for material on the years Hendrik lived in Greenville. Other institutions of particular assistance were the Holland (Michigan) Public Library, the International Institute of Social History in Amsterdam, the Labadie Collection in the Harlan Hatcher Library at the University of Michigan, the Hengelo Museum in Hengelo, the Netherlands, and the Dutch consulate in Holland, Michigan.

Ross Gregory and Larry ten Harmsel of Western Michigan University and Marcie Anderson of Seattle offered extensive editorial help, as did my editor at Eerdmans, Reinder Van Til. Chuck Van Hof of Eerdmans provided a final sounding board.

Also reading the manuscript critically were Herbert Brinks of Calvin College, Phillip Mason of Wayne State University, James Hoffman, Joan Hoffman, David Dekker, Frank Lyman, David Kagan, Bill Smith, Mary Dechow, Marlan Buddingh, José Calderon, Philip Knoll, Jill Rodin, Dave Lukens, and Jean Reifel. Portions of two chapters appeared in the *Grand Rapids Press*. Harold Hans, my former supervisor, allowed me time to complete the manuscript. The staff of the Meijer Word Processing Department was an invaluable help, and many friends within the company offered encouragement.

Without the editorial judgment and love of my wife, Deborah, however, all other aid would have fallen short.

—HENDRIK G. MEIJER

Introduction

In the late 1950s, Hendrik Meijer was already in his seventies, a tall man with white hair, a broad smile, and a gaze that took in everything from a scrap of paper in the cereal aisle to a shoplifting suspect at the cash register. He carried himself with a bearing that never succumbed to old age. His temperament was such that he might explode over a minor irritation, yet when fire destroyed a store he would say calmly, "We will build another."

In his last years he was a familiar figure to people who worked and shopped in Meijer stores. He was walking through one of his supermarkets in Grand Rapids one day when a butcher stopped him. The butcher, like Hendrik a Dutch immigrant, asked my grandfather if he would sponsor the immigration of a friend from the Netherlands. It was a familiar request for a Grand Rapids employer, particularly in the years after World War II. Hendrik had already helped several of his countrymen immigrate.

"Bert, a friend of yours is a friend of mine," Hendrik told the butcher. "I'll sponsor him." The butcher thanked the older man, then hesitated. Grand Rapids was, and still is, a conservative, sometimes pious place. "I have to warn you, Mr. Meijer," he said. "This man is not a Christian and he doesn't attend church." At that, Hendrik leaned toward the butcher and said, "You know Bert, if what you say is so, I'll not only sponsor him, I'll give him a job when he gets here."

Hendrik Meijer's prospects had been far less certain in June of 1907 when, as a twenty-three-year-old factory worker carrying a book of anarchist verse, he left the Netherlands for America. He was engaged to my grandmother at the time, but for the next five years kept her in suspense, while she waited for him to settle down and ask her to join him. Hendrik worked as a molder in foundries for much of that time, but dreamed of driving trolleys or farming out west or cutting hair. Eventually he became a barber, and sent for my grandmother after he had found a steady job. Hendrik and his wife had two children and a placid if sometimes restless life in a small town.

In his late forties, Hendrik built a building next to his barber-shop that he planned to rent out, to provide an annuity for his old age.

He was fifty years old when the Great Depression changed his plans. Unable to find a tenant for his new building, and watching his business in the barbershop evaporate, he could not afford even the interest on his mortgage. Finally, with his resources dwindling, he bartered his violin to a plasterer for finishing off the interior of the vacant storefront; and there, in 1934, he opened a grocery store. With the help of his wife and children he turned that first store into a supermarket. The supermarket led to a chain of supermarkets, and when Hendrik was nearly eighty years old the chain gave rise to a new form of mass merchandising, a hybrid of supermarket and discount department store called Meijer Thrifty Acres.

Even the first step in that evolution was far beyond the imagination of a boy who had gone to work in a Dutch cotton mill when he was thirteen. And Hendrik Meijer was hardly a character from a Horatio Alger story. He was a socialist and anarchist, bent on nothing more than escaping the only life he knew. Escape—and then what? There lay the irony. The young rebel who had scorned capitalism would come to embrace it. The possibilities of American life raised hopes, the Depression dashed them, and the desperation that resulted gave to a settled, modest life an unexpected second act.

In 1882, the year before Hendrik was born, Emile Zola published *Au Bonheur des Dames* (Ladies' Delight), a *roman a clef* about Aristidé Boucicaut, the founder in Paris of Au Bon Marché, the first great department store. Perhaps Hendrik read the story while confined to the stockade in the Dutch infantry; perhaps between shifts in the spinning mill of the *textilfabriek*; perhaps even in Holland, Michigan, on a Sunday in winter when it was too cold to walk along the lake and everyone else was in church. In any case, he read the book decades before he became—almost accidently—a retail merchant. Yet *Ladies' Delight* was a story he never forgot, a primer, in its way, for an old man who became a mass merchant.

Boucicaut was among the first merchants to break with the tradition of catering to the rich few. "A humble clerk," according to business historian Miriam Beard, "who created the first really modern department store, to offer wares to the masses. . . . The idea of selling cheaply for cash was developed as never before." Rich and poor alike converged *en masse* upon his great department store's dramatic displays and overflowing sale tables. Yet Boucicaut was also a high-minded entrepreneur who set new standards in employee relations as well as in selling merchandise. He married a young clerk who succeeded him upon his death. "The pair were pioneers in humanitarian enterprise and not only stimulated the mass consumption of goods," Beard observed, "but sought to form new patterns in mass management."

In his later years Hendrik loaned Zola's book to a brother-in-law who ran a tailor shop in their native town of Hengelo. He asked his brother-in-law, whose trade was declining as men began to rely increasingly on ready-to-wear clothing, what he thought of the novel. The brother-in-law had found it a nice love story; the rest was lost on him. The tailor shop has long since ceased to exist, but there may be no truer offspring of Au Bon Marché than the Meijer stores first known as Thrifty Acres.

Hendrik Meijer was not a famous man; yet twenty years after his death, his name—its odd Dutch spelling with the silent *j* routinely mispronounced—is synonymous with a unique retail institution. Where else might one buy lettuce and lingerie, a turkey, a tennis racquet, and a toaster, put them all in a shopping cart and pay for everything at one cash register? With an inventory of more than 100,000 items and an assortment of services, each Meijer store qualifies as a noisy, bustling world unto itself, a regular bazaar in an age of mass consumption. And Meijer remains a family company, as close to its origins as the scale of a large corporation allows. Its place in the lives of the people it serves has been acknowledged in unusual ways. Second graders in a Kalamazoo Sunday school once composed a prayer that concluded:

> I will thank God at football games, parades,
> Thrifty Acres, and everywhere.

Part I

The
Immigrant

Chronology

1883 Hendrik Meijer born December 28 in Hengelo, Overijssel, the Netherlands

1886 Gezina (Zien) Mantel born July 11 in Hengelo

1896 Hendrik completes sixth grade of primary school, begins work in cotton mill

1903 Conscripted into Dutch army (active discharge in 1906)

1905 Meets Zien Mantel in Hengelo choral group

1907 Sails for the United States with father and one sister, arriving in Hoboken, New Jersey on June 24

1910 Returns to Hengelo to spend summer with Zien

1911 Travels to Yakima, Washington; attends barber school in Chicago

1912 Finds job in Greenville barbershop; Zien arrives in Hoboken October 28; Hendrik and Zien marry November 11

1914 Opens barbershop in North Greenville

1916 Daughter Johanna born April 9

1919 Son Fred born December 7

1923 Hendrik constructs building in North Greenville for new barbershop and other tenants

1928 Builds twin storefronts next to barbershop for rental property

1934 Opens grocery store in vacant storefront

1937 Doubles size of store with expansion into storefront next door

1940 First attends meeting of Super Market Institute; expands store again to include 1923 barbershop building

1942 Cedar Springs store opens

1946 Ionia store opens; Greenville store burns

1949 First Grand Rapids store opens on South Division Ave.

1952 Family moves to Grand Rapids when offices are opened with new store at intersection of Michigan and Fuller on city's northeast side

1960 Proposed merger with Plumb collapses; Johanna and Don Magoon leave company; premium stamp program is dropped in favor of lower prices

1962 First Thrifty Acres discount department store opens at Kalamazoo Ave. and 28th St. in Grand Rapids June 5; Muskegon and Holland stores follow in fall

1964 Hendrik Meijer dies May 31 in Grand Rapids

1978 Gezina Mantel Meijer dies February 28 in Miami

I learned early that the richness of life is found in adventure. Adventure calls on all the faculties of mind and spirit. It develops self-reliance and independence. Life then teems with excitement. But man is not ready for adventure unless he is rid of fear. For fear confines him and limits his scope. He stays tethered by strings of doubt and indecision and has only a small and narrow world to explore.

—WILLIAM O. DOUGLAS,
Of Men and Mountains

1

The
Old Country

I

The history of the Nineteenth Century may be summed up in three words . . . industrialism, militarism, socialism.

—*Edmund Wilson, quoting Michelet*
in To The Finland Station

The soot and promise of the industrial revolution reached the Netherlands midway through the nineteenth century, when steam power was harnessed to looms in the textile-producing region of Twente, near the German border. In 1851, the year Hendrik Meijer's father, Frederik, was born, English engineers installed Twente's first entirely steam-driven mill. In the village of Hengelo, where two railroads crossed a river, the brothers Stork built a machine shop alongside their weaving sheds. And as Hengelo became an industrial center, farmers' sons like Frederik Meijer flocked to jobs in its mills and factories. Subjects of the early works of Vincent van Gogh—a gaunt weaver bending over his loom, the peasant family seated around a plate of potatoes—would have been at home there.

Hendrik Meijer was born in a brick flat on Hengelo's Haaksberger Straat, almost literally in the shadow of the Stork works, on December 28, 1883. The only son of Frederik Jan and Maria Loois Meijer, Hendrik was the third of seven children. (Two sisters, one older and one younger, died in infancy.)

In 1890 a committee of inquiry appointed by the Dutch parliament visited Hengelo to study the effects of a labor law that had been enacted the year before. The law, limiting the working day to eleven hours for women and boys under sixteen, showed that even the more conservative of the King's ministers were not indisposed to social reform. A clergyman in the delegation was therefore surprised to discover among Hengelo's factory workers not contentment but growing militance. His colleagues could not explain why. Hengelo at the time claimed the lowest unemployment in the region. Its mill owners were as enlightened as any in Enschede or Deventer—indeed, in smaller towns working conditions were often far more oppressive. Some employers tried to control workers' educational and social contacts to minimize the spread of radical ideas.

Perhaps Hengelo was rife with socialist agitation because of its tolerance, not in spite of it. In the market square and along the cobbled streets, workers talked of strikes and even revolution. Socialist ideas, spread by rabble-rousing unionists, were gaining momentum all out of proportion to the town's economic circumstances, the minister reported when he returned to The Hague. Unable to blame the industrialists for this condition, the preacher thought he discerned a more sinister source of discontent. A number of workers, he had observed, had loosened their ties with the church. There lay the blame, he concluded; these were men who no longer believed in God.

The most militant workers were following the lead of a fiery clergyman's son from Friesland who had traded the ministry for the revolutionary gospel of Karl Marx. His name was Ferdinand Domela Nieuwenhuis, and in 1891 he published his first tract, "My Divorce from the Church."

Frederik Meijer belonged to Nieuwenhuis's generation. He came from a farm family more prosperous than that of his wife, Maria, and his parents had been none too pleased with the match. Maria was a short, slight, vigorous woman, the second youngest of eleven children and nine years younger than her husband. She had gone to work in the Stork spinning mill when she was eight years old. Foremen in the mills were paid according to the pieces their workers produced. A section of cloth torn or snarled in the spinning was subtracted from the foreman's wage as well as from the worker's. So the children hid their mistakes. They concealed the torn fabric under their long dresses and later smuggled it home, where it provided material for clothes or bedding.

When Hendrik's father settled in Hengelo, Twente's mills boasted nearly 9,000 steam-driven looms. Years of furious growth had taken a toll no one anticipated. Beggars may have disappeared, but workers knew poverty as the accepted standard of living. In *The Netherlands*, Dutch historian Hendrik Riemens described them as a class of "men, women and children dragged through days of interminable labor for just enough to buy a skimpy diet of potatoes and salt pork, with gin to make life tolerable." Across the border young Friedrich Engels surveyed the sullen faces and stifling air in German mills and wondered who would not turn to drunkenness, even violence, after crouching all day above a loom, breathing more dust and coal smoke than oxygen.

The Stork works produced steam engines that powered ships as well as textile mills. Frederik Meijer worked on a crew that repaired boilers, sometimes working inside the great chambers while they were still hot, with a keg of beer waiting by the door. After thirty years of hammering and pounding, Frederik was deaf in one ear. And among his son's most vivid memories was the day he met his father on a footbridge that crossed a canal outside the foundry. Frederik was coming from the shop with one hand covering an eye that had just been blinded in a boiler accident.

Hendrik grew up in a bleak quadrant of single-story flats intersected by railroad tracks. Many of the houses were little more than hovels. In the flat next door lived a family of orthodox Jews. Forbidden to work on their Sabbath, early every Saturday morning they rapped on the flimsy wall that separated the two dwellings. At the signal, Hendrik would light their stove and receive a handful of raisins in return. The boy performed other errands that contributed to the family's income. One afternoon he was hauling meat by dogcart up the tree-lined brick toll road from Hengelo to the neighboring village of Borne. Coming home that night, he fell asleep in the cart while the dog kept walking. When they reached the toll gate, the dog passed underneath easily, but the youngster sat up with a start when his cart collided with the barrier gate.

Slender to the point of scrawny, with a shock of red hair, Hendrik wore the customary wool cap, wooden shoes, and short black pants of his age and social status. In primary school he displayed a great enthusiasm for reading. More than once, because pupils were not permitted to remove books from the classroom, he spirited them home in the seat of his trousers. He attended six grades of school, but failed his final year and had to repeat it. For the rest of his life he suspected an unspoken motive behind the teacher's decision. It was apparent that the brighter youngsters were more often the ones who were failed, thus giving them a year's reprieve from the mills.

Hendrik was baptized in the Reformed Church. Although he pumped the organ for the choir on Sundays, he was precluded from singing because he came from a working-class family. His parents had never been particularly devout. The presence of the minister at dinner one night, in fact, caused a moment of suspense, since the family customarily did not pray. When Hendrik's mother lowered her head quite solemnly and said, "Let us pray," the call caught the boy and his sisters off guard and they could not suppress their laughter.

As a rule, however, laughter did not predominate in the Meijer household. Once Hendrik started in the cotton mill, his mother collected his pay. Sometimes he hid it—behind the mantel clock, for example—but his mother always seemed to find it. She claimed the family needed every penny, but the refrain grew hollow: she was often drunk, and so was Hendrik's father. They drank and fought, and home became a bitter place, particularly just before payday, when the family found itself close to the edge once again. The guilders had gone for gin or beer, and dinner was boiled pork or pea soup—mostly, as Hendrik remembered it, pea soup.

Schooling ended for Hendrik when he was thirteen. The bricks of the great smokestacks ceased to be a place for him to warm his hands in winter on the way to school. He became an apprentice spinner in a labor force that ranged from children his age to grandfathers who had spent their lives in the mills' tubercular haze—ten or eleven hours a day, six days a week, with three days of vacation a year. At noon the men would send boys to the tavern for pails of beer to wash down the cotton dust. Shuttlecocks rattled and roared in poorly lit, poorly ventilated halls. It was not always easy to breathe. These were the years against which Hendrik was to live his life in reaction. Fresh air, a long walk in the early morning—these would come to exert an almost hypnotic appeal.

Escape from the mills came for Hendrik in 1903. The nineteen-year-old weaver was drafted as a private in the Queen's infantry and assigned to the barracks of the Fifth Regiment in Amersfoort, midway between Hengelo and Amsterdam.

Radical workers scorned the monarchy, and the army was its most contemptible extension, a lightning rod that provoked the opposition of socialists, anarchists, pacifists—all who saw it as defender of a reactionary system. (Indeed, as recently as 1901 young Dutchmen of wealthier circumstances could buy substitutes to fulfill their military obligations.) Domela

Nieuwenhuis called the army "the last stronghold of capital-ism." Young workers, he wrote, "are compelled at a certain age to bid farewell to home and parents, work and friends, to be clothed in fool's dress with red or yellow ornaments, and to be taught the trade of slaughter."

Like many of the more intellectually curious young con-scripts, Hendrik shared that scorn. But he also found something unexpectedly agreeable in military life. Here was well-fed discipline, in contrast to the near squalor of a worker's flat. Here was pride for the asking; back in Hengelo that too had been in short supply. This confidence derived in part from small things: boots polished to a shine, a well-pressed uniform, an invigorating march with chest out and back straight. Precisely because of its custom and ritual, there was room for self-respect in the army—more room, perhaps, despite its dedication to the "trade of slaughter," than could be found in the lint and haze of the weaving sheds.

Private Meijer took a lasting pride in spit and polish. Dur-ing one inspection his captain berated another private for a sloppy uniform. "Look at this man," the captain said, point-ing at Hendrik. "He was drafted and you're a career man—you enlisted in the army. This man has his buttons polished and his boots shined; his pants are pressed. And here you are; you enlisted, and you're a slob."

Long marches across the moors were a vast relief from the mill. Hendrik responded to his duties with vigor, if not always with enthusiasm. Yet there was no denying the aversion he felt for the armed forces of a monarchy still training troops for colonial garrisons. He belonged quite consciously to the work-ing class—"the people" of the urban proletariat—whose aspira-tions collided with the capitalist status quo. He certainly did not want to stand across the barricades from other workers.

The army's inflexibility also caused problems at a practical level. Hendrik sang in a choral society in Hengelo, and was determined to join an overnight concert trip to sing in the court-yard of a castle in Bentheim, across the border in Germany. But his regiment had been placed on alert because of the threat of violence during a railroad strike. All leaves had been short-ened or cancelled; troops occupied railway stations around Amsterdam. Hendrik badgered the captain for days before receiving a special leave—for one day only.

One day was enough for a short visit to Hengelo but not for a concert trip across the border. As he knew he would all along, Hendrik returned to the barracks two days later. He had been absent without leave, and the captain was furious.

"I missed my train," Hendrik told him.

"How many?"

"Several."

"You knew you couldn't be back in time," the captain said, and he sentenced Hendrik to a week in the stockade. According to Dutch military custom, the soldier receiving the punishment was expected to salute and thank his superior officer for the sentence. When Hendrik saluted, he could not suppress a smile. That doubled the sentence.

Word of his imprisonment alarmed Hendrik's family. But apart from the diet of bread and water, Hendrik himself was less distressed. During the day he was released to train with his company, and when he settled in for the night with a stack of books, he found little cause for complaint. Nor was he deterred from passing out anarchist pamphlets and putting up posters protesting Holland's colonialist policies in the Dutch East Indies. In the barracks men sang the socialist anthem, the *Internationale,* and made up mocking songs about their Calvinist prime minister, Abraham Kuyper. But these acts escaped detection. In fact, such was the private's general demeanor that upon his release from the stockade the captain asked him, "Why didn't you put in for corporal? The notice was posted."

But Hendrik said that he had no interest in becoming an officer, even a noncommissioned one. Besides, he told the captain, he hoped to join the bicycle corps. However, the captain ordered him to apply for the promotion, which he did reluctantly. He was reluctant because he had no desire to extend his service and wished to do nothing to jeopardize his easy camaraderie with the other men. But he was promoted in spite of himself, only to discover that exercising authority did not automatically destroy the camaraderie. It spiced it, instead, with the flavor of respect.

One of his responsibilities was the laundry detail. As a corporal, he wore white gloves. Under his supervision, a private carried the heavy basket of soiled uniforms from the barracks. One day four of his men were playing cards by the cots when the new corporal stood in the doorway.

"Who's going to help me?" he asked.

"Aw Henk, don't break up our game," said one. "Get someone else."

Hendrik watched them play a hand. Then, after a pause, he said to one, "I'd like you to come with me. Let's go."

The soldier promptly put down his cards, as though he had just been waiting for Hendrik to show a little leadership.

Indeed, the camaraderie remained intact. As they returned to the barracks from the laundry in another quarter of the city, the private handed Hendrik a cigar. Smoking on duty was against regulations, but they were on a public street, away from the fort. They lit up the cigars and were enjoying the stroll when suddenly the captain—the same officer who had sentenced Hendrik to the stockade and then ordered him to apply for promotion—came striding toward them from the opposite direction. The two men held the cigars behind their backs, but their gestures were transparent. Said Hendrik, "I put the cigar from my right hand to my left hand, put it behind my back, and saluted with the right hand." A smile flitted across the captain's face as he returned the salute and walked on by.

Hendrik's two years of service were nearly over when the captain ordered him to report for sergeant's training, and his final weeks of duty were spent training for a promotion he would never accept.

II

A working class hero is something to be.

—*John Lennon*

Much as he disliked the idea of the army, Hendrik had made his peace with it. Back in Hengelo, where he remained on reserve status, he received a letter from his former captain that urged him to reconsider a military career. The captain told the young veteran he would make a fine officer—this from the officer who had sent him to jail. Hendrik declined. He had no desire for a soldier's life, even as an alternative to being a weaver. But someone in a position of authority had shown an interest in his future. He was grateful for that—and for the upright stride and martial bearing that remained a source of pride all his life.

Whatever its evils, the army had provided a diversion that made a return to the mill town a dreary prospect. More often now, his mother's drinking made her hostile. Hendrik's older sister, Griet, had once come home to find Maria Meijer passed out on the floor. Griet had married, and the younger sisters looked to her for the support and affection their mother could not supply. Their father had grown more withdrawn. So Hendrik went to live with Griet and her husband.

The long hours at the treadle made leisure precious. While in the army, Hendrik had joined a choral society, which met once a week near the socialists' hall on the Anninksweg, a narrow street on the edge of Hengelo. From dues of ten cents a month, members financed weekend concert outings such as the one that had earned Hendrik his sentence in the Amersfoort stockade.

A six-foot-tall tenor, he stood in the back row, broad-chested but so slender that friends called him The Beanpole. In front of him stood a small soprano who was three years younger than he. Gezina Mantel, known to her friends by the diminutive Zientje, or simply Zien (pronounced *zeen*), lived with her parents and three brothers across the street from the music school. One night as the singers were putting on their coats, Hendrik asked Zien if he might walk her home. Shy and blushing, she wondered aloud whether he did not think she could find her way. But he insisted, so she let him accompany her across the cobblestones. A few weeks later he invited her to the circus and gave her a small bottle of perfume, unaware that she was allergic to the contents.

Meeting the Mantel family was an event of lasting consequence for Hendrik. In contrast to the instability of his parents' household, the Mantels offered a model of domestic harmony. First of all, they were teetotalers; his family had been torn apart by alcoholism. And they were leaders in the labor agitation for which Hengelo had acquired a reputation. Hendrik was in his early twenties, an intellectually impressionable age, and military service had done nothing to lessen his own socialist—even anarchist—sympathies as a son of the working class. His acquaintance with the Mantels brought those sympathies into flower.

The Mantels were independent-minded West Frisians from the harsh coast of the North Sea. Zien's father, Gerhard Mantel, was a descendant of shipbuilders and sailmakers. His grandfather had settled in Twente in the 1820s as a weaver on a hand-powered loom; his father was a pipefitter at the Stork factory, a wiry, agile man who even in his sixties clambered through the pipes to repair a steam vent. Gerhard had once worked in the Stork mills himself. Like his father, he might have been expected to spend his life there. But in 1883, the year Hendrik Meijer was born, he helped organize the town's first industrial union. And his political passions cost him his job.

Mantel was a tailor and his wife taught sewing when Hendrik met them. Tailoring was only Mantel's most recent trade, however; before that he had been a shoemaker, and before that a weaver. He belonged to the first generation to grow up in the shadow of the big mills. For the men and women drawn to jobs in the mills, technological progress brought with it cramped and inadequate housing, unhealthy working conditions, subsistence wages—and an increasingly fervid desire to share in the fruits of that progress. Convinced that their time was coming, some workers were prepared to take matters into their own hands. "The last third of the nineteenth century," wrote Samuel P. Hays in *The Response to Industrialism, 1885-1914,* "was an era of popular schemes for remaking society, of simple solutions to complex problems. . . ."

Gerhard Mantel was eighteen years old when the charismatic preacher from Friesland, Ferdinand Domela Nieuwenhuis, embarked on a crusade for change that swept like a beacon into the brick flats of Hengelo's working class. A tall, spare man with a stiff demeanor, Nieuwenhuis rejected the church to seek salvation in a Marxist Eden. Preaching a utopian gospel of socialism and brotherly love, he wrote anarchist-pacifist broadsides in his influential journal *Recht voor Allen* (Justice for All). His acquaintances included the leading radicals of the era, from Peter Kropotkin to Emma Goldman, all of whom came to be revered figures in the Mantel canon.

Dutch society posed a stiff challenge to the would-be revolutionary. Socialism, like the industrial revolution that was its seedbed, arrived late in the Netherlands. Trade unionism did not exist until people like Mantel began to organize meetings and talk about strikes during the last quarter of the nineteenth century. And the liberals of the upper classes still acknowledged the nation's traditional reputation for tolerance. This was not St. Petersburg or Vienna. Working people had a hard time of it, but oppression was hardly pervasive. (The Hague had abolished capital punishment in 1870 and was becoming the favored setting for high-toned gatherings like international peace conferences.)

Yet class divisions remained rigid, and few workers had the right to vote. At the same time, the steam-driven mills brought an influx of young workers to such cities and towns as Hengelo. A restless new urban proletariat faced a housing shortage and often had no choice but to live in flats owned by their employers. The concentration of labor encouraged unionism; and as the workers sought political power, socialism became their rallying cry.

Nieuwenhuis first visited Hengelo in 1885, a year before Gezina Mantel was born. He called on Gerhard Mantel, who risked his job at Stork to attend a rally the next day in neighboring Enschede. Nieuwenhuis was also an unexpected guest of Mantel's Hengelo unionists at a meeting that weekend on workers' voting rights. He gave a short speech condemning the "slavery" of the millworkers, but the meeting was poorly attended. "How different it would have been had they known that Niewenhuis would be there," one of Mantel's cohorts wrote later, "but they were scared to announce his appearance." Stork did find out about Mantel's role, however, and fired him the next day.

Six weeks later, Mantel left Hengelo for The Hague as Twente's first delegate to a national workers' rally. Early on a Sunday morning he walked to the station, where nearly fifty workers sang labor songs in a festive farewell. "For a moment," a Hengelo comrade recalled, "their conditions of enslavement were forgotten." In The Hague, the socialist protesters marched through the streets and threatened revolution if their demands for voting rights got no response. It was a heady moment for the movement, but in Hengelo a band of Stork partisans—thugs, it was said later—awaited Mantel's return. His arrival nearly touched off a brawl, before a brawny comrade escorted him from the station.

An international depression in the late 1880s retarded the progress that people on the lower rungs of the economic ladder had begun to expect. Socialist rhetoric became more strident. "This is a time of passion rather than of reflection," declared socialist writer Albert Verwey. "People have things to say that brook of no delay, and their movements are the movements of people proceeding to sudden action." The depression increased the migration of jobless workers to industrial towns like Hengelo at a time when the mills could not accommodate the influx. Unemployment rose to alarming proportions.

Against this backdrop, Mantel joined with another follower of Nieuwenhuis, Gerrit Bennink (who was married to Hendrik Meijer's aunt), to open a socialist hall on the Anninksweg, near the house where Mantel later set up his tailor shop. In a nation as compact as the Netherlands, the radicals comprised a close-knit—though seldom harmonious—fraternity. In their little hall the local radicals chose delegates to national congresses and planned strikes and demonstrations. There they debated and lectured, preaching their visionary social gospel and sharing tales of exploitation and frustration with audiences that generally consisted of one another. The day of revolution always seemed to be just beyond the horizon. Yet, as A. J. P. Taylor observed in *Europe: Grandeur and Decline*, "This did not take the zest from a lifetime of planning."

In their propensity for religious dispute and schism, the Dutch display an exaggerated sense of freedom. With messianic fervor, Nieuwenhuis put forth a creed in which all responsibility for thought and action belonged to the individual—anarchism in its purest form. He broke with the more politically realistic Social Democrats in 1897, and, finding their willingness to compromise with the conservatives and monarchists contemptible, wrote a fiery pamphlet, "Socialism in Danger." All political parties had become, in Nieuwenhuis's view, enforcers of the status quo—"one great reactionary party," from the pope to the Social Democrats.

Nieuwenhuis could claim no more than five thousand followers in all of the Netherlands. Yet in spartan meeting rooms like the one on the Anninksweg they talked of revolution as though it would strike suddenly, like a bolt of lightning. To hasten the day, the anarchists campaigned relentlessly. Nieuwenhuis boasted, "We dispose of great quantities of propaganda leaflets."

Like Nieuwenhuis himself, Mantel and his wife had been religious people. Zien's mother had attended three services each Sunday. Their church—or, more accurately, their faith—was *Minnessen*, or Mennonite. They were followers of the sixteenth-century Dutch Anabaptist Menno Simons, a radical priest who went into hiding to escape persecution and was rebaptized upon his confession of faith. Anabaptists, who flourished among the urban lower middle class—tailors, bakers, shoemakers, carpenters—espoused the conviction that "among the Brethren all things should be in common." Although later Mennonites were a moderate offshoot of their revolutionary forebears, some still clung to vague notions of communist cooperation. There prevailed among them what Max Weber called "an invincible antagonism to any sort of aristocratic way of life."

Mrs. Mantel was fond of quoting a revered preacher who expressed the Minnessen creed, which was derived from the Sermon on the Mount, as "my yes is my yes; my no is my no." Mennonites believed that the word of God was internal. The state permitted them, for example, to affirm instead of to take oaths. Called to testify in a neighborhood dispute, Mrs. Mantel refused to swear on a Bible. There was no need for that, she told the magistrate; her word was her bond. The magistrate allowed her to proceed. The Minnessen practiced adult baptism in accordance with their belief that only men and women mature enough to follow the dictates of conscience were justified in considering themselves reborn.

After Mantel was fired, the church's young preacher—an unfortunate successor to Mrs. Mantel's favorite—was sent over by the mill owner with an offer: Mantel could have his job back if he abandoned his agitation. The preacher did not get far. Mantel refused to return under those conditions, and his wife became so indignant at the pastor's obsequiousness on behalf of the capitalists that she quit the church. To their other causes the Mantels added unrelenting opposition to what they now condemned as the hypocrisy of religion. They found a substitute for Christianity in "the religion of humanity." A quarter of a century later, when Zien set up housekeeping in America, her hostility toward religious ritual remained so intense that she was even reluctant to adopt the Christmas customs of her new country.

Zien was two years old in 1888, when the socialists opened their hall and her mother declared that she would never set foot in church again. Her father, unable or unwilling to work for the families who controlled Hengelo's industry, chose to become a cobbler. It was a trade he could practice in his home, where his politics were his own—a trade where he was neither employer nor employee. In exchange for room and board, a young man who had been taught shoemaking in a government orphanage showed Zien's father how to make shoes. But Mantel took up the trade too late. Factories were already mass-producing shoes far more cheaply than he could make them. After two marginal years, he abandoned shoemaking and took a job in his brother's tailor shop, the largest such establishment in Hengelo. Mantel's brother was the enthusiastic outfitter of the town's sports clubs and bands; he prided himself on his uniforms and catered to the bourgeois establishment. Gerhard preferred simpler suits and skirts and made no secret of his hostility toward the establishment. There was not enough room in one shop for two men with so little in common. So with his teenage sons, Wilhelm and Ferdinand, Gerhard Mantel set up his own shop. Once again he went to work in his parlor, in a shop rather grandiosely named "De Toekomst" (The Future).

In 1891, Mantel's comrade Gerrit Bennink founded *Recht door Zee* (Justice through You), a Twente counterpart to the newspaper Nieuwenhuis published in Amsterdam. The little weekly, "dedicated to the interests of the oppressed and disenfranchised," chronicled labor disputes and meetings of the local organization and nurtured its readers' dreams of impending revolution. With naive faith and overblown expectations, many socialists believed that when all workers had the right to vote, the salvation of the working class would be at hand. As A. J. P. Taylor observed, "Universal suffrage . . . became everywhere the most concrete expression of the revolutionary program." A Dutch law passed in 1887 gave the vote to all men at twenty-three years of age, provided they could show "signs of capability and prosperity." Yet the new law still restricted the franchise. Parliament debated interpretations of "capability," and radicals demanded to know what signs of "prosperity" could be expected in a worker's crowded flat. Certainly there was no prosperity on Haaksberger Straat and precious little on the Anninksweg.

The Mantels remained loyal to Nieuwenhuis and his search for the proletarian grail. They wanted to overthrow the monarchy, not make accommodations with it. Their utopian ideals became a substitute religion, and in their living room hung green felt plaques with quotations from the martyrs of the revolution. Next to a portrait of Kropotkin, the legendary Russian anarchist, were the words, "Everything must go that debases mankind: the State, the Church and the Extortionists [exploiters of the worker]." Another plaque read, "Man has just so much freedom as he allows himself to take." Nearby was the portrait of another hero, the Spanish radical Francisco Ferrer, a teacher executed after an abortive revolt in Barcelona.

In 1898, at the age of eighteen, Princess Wilhelmina ascended the Dutch throne. When she traveled through Hengelo after her coronation, Mantel and his comrades stationed themselves along her parade route, blowing whistles and jeering from the rooftops to compete with the music of the royal procession. The protesters scrambled from roof to roof to elude the police. And when the Queen's birthday was celebrated, the Mantels kept Zien home from school.

The Mantels' political zealotry went hand in hand with a host of puritanical obsessions. They believed that tobacco and alcohol were, in the words of Nieuwenhuis, the "material means of brutalization" of the people. "No man can be free who's slave to drink," he had written. The Mantels were vegetarians as well; and while younger anarchists talked of bombs and violence, they remained passionate pacifists. All this was of a piece with the traditional asceticism of their discarded religious faith. They were tailors, but they dressed austerely, as Mennonites might; and simplicity marked every facet of their lives, from their diet to their home and its furnishings. Parents of a large family, they became outspoken advocates of birth control and the right of abortion. They organized chapters of a Malthusian society to draw attention to the catastrophe which they believed unbridled population growth would inflict on the world. They were apocalyptic visionaries of a peculiarly modern sort.

A younger Mantel daughter, stricken with spinal meningitis, died in her sister Zien's arms in 1901. Not long afterward, a two-year-old brother died suddenly in his sleep. Zien and her three surviving brothers would walk to their school in the neighboring town of Enschede, warming their hands in the winter on the broad brick chimneys of the mills along the way. Their father's tailor shop prospered in a modest way, and the family enjoyed a measure of middle-class security. They were diligent workers, and the scrupulous truthfulness practiced by the Minnessen lent itself—perhaps somewhat ironically in their case—to that cornerstone of the capitalist ethic: "Honesty is the best policy."

Zien was working for her father as a seamstress in 1905, when Hendrik Meijer walked her home from choir practice. Later, when Hendrik met Gerhard Mantel at a birth control clinic operated by one of the radical groups, the younger man explained to his future father-in-law that he was there to get information for his sister, who was getting married.

III

> But when I become a man
> then will I stand firm;
> I ask for and I demand
> a free, a human life.
>
> —Hendrik Meijer, ca. 1907

In Russia, 1905 was the year of Bloody Sunday, when Cossack cavalry massacred protesters outside the czar's palace in St. Petersburg, of the mutiny aboard the battleship *Potemkin,* and of demonstrations against the Russian government in which more than two million workers took part. To European radicals these events portended momentous and irresistible change. Strikes spread to Austria, Germany, Bulgaria, Italy, and France. The new century's agenda was clear, and great things were expected.

For Hendrik Meijer, however, revolution remained in the realm of the imagination. In his black worker's shirt and baggy trousers, his tour of duty in the army behind him, he once again wove cloth in the Stork mill.

In the summer of 1906 he was called away from the looms again for a season in the army reserve. For two years, to make military life tolerable, he had made his peace with the army. But now he was twenty-two, not nineteen, and the months in the mill—as well as in the company of the Mantels—had done nothing to soften his convictions. "He was . . . a rebel," recalled his nephew, Fred Veltman. In the months that followed Bloody Sunday, Hendrik's sympathies were with the workers, not the army.

The new century failed to inspire revolutionary unrest in the Netherlands, but neither did it bring great progress. Workers were organized, and the franchise had been extended; but change came slowly. Indeed, it often seemed not to come at all. While Nieuwenhuis led his followers off into deluded utopianism, the Dutch lower middle class—the farmers and the shopkeepers—was roused by the charismatic eloquence of a new prime minister, who mixed strident Calvinism with demagoguery. Abraham Kuyper called on his followers to rout the radical and godless forces of evil. The evangelical character of Kuyper's Protestantism reinforced the young radicals' hostility toward religious institutions. But he drew into the mainstream of Dutch political and cultural life the rural and small-town Calvinists whose interests lay with neither the liberal traditions of the faded Dutch republic nor the noisy rabble-rousers on the left. From this Calvinist milieu came the Boers in South Africa and the pious pioneers who organized immigration to America.

When workers threatened protests, Kuyper threatened to call out the troops. Such a prospect at once horrified and excited a young revolutionary like Hendrik. His letters to Zien reflected that reaction: "I dreamed last night that we were in Russia already," he wrote from Amersfoort. "I saw them put up the barricades." He quoted a stanza from a barracks tune his comrades were singing:

> There will come a time
> When we leave this mess;
> Damned be the regiment
> But never the soldiers!

At night in their bunks young soldiers debated the future of the proletariat. Followers of Nieuwenhuis took issue with pragmatic socialists, or argued among themselves over individualism versus collectivism, pacifism versus the revolutionary deed. The sources of debate were limitless. *Recht door Zee* kept Hendrik informed of the strikes and protests back in Twente; but the news from Amsterdam was disheartening. Since Kuyper had come to power, none of the improvements in voting rights or working conditions endorsed by the liberals and even by the Queen had come to pass.

On his last weekend in uniform, Hendrik visited a socialist leader who lived near Amersfoort. He noted in a letter to Zien: "That will be the last Sunday that we serve under the monster of militarism. After that, I'll enroll with her mother, capitalism." Hendrik was in no way excited about this return to "capitalism" and the prospect of a weaver's life in the mills. It was not a life but an existence that had taken its toll on his family and friends. Tuberculosis was common among men who spent their lives breathing the lint-filled air. And his father had lost an eye and much of his hearing.

Hendrik quickly became convinced that the doors of advancement in Hengelo were closed to him. When he asked for a transfer out of the weaving sheds and into the machine shop or the boiler factory, his request was denied. "I didn't cause any trouble," he said years later. "I got along in every way, and yet I couldn't get a promotion. I don't know why." And he never did find out why. His employers may simply have wanted to keep him where he was. But he suspected another motive, which he traced to the day a company supervisor visited Frederik Meijer at home and noticed Hendrik reading a socialist newspaper. And then, of course, there was his intimacy with the Mantels.

The army had given Hendrik a glimpse of a world outside the mill. Now he began to wish for more. British experts were often called on to teach Dutch workers how to build and maintain power looms. When a pair of engineers arrived in Hengelo to install new equipment, Hendrik was assigned to work with them as a pipefitter's helper. He was still going for beer at noon, and once, stumbling home, he dropped a letter for Zien into the gutter. In light of the Mantels' strict code of temperance, the moment seemed to crystallize his dreary circumstances. The Englishmen talked of places where a young man like himself might find a better future. They talked about America. The year was 1906, the same year popular Dutch novelist Louis Couperus published the story of an opera singer who abandoned the Netherlands for a new life in Paris. "I couldn't breathe," his heroine said. "The gray skies hindered my breathing, and the houses stopped me from producing my voice properly." Whether or not Hendrik read the book, the singer's yearning mirrored his own.

Still more compelling was the shriek of the whistle of the express train that roared through Hengelo. The second- and third-class cars were crowded to overflowing with Russians and Poles, many of them Jews, en route to Rotterdam and the voyage to America. Women in kerchiefs held babies in their arms; families carried bundles of clothes with their possessions tied up in old sheets; children with round eyes stared out at the flat Dutch landscape. A sea of faces, bound for America—it was a persuasive picture. "I told myself," Hendrik recalled half a century later, "that some day I would make the same journey."

America belonged to the imagination, a place pieced together from books, postcards, gossip, and the letters of friends of friends. Hendrik read the *Last of the Mohicans*, with its exuberant descriptions of the great wilderness. With the Holland-America Line employing more than two thousand agents, passage could be easily arranged. Newspapers listed sailings and fares, and each departure of a friend or co-worker inspired fresh ambitions.

Hendrik told his older sister and brother-in-law, who also talked of emigration, that whatever they chose to do, he was not going to stay in Hengelo. If it was not to America, then he would go to Germany. (With radical verses in his rucksack, he would have had something in common with an Italian socialist who was born the same year he was. Said Benito Mussolini of a job-hunting foray in Switzerland, "I carried my bible in my pocket: Marx.") Other men from the Hengelo mills had found work in German factories or, better yet, followed the harvest, roaming about in a manner that the Germans called *die Wanderschaft* (literally, "on the tramp"). Hendrik's mother, whose sympathy he must have thought misplaced, was afraid he would become a hobo. But a foreign adventure had powerful appeal. A popular narrative poem of the day described a young man's nomadic ramble through Italy, where he fell in love with a nobleman's daughter. And there was a Dutch expression current at the time: "See Naples, *then* die."

Hendrik had already fallen in love—with the little soprano who saw the world much as he did. They sang together. They took long walks through the gardens and forests of the baronial estate of Twickel, west of Hengelo, where his mother's family had once labored. It was not easy for Hendrik to tell her of his ambitions. Nor was he certain of his plans. He talked of Germany and *die Wanderschaft*, but also of more distant places, of South America, or perhaps the Carolinas, where another textile industry flourished.

After much procrastination, he explained to Zien that he had saved three hundred guilders and intended to go away, to Bavaria, for a few months. Zien did not know how to respond. After two years of courtship, she had thought he might be about to ask her to marry him. And for Hendrik there was the nagging thought that although a season in Bavaria offered a respite from the mill, it was no real alternative. He had not forgotten the advice of the English engineers, nor the whistle of the emigrant train that roared past the mill.

When he resigned from the weaving mill of the Stork works on June 1, 1907, he told Zien he had changed his mind. He was going to America. Here was shocking news for a young woman whose thoughts had turned to marriage. It was one thing to hike into a neighboring province for the harvest; it was quite another to cross the Atlantic. Zien did not know what to say; so she said good-bye. It did not have to mean that, Hendrik said quickly. He told her that he did want to marry her. He could not tell her what would happen in America—whether he would stay there for good or come back to Hengelo. It depended on the work. If he stayed in America, he would come back for her, or she would join him—someday, when he was settled.

Before he left, he gave her a thick gray album for postcards and vowed to fill it. "That way," he promised, "you'll always know where I am."

Bewijs van Ontslag.

Naam _____ *Mijer*

Voornaam _____ *Hendrik*

Geboren te _____ *Hengelo (O)*

den _____ *2en December 1883*

heeft van _____ *af 3 April 1905*

tot _____ *1 Juni 1907*

tot onze tevredenheid bij ons gewerkt en is op

zijn verzoek ontslagen.

Koninklijke Weefgoederen Fabriek
voorheen C. T. STORK & Co

Hengelo _____ *1 Juni* _____ *1907*

Hendrik's notice of resignation from the Stork factory indicates that he was employed there from April 3, 1905—after his military service—to June 1, 1907, when he left the company voluntarily.

2

The
New World

You see, Meijer, it's not always easy to be free.

—*Gezina Mantel, 1907*

In the record year of 1907, seven thousand Hollanders were admitted to the United States. Better than half were bound for Michigan, and the largest percentage of those for the city of Holland—"De Kolonie" its founders called it—the original Dutch settlement at the mouth of the Black River on Lake Michigan's eastern shore.

An immigrant's life was unsettled enough without severing all bonds of kin and culture. Holland, Michigan had a Dutch-language newspaper, a score of Reformed churches, a Reformed seminary with its roots in the stern convictions of the community's founders, and, for transient immigrants headed farther west, steamer service to Chicago. Dunes that sheltered the little city from the lake brought to mind the windswept coast of the North Sea, while the rich black muck farther inland suggested the peat bogs of the Dutch countryside.

Nearby settlements took their names from places back home: Borculo, Drenthe, Graafschap, Vriesland, even Overijssel, Hendrik's native province. Many settlers still wore wooden shoes and remained faithful to the strict customs of their native districts.

But Michigan might as well have been Manchuria, so remote was it on the June day in 1907 when Hendrik Meijer, accompanied at the last minute by his father and twenty-year-old sister, Anna, boarded a train bound for the harbor at Rotterdam.

The *S. S. Nieuw Amsterdam* was the newest ship in the Holland-America fleet, commissioned only the year before and outfitted to accommodate 417 first-class passengers, 391 in second class (including Hendrik, his father, and his sister), and 2,300 in steerage. With one of the largest steerage capacities of any vessel afloat, it had been designed expressly for the transatlantic immigration trade. "We were amazed by the size of it," Hendrik noted. "They were busy loading, painting, scrubbing, etc." Although he was twenty-three years old, Hendrik had never seen a seagoing vessel. Indeed, he had never seen the sea.

At 4 a.m. the ship eased away from the dock. On the pier a handful of well-wishers waved handkerchiefs as the *Nieuw Amsterdam* receded into darkness. After that, Hendrik wrote, "most people went to bed, but I stayed up to take a last look at the Netherlands' narrow shore." At dawn he sighted the steeples of the Hoek van Holland, and after that, "all we could see was sea and sky, gulls, and once in a while a steamer or sailboat." The sandy, yellow-green water near the coast gave way to the deeper blue-green of the North Sea.

Rigid class distinctions followed the immigrants aboard ship. At breakfast first-class passengers were summoned to their dining room by a horn. In second class a bell clanged, while on the third-class deck a cook's helper clapped a wooden spoon against a pan, as though, Hendrik wrote, "it was feeding time for animals."

Late in the afternoon the ship approached Bologne on the coast of Brittany. It looked like a green and pleasant town. "I could have stayed there a couple of weeks, by the looks of it," Hendrik observed. As the band played *La Marseillaise,* a small boat came alongside to put aboard passengers and pick up a mail pouch. French fishermen rowed out, gesturing and shouting, begging passengers for tobacco or cigars. An hour later the *Nieuw Amsterdam* was steaming out to sea again, setting course for Hoboken, New Jersey, as the band struck up an American tune.

The passage was difficult. "No wonder," Hendrik observed, that a ship that "danced on the water like a feather must make everybody sick. I was pretty sick too. I ate practically nothing for a day and a half."

But he wasted little time observing the sights and sounds and smells of his fellow passengers. "After a while I went to the third-class [steerage] deck, although I was not allowed there," he wrote. Here were more than two thousand peasants and factory workers—more Poles and Russians, Jews and Slavs, than Hollanders—sharing forty toilets and about as many washbasins. There were only two showers. "I crawled very quietly over the rail," Hendrik continued in his first letter to Zien.

> I cannot describe the smell. . . . I hope you don't mind that I tell you exactly how it was. They looked and lived like animals. They were lying around like animals on deck; you could see that the lice bothered them. And they would rather sit next to the toilet than on it. All day long someone kept watch in the bathrooms.
>
> This even happened on the second-class deck. Potatoes were eaten peel and all. They ate the herring before it was cleaned. Lemons, with peel, were cut in pieces and eaten. All day long they sat with their teapots in their laps. There is a terrible smell when you go below.

"You cannot believe the things that happened on such a sea hotel, and I have seen it," Hendrik added. "You meet all kinds of people." One had run away; another had had problems with his business. "I met a neat-looking man with a woman, both about 28 to 30 years old, who told me he had lost 6,000 guilders in a leather company. An architect was going to San Francisco to work as a carpenter because he could not make a living in the Old Country. I also met a comrade from Amsterdam. . . . He gave me a book of poetry, one of the first editions of *Naar de Vrijheid [Toward Freedom]*. . . . There was a baby born on the third-class deck. Sometimes church services were held. The Jews and the Catholics and other Christians sang together. Everyone in his own way gave thanks to the same Father."

After the rush of new impressions, however, "lots of people got bored."

> We were trying to keep busy. Twice a day they played music for an hour. Every other day there was a concert with beautiful music. There were also Hungarians on board with violins and zithers, and they played dance music.
>
> In third class they played a harmonica and everyone danced. . . . Sometimes we didn't see anything for two days. We passed three icebergs. . . . One man had a pair of binoculars. He looked at the iceberg and said, "There's an ice bear sitting on it." Someone else said, "Let me see that." "Yes," he said, "he's mailing you a letter." . . . We could usually see big fish at night—they said they were whales. Some fish were swimming alongside the ship, jumping up and down. Some were very, very big, and water was coming out of their heads. We had a lot of fog, too. The foghorn blew constantly. For a while we heard two foghorns, so there was another ship nearby.

The ship's bulletin reported a hurricane one hundred miles to the south.

The agents of the Holland-America Line had claimed that prices aboard ship were reasonable. Not true, Hendrik wrote. "Everything is very expensive. Twenty-five cents for a shave; a boy ordered a cigar for 10 cents and had to pay two and one-half cents extra. One bottle of lemonade costs 25 cents. . . . The waiters don't make much in wages and have to beg for tips."

After a week at sea they approached the American coast. For hours before the first sighting, the cabins filled with anticipation. "We were sitting in the lounge Sunday and heard people screaming on deck," Hendrik reported. "When we went up to look, we saw big lights—it was the first lightship that we passed. We knew now that we were close to land. . . . We were going very slowly, and at about 11 a.m. we saw land. We passed several of these lightboats . . . also several warships. We passed the Statue of Liberty . . . "—and here he added, somewhat cynically, "I don't know what it means. . . ." Certainly he had not read the verse an earlier immigrant, Emma Lazarus, had written the year he was born about "huddled masses, yearning to breathe free."

They sailed past sumptuous summer homes along the Long Island shore, past Battery Park on the southern tip of Manhattan, and up the mouth of the Hudson River. Passengers struck up musical accompaniment as the ship entered the harbor. Hendrik had risen early to shave and wash. Passengers anxiously rehearsed their responses to the questions they expected from American immigration officers. Doctors were brought aboard and everyone had to be examined. "I stood close to the door and noticed that several were put aside," Hendrik wrote. "Nyhuis and Schouwink were refused. Then it was our turn. The doctor asked me if I could speak English. 'A little bit,' I said." (This was hardly true, for he spoke virtually no English.) "He asked me if my father was deaf. I said yes. He had not even seen my father. I could leave, he said, and then it was my sister's turn. She was OK too, and my father was also all right."

The Hoboken dock bustled with noise and confusion as baggage was unloaded and voices called out in strange languages. Hawkers sold fruit and baked goods at exorbitant prices, and the poignant moments of leavetaking began. Friends wondered if they would see one another again. With the ship in its berth, first- and second-class passengers who had passed the physical examination were permitted to disembark. (Steerage passengers remained on board to be processed the next day at Ellis Island.) "We were waiting for Schouwink," Hendrik continued,

> but he was refused a second time, and Nyhuis as well. We could not wait any longer; they had to wait until the next day to be re-examined at Ellis Island. I walked over to them to say goodbye. It didn't look too good. They were afraid of the worst. I shook hands with them and wanted to leave, but Nyhuis grabbed my arm and said, "Please don't forget me," and I shook hands with him again.

In the customs building the immigrants took their places in long lines according to the first initial of their last name. "We stood under the M, where they would put your trunk and belongings," Hendrik wrote.

> I don't have to tell you what a busy place it was. I opened my trunk to put my coat back in, and when I went to close it again, my friend from Amsterdam who shared the cabin with me put in a coat that belonged to one of the Hungarians who had a trunk next to mine. I didn't know it was his, and a while later he [the Hungarian] asked me about his coat and pointed to my trunk. I opened it again—it was sealed with screws—and took out the coat. He was so happy; he shook my hand. He knew I hadn't done it on purpose.

After resting a few hours at the familiar-sounding Hotel Van Wyck in Hoboken, Hendrik and his father and sister boarded a streetcar for Grand Central Station. "We could not see much of New York," Hendrik noted, "but there were people skating in the streets—not on ice skates, but on a board with four iron rollers. You cannot do that in Twente, Zientje; you have to do it on paved roads."

Their train left New York that night. Hendrik draped his jacket over a suitcase for a pillow and sleep came easily. "The conductor told us we would pass Niagara Falls at about 10 a.m., but no such luck. We passed Buffalo, but no waterfalls." At Buffalo they changed trains, and the new train was put aboard a ferry across Lake Erie to Detroit. From there they rolled on through the dark Michigan countryside. The quiet depots along the way—Plymouth, Howell, Lansing, Ionia—slid by indistinguishably until they reached Grand Rapids, shortly after midnight of the second night. After another change of trains and another hour, the cars lumbered into Holland, the Dutch enclave on Lake Michigan.

"I've told you everything in short form," Hendrik concluded. "When you first see the houses it's a little strange.

Most are built of wood. . . . Each house stands alone. Except on the main streets, they're never connected. . . .''

In Hoboken, Hendrik, like the others, had answered questions regarding his age (twenty-three), marital status, literacy, amount of money in his possession (seventy dollars was the average for Dutch immigrants in steerage; Hendrik may have had a bit more), health, occupation, and whether or not he had a prison record. He gave no indication of his anarchist sentiments, nor did he list any affiliations—a good thing, since the most recent immigration law outlawed such radicals. As for a destination, it was not uncommon for immigrants to name a place and then never go there. But Hendrik knew of others from Hengelo who had already come to Holland.

On the train Hendrik helped a Hengelo couple with their crates and loaned the man a dollar. The couple was meeting relatives in Holland and would have a place to live. At the time the Meijers did not know where they would stay. When Hendrik remarked, as they rode the train across Michigan, that he would be glad when the trip was over, the man mumbled noncommittally that there might be a problem with accommodations. But Hendrik had not been hinting for a place to stay, and he was indignant at the uncalled-for refusal to be hospitable. "I always told you I wanted to be independent," he told Zien. "We went to the hotel and our friend . . . did not pay any attention to us anymore." Neither, however, did he pay back the dollar.

Hendrik and his family spent their first night in the Holland Hotel, which sent a carriage to meet incoming trains. But the hotel was expensive, and they left the next morning without breakfast and took lodging with an acquaintance. Four days later they moved into the unfurnished upper flat of a house another friend had rented. They used orange crates for a makeshift kitchen table, and Anna bought a used clock for fifty cents. That, in an anxious, breathless week, was their introduction to this land of wooden houses.

Hendrik enrolled immediately in an evening English class taught by a student at Hope College. But language was hardly a barrier. Most of the townspeople were of Dutch descent, and many were recent immigrants. By 1907, in fact, 10 percent of all the Netherlanders who had ever immigrated were residents of Michigan. In the sixty years since the founding of De Kolonie, Holland's inhabitants had created a bustling town envied by its neighbors for its energy and sometimes patronized for its sober-sided piety. "In the span of one lifetime," wrote Henry S. Lucas in *Netherlanders in America*, "the immigrants from the Netherlands had cleared the forests, laid out their farms, built their houses, barns and churches, and founded a community unique in the annals of American immigration."

It was a pious place, established in 1847 by a party of religious dissenters, "Seceders" from the Dutch Reformed Church. Many had suffered hardship in the Netherlands, particularly as a result of a potato famine in the mid-1840s; but religious discontent was at the heart of their decision to leave. They could not abide a Reformed Church that abandoned the catechism and even rewrote the hymn book to emphasize merely rationalist beliefs. For many of the Seceders, the economic crisis was simply the last straw.

The serious-minded society they had established sixty years earlier still prevailed in 1907. And their hero in Hendrik's time was that same Calvinist preacher who was the nemesis of Nieuwenhuis and the Mantels, Abraham Kuyper. He had risen to power in the Netherlands by exploiting the same vein of conservatism that characterized the religious beliefs of the settlers in western Michigan. Like Kuyper's followers, the immigrants were often farmers, inclined more to quiet domestic life than to politics. "Nobody walks the streets on Sunday," Hendrik reported to Zien a couple of weeks after he arrived. "Everybody (except me) sits in one of the 20 to 25 churches." So thoroughly Dutch was the community that the local newspaper found it noteworthy in the summer of 1907 when the county clerk published a jury list without a single "van" among the surnames.

By the time Hendrik arrived, however, the character of Dutch immigration was changing. Farm families had given way to immigrants like Hendrik—often single and in their teens or twenties, disillusioned with factory life and troubled by family problems. Both conditions influenced Hendrik's decision, but a third factor that motivated many young men to immigrate cannot be overlooked: a yearning for adventure.

*   *   *   *   *

Hendrik's first job, wheeling barrels of pickles at the Heinz factory, left his overalls stiff with salt brine. The pay was poor and the work unappetizing. After ten days he stopped by a furniture factory, where the foreman told him he could start work the next day. After all his frustration with the rigid hiring practices of the Stork mills, everything in America seemed so casual; Hendrik was amazed at the ease with which workers moved from one job to another. He wrote Zien, "You just walk off the job here, and the next day you pick up your pay for the days you worked."

The job at the furniture factory also proved shortlived. As Hendrik wrote, "I was walking down the street and somebody called to me and asked if I had a job." When Hendrik expressed interest, the caller said, "Come along with me," and Hendrik found himself working at another furniture factory. "After half an hour I wanted to leave again. I had put on my hat and coat, but there came the boss. He talked me into staying, and I stayed for one day, working at a saw for $1.50." The day stretched into four weeks, and Hendrik's father found a job there too.

Accustomed to a milder climate, the new arrivals found their first summer in Holland unexpectedly sweltering, with thunderstorms more violent than in the Netherlands. "They say that's because of the lake," Hendrik wrote. "We only live two minutes away." Electrical storms produced a power failure that stalled the trolley on the Grand Rapids line, and on Lake Michigan several boaters narrowly escaped disaster. When a chimney in Hendrik's neighborhood was struck by lightning, the poor woman of the house, according to a newspaper report, "fell into a swoon" after choking on sulphurous fumes.

In the boiling heat of the furniture factory Hendrik had a run-in with an American co-worker. "I stood in front of him with a stick in my hand because he was bothering my dad," he told Zien. "My boss grabbed me, so I took my coat and hat and told him I didn't want to work with the American anymore. Everybody was on my side, and the boss had a nice talk with me and asked me to stay until I went to the foundry [where Hendrik had already lined up another job]." When he left the furniture factory to become a molder, he gave his boss notice. "Usually you just leave without saying anything, but my boss is a nice guy and I wanted to be good to him," he explained. "I told him the reason I wanted to leave (better pay) and he said, 'I can't blame you.' "

Summer in Holland could be idyllic. The beaches attracted wealthy Chicagoans, who came by train or ferry to stay in the big Victorian "cottages" at Macatawa Park. The Meijers' upper flat on West Tenth Street stood just two blocks from Lake Macatawa, which was connected by a channel to Lake Michigan. The city had grown up along Macatawa's eastern and southern shores, with factories directly on the lake. In 1907 incandescent lights illuminated the main streets, and telephones had been installed in many of the commercial buildings. The old wooden sidewalks were being replaced with cement ones, but the automobile remained chiefly a toy of the well-to-do.

Holland residents marked the Fourth of July with bunting and speeches and a big parade through the business district on Eighth Street. They greeted the occasion with the special enthusiasm of newcomers eager to share the American experience—and often with an eye to profit. In fact, Holland surpassed neighboring towns in its display of patriotism. "The Dutch have the reputation of being exceedingly thrifty and putting every cent to account," reported the newspaper in a neighboring town. "It must be calculated that they can see dollars ahead for every cent they invested in the celebration of the Fourth." The city's festivities were kept notably sober, however; visitors from nearby Grand Haven complained that "Holland had the lid on and drinks were few and far between."

During the popular Venetian Festival in August, handsome boats from the yacht club sailed out on Lake Macatawa at dusk surrounded by dozens of dinghies and rowboats. On a sultry Saturday night Hendrik watched the boats assemble in a great regatta, with lanterns strung from their masts and flagpoles, their colored lights dancing on the water. "It was something special," he reported. "The streetcar to the park was full and did not stop on the way to pick up more passengers." Along the shore were roller coasters and other amusements Hendrik had seen only in pictures. Now a member of the town band, he played clarinet in a group that serenaded the crowds.

Holland was, in many ways, a typical American town. Its Dutch-born sons had acquitted themselves with valor in the Civil War. They had evolved a curious tongue called "Yankee Dutch," a dialect which provided no end of amusement for native speakers of English. And the Hollanders applied their severe Protestant idea of a man's "calling" to the American republic at large. They absorbed the spirit of manifest destiny as readily as they organized baseball teams and congregated for Thanksgiving services. They felt that they had a stake in a great democracy and thus had little patience for rabble-rousers. "We will not accept socialism, with its unworkable demands! Still less anarchism, with its wild dreams and demonic tools!" declared *De Grondwet* (The Constitution), the Dutch-language weekly newspaper.

The immigrant tide brought a demand for more housing, and Holland's real estate developers opened new subdivisions, tempting immigrants with astonishingly easy terms of credit. "If you have $50 down you can sign a contract just as though you were buying a sewing machine in Hengelo," Hendrik informed Zien. "Most people get into financial worries right away, and it takes them years to get out. . . . They don't know the value of the dollar." Brower's Furniture Store, for example, advertised itself as "the store that saves you money. The store that grants you credit."

If credit was easy, economic security was more elusive. The new immigrants were greeted by the Panic of 1907, in which thirteen New York banks failed, along with several railroads. As Walter Lord noted in *The Good Years*, "Stocks fell because no one had the money to buy them. Building plans were postponed because no one had the money for construction." Hours were reduced at the foundry where Hendrik worked, and to maintain an income, he ran errands for his boss, installing windows and cleaning up around the shop. He had no family to support: his father and sister (who worked as a maid) had wages coming in, so Hendrik took the downturn with good cheer. After all, he wrote to Zien after a week of odd jobs, "You have to know a little bit about everything in America."

Zien, however, was irritated by news back home that Hendrik had sent a considerable sum to his mother, who, she reminded him, was likely to spend anything she received on liquor. He should be saving for his own return trip, if not for her passage, she wrote. Hendrik tried to assuage her fears. He said that he had not sent much money to his mother, but that one sister to whom he had sent a money order had passed that on to Mrs. Meijer.

As for his mother's condition, Hendrik showed little sympathy. His letters seldom mentioned her, and then only with hostility. Her drinking grew worse after she was separated from her husband. "I suspected it," Hendrik wrote to Zien, "but I'm not going to worry about it. . . . She is responsible for her own deeds. Father could not believe it at first; it seems as though he has been blind all this time."

Hendrik's father was a night watchman at the furniture factory. He was staying off the bottle, but he was lonely. He talked about having his wife come over; but Hendrik was afraid that if she did, his father would go back to his old ways. He was willing to send Maria Meijer a little money, but not to help her immigrate; he was adamant on that point in a letter to Zien.

"This is it . . . ," he wrote after one report from Hengelo. "If she writes 1,000 sob letters she'll get nothing." His father authorized the magistrate in Hengelo to transfer custody of the two youngest children, Tonia and Rika, to his oldest daughter Griet and her husband Engbert Snuiverink—until the girls could immigrate. Thus, bringing over his two other younger sisters became Hendrik's first priority. "Mother does not have a chance yet [of immigrating], Zien, I'll see to that," he added. "She is accusing me of all sorts of bad things, but I don't think she is thinking straight. . . . She was also going to tell the Mantels what kind of a guy I was, so some day you can expect undesirable company. Father's mad at the way she's treated me, and that's only a small part of it."

He told Zien that his plans for bringing his two remaining younger sisters to America depended on his income. "Father and I have not missed a day," he noted proudly. "Father gets homesick for those who stayed behind. It's no wonder, because we've been here five months already."

Payday came at the end of the week. "They give you a check and you take it to the bank to cash it," he wrote. "The banks are very busy here on Saturday." And Saturday night, for the less piously inclined, usually meant a vaudeville show or even a moving picture. Sunday, however, was a different story. "There is not much to do here on Sunday," Hendrik observed. "You can see large groups of people going to church—not because they're so devout, but out of habit, because everybody does it."

The Panic of 1907, combined with the inevitable inability of America to live up to everyone's expectations, took its toll on immigrants. Other Hollanders who had come over during the summer were having trouble finding work. "The Americans call it a depression," Hendrik noted. "It happens every twelve or thirteen years. [The last slump of such magnitude had been the Panic of 1893.] You'd better hold on to the things you have with both hands. It was a good thing we left the two [sisters] in the Netherlands."

Others who had come over with Hendrik were out of work and hungry. Hendrik received a letter from a friend in Paterson, New Jersey. "He does not like it there," he told Zien. "He might go back to the Netherlands. . . . But it is too soon to go back, don't you think? The first year is the hardest. You have to put aside the nice things you enjoyed in the Netherlands. But there are other nice things here. It is just the beginning, and as a single person I would not think of going back to the weaving rooms. . . . For me each tread was a curse." One acquaintance had returned to the Old Country three times, intending each trip back to be permanent. Finally, coming back to Michigan the third time, he declared, "I don't like it [there] anymore." Thus was he cured.

Another friend looked for a job in Grand Rapids and Fort Wayne and returned to Holland empty-handed. The man's wife had recently joined him from the Netherlands. "In the days before his wife was here he spent all of his money, just the same as all his friends did," Hendrik told Zien. "We warned him many times, but he kept saying, 'Oh, it'll be OK.' When his wife came over here, she had to borrow the money [for the trip]—and then she found herself over here in an empty house, with no chair to sit on, no table to put anything on. You'd have to feel awfully lonely."

Some immigrants were reluctant to admit their desperation. One night Hendrik encountered an unemployed acquaintance who had arrived in Holland, Michigan only a few days before he had. "I asked him if he had a place to live," Hendrik wrote. "He said, 'I sleep in restaurants.' But we found out that he slept in police stations, Zientje. He said he had sent $40 to his mother—he didn't want her to know how bad off he was."

In Hendrik's eyes, blame for the Panic rested squarely with America's industrialists. A few of these men had amassed huge fortunes, while most American farmers and wage earners considered themselves fortunate if they made a living. Radicals chafed at the paradox of poverty amid progress. Observed Hendrik, "The capitalists are saying they have overproduction, but we all know better. They had better open the doors of the warehouses. . . . The trustmen like the Rockefellers, the Vanderbilts and the Pierpont Morgans are at fault. They take all the money out of the banks, the banks panic, and then the people hear about it and take out what little money they've got because they get scared—so that leaves no money to go around, and the saying is, 'no money, no work.' Then the production stops."

Nor was this an exclusively radical viewpoint. Hendrik's conclusion was characteristic of the public's attitude. "These few were the enemy," wrote Henry F. May in *The End of American Innocence*. "Powerful and corrupt individuals had perverted the country's institutions and dammed for their own benefit the rivers of progress." Theodore Roosevelt complained of stock manipulators and "the dull, purblind folly of the very rich men."

The festivities of the Christmas season often brought on an immigrant's loneliest moments. Hendrik too felt the touch of homesickness, writing Zien, "I did not dream last year that I would be here now." He sent her his silver watch chain, which a jeweler had fashioned into a bracelet with an American quarter as a charm.

The ragged fringe of ice on the Lake Michigan shore and heavy, frequent snowfalls gave winter a different meaning in Michigan. It snowed in Hengelo, but seldom with much accumulation. Holland, Michigan, however, drew the full force of storms blowing in off Lake Michigan—the lake effect. "If you could hear that wind and see all the snow—and it's still snowing—then you would say that winter in the Old Country is nothing compared with this," Hendrik wrote to Zien. "I sank hip-deep in the snow in some places tonight, and you know, with my long legs that isn't easy."

The molder's trade, with its sand and smoke and plumbago for blacking the core in a hollow casting, was tough and dirty work. Yet Hendrik preferred the rough-and-ready foundry crew to the men he had known in the furniture factories, "hypocrites" who were interested in which church he attended. In an early photograph, Hendrik and three other foundrymen are leaning against an upright casting. All four men are wearing overalls. Hendrik, his cap pushed back on his head at a jaunty angle, rests a shovel on his shoulder and looks into the camera with a sly smile. The wall behind the men is corrugated metal. There are wooden molds on the floor in the foreground, with castings in progress. More molds are stacked along the walls, with bellows and buckets scattered about.

The molders may have been more tolerant, but they were also a rowdy crew. One co-worker had been a foreman at another foundry before he punched his boss. And their pastimes ran to drinking and gambling. Hendrik's aversion to alcohol had been reinforced by the Mantels, who wore the blue buttons of a Dutch temperance group. Zien's mother sent Hendrik a copy of Zola's *L'Assoimoir* (The Dram Shop), a story of the degradation to which the bottle led. Wrote Hendrik, "It explains how a person can fall into temptation and get used to that kind of life. . . . The foundrymen are known as drinkers, but they won't get a chance to waver me." As he noted in another letter, "Almost every night they go to the bar for a barrel of beer for a dollar. There are five of them, and they finish off a barrel. . . . On Saturday night, the guy who is treasurer of the group pays the bill. But I'll spend my hard-earned money in other ways."

He also reassured Zien that he had not neglected the struggle for political change. Within weeks of arriving in Michigan, he had joined a radical group. Although their bark was vastly more threatening than their bite, and their numbers were insignificant, Holland's handful of radicals reflected an element of dissent largely ignored by students of Dutch immigration. "Neither among the Dutch farmers . . . , who are as determinedly independent and individualistic as farmers can be, nor among the Dutch factory workers in Grand Rapids and Holland, Michigan were there any socialists," wrote Henry Lucas, the leading historian of Dutch immigration. He may have been right about the farmers. About the factory workers, however, he was surely mistaken.

Hendrik was disappointed to discover that his fellow workers were more inclined to pragmatic socialism than to the utopian anarchist creed of Domela Nieuwenhuis. Their debates produced a split between socialists concerned chiefly with economic progress and those, like Hendrik, who espoused broader ideals. "We have met three times already," Hendrik informed Zien.

> We had such good discussions, on total abstinence, anarchism, etc. I asked a gentleman of Dutch descent if he had heard of anarchy. "Yes," he said, "but only that those people throw bombs." He is president of the American branch of the socialists. I asked him how he would arrive at socialist unity. His answer was that the economic battle should be the main goal, and that the actions of parliament were of minor importance. His views are the old socialism [that is, of Marxist determinism]. We had a long discussion about total abstinence. I was supported by three people from Zaandam and one Amsterdamer; all four were anarchists. We decided to form a group. We were asked to distribute brochures among the Hollanders. People need it here, because they are all hypocrites.

Hendrik's conservative neighbors were mainly preoccupied with home and church activities or the prospects of the town's baseball club. After visiting a housewife he and Zien had known in Hengelo, Hendrik reported, "Sometimes we discuss things, but one thing is for sure, she knows as much about socialism as cats know about the stars."

The same woman blamed Hendrik when her husband had trouble holding a job. The man had had an accident and, after looking for other work, was digging ditches. "If he would have kept his mouth shut about socialism, none of this would have happened," she told Hendrik. Such nonsense was all right for a bachelor, she added, and at Hendrik's factory no one seemed to care. It was different for her husband. She implied that Hendrik was somehow responsible for his plight. "In the Netherlands," she said, "your *friends* help you when you're out of work, but not here." Hendrik told Zien that he had described Gerhard Mantel's experience to the woman, and how in the Netherlands people also lost their jobs because they spoke out politically.

A typical meeting of the socialist group drew perhaps a dozen young men—all of whom spoke Dutch—and began with the singing of the anthem of the French Revolution, *La Marseillaise*. ("That was always the tune," wrote Walter Lord. "In this confident era when political and social patterns seemed so firmly set, men had to go back more than a hundred years to find the music that could express their anger.") Fifteen people showed up for a lecture on the Panic, and Hendrik noted, "That's good for a city like this."

The *Holland City News* adopted a tolerant, if somewhat patronizing, tone when it announced the visit of a socialist organizer: "Many strong protests have been made against her statements. But whether her statements are rash or not, Mrs. Lewis [the socialist] is a good speaker and the citizens of this city are intelligent enough to listen with comparative immunity to any speaker. If Mrs. Lewis' words must be taken with a grain of salt, Holland can furnish the salt." Such was the tolerance of the Progressive Era, even in a small town with puritanical values. But Holland's inhabitants were no different in this respect from Americans elsewhere. As John Higham noted in *Strangers in the Land*, "A people with great expectations of building a better society could perhaps afford a certain nonchalance toward radical critics of the present one. . . ."

Upon reading of Hendrik's activities, Zien replied, "congratulations on the club you organized." She was impressed with his display of initiative—and his request for books about communism and "individualism"—but she was also beginning to grow concerned about where *she* fit into his plans, and she was terribly sensitive to casual comments she had heard in Hengelo. "They are still thinking you will come back here," she wrote in December. One friend "said you were always so involved in all the movements here—that was your life. So he said you will come back, even if you could do better over there." It was someone else's prediction, but it may have been Zien's hope as well. With it she implied a question she might otherwise have had to bring up directly: What *were* his plans?

"I've been thinking a lot about that question too," Hendrik replied.

> But there's no decision yet. Often I think about what I read in *The Revue* [a Dutch periodical], and I can't wait until *Recht door Zee* comes again to read about the organization and the things going on in Hengelo, and I'd like to be a part of it again and help them fight for the things we stand for. *You*—and that—are so close and important to me. But then I think about the weaving mill and that brings back memories too. How often, on a Sunday evening, did I not say, "And now tomorrow I have to go back to that terrible, damnable factory again?" And I was always the last to go inside.
>
> Now I work in a factory again. And I have a job that takes a lot out of me physically. But I like it so much better here, and I feel at home. The mill was the same thing day in and day out. You are a weaver from birth until death, in one and the same place all the time until you reach your final resting place. I see those terrible factories here too. Like the tannery—I see those workers come out with red around their eyes and tubercular faces. And they carry a smell with them—I couldn't stand that. Then I think how sad it is that they don't know their own luck, and I wish I was so dumb. Maybe I would be happier and not always get so upset by everything I see that's no good and could be so much better.

Zien sent Hendrik a socialist newspaper with an article that reflected her feelings—and supported her case for remaining in the Netherlands. The writer accused emigrant radicals of running away from the problems of Dutch society and the issues for which their comrades fought. Hendrik felt compelled to respond to what he took as a criticism of his own decision to leave: "You said, 'Read this carefully, Meijer.' But I would ask if there's anywhere in the world we can go without coming into conflict with society? I don't know if you agree with me, Zientje, but that doesn't matter. We have disagreed before, so one more time makes no difference."

Hendrik applied for a job at the relatively new Holland Furnace Company, but the position went to an American with more experience whom he knew from the socialist group. One night the American stopped by. "The boss had sent him to

ask if I wanted to work there, and that if I wanted to, I should
be at the factory Tuesday morning," Hendrik told Zien.

> I told him I would be there, and when I got there yesterday, the
> boss told me he would give me a quarter dollar a day more [to
> come and work for him]. In the afternoon I went in to work at
> the old factory and told my boss I was not coming back the next
> day. He asked me how come, etc. Then, sometime later, he came
> back to ask me if I would stay if he gave me a quarter dollar a
> day more too. I don't like to be bought, so I turned him down.
> He got so mad after I told him that that he walked to the
> telephone and told the boss at the other factory not to hire me.
> This morning I went there not knowing anything, and when I
> got there the boss told me what had happened. He said, "The
> president told me not to hire you *today*, but come back tomor-
> row and I'll give you work. . . . I asked your co-workers about
> you and they said you were all right."

The incident ended happily enough, but Hendrik was indignant. "So I was a victim of all this," he wrote. "This is
America, Zientje."

No episode in American history aroused anarchists
everywhere more than the execution in 1886 of six of their comrades (mostly foreign-born) for conspiracy in the bombing that
killed several policemen in Chicago's Haymarket Square.
Nieuwenhuis impressed on Dutch anarchists the significance
of the executions. He urged the Hollanders to wear black arm-
bands every November 11 on the anniversary of the hangings.
The Mantels revered the date with all the solemnity of a
religious holiday—at a time when Americans generally
regarded the event with horror. Actions that to some
symbolized a *battle for* freedom were seen as a *threat to* freedom
by others. As John Higham has observed, "For years the
memory of Haymarket and the dread of imported anarchy
haunted the American consciousness." In Holland, Michigan,
however, Hendrik's organization held an open meeting to
mark the anniversary.

"But it is the same here as in Hengelo," Hendrik wrote.
"Only a few people showed up." Hendrik collected two dollars
in donations for the Anarchist-Communist Congress and sent
Zien a button from the American organization. Anarchism was
hardly a socially acceptable philosophy in the United States
at that time. Hendrik had a Dutch-English booklet on citizenship from the Ottawa County Clerk which contained the warning: "Any person who is an anarchist or a member of any

society teaching disbelief in organized government . . . will be denied citizenship." (Only one other group faced the same threat: polygamists.)

For Zien, Hendrik's commitment to social change was inseparable from his commitment to her. If his fervor flagged, it reflected on his devotion to her. She wondered why he had not yet made a pilgrimage to Chicago. "You are so close by . . . and everyone always talks about the martyrs over there," she said. "If I were you I would visit that city." The thought of going to Chicago had certainly occurred to Hendrik, but as much out of curiosity about this fabled American metropolis as out of homage to the Haymarket martyrs.

*   *   *   *   *

Hendrik was pleased with his job at the Holland Furnace foundry. To Zien he emphasized the progress he had made. "Today you have your choir concert . . . ," he remarked. "How I would like to be there once to hear you. . . . But then I read in *Recht door Zee* how a weaver, with tears in his eyes, has to tell his wife that he made only three guilders and fifty cents that week, and that he worked and slaved for it—then I think how lucky it was for me that I took the step to come over here. . . . And if I ever come back to Hengelo sometime, I'll always be free, because I know now that I can work when I have to, and that I can do more than just weaving."

When his father lost his job and threatened to go back to the Old Country, Hendrik would not hear of it. "There are plenty of people going back," he told Zien, "but when they are standing between all those buildings again in Hengelo, then they will think to themselves what a stupid thing they've done. I don't want to tell anybody to come to America, but once you're here it's dumb for a weaver to go back. The times won't stay the way they are now; they will get better."

Hendrik had reason to feel good about the future. "The factory where I work makes furnaces in three sizes," he wrote. "They are placed in a basement and heat the whole house with either water or air. One of the biggest shareholders bought the patent, and now no one in the whole USA can make the same furnaces. This way they can ask good money for their products. . . ." Even an accident at the foundry left him undaunted. "I'm happy I didn't get hurt more than I did," he told Zien after burning his foot. "I had my pan too full of molten iron and some of it spilled out onto my shoes as I was carrying it." Zien was not surprised by the mishap. "When you were a weaver," she said, "you had to be careful not to get a spool of thread thrown at your head."

One warm and sunny April morning the foreman told the foundry crew, "Boys, you can go home now." The castings were bad and could not be used that day. "I was laughing inside," Hendrik wrote, "because a day off is fine with me. So when I came home I started singing." Memories rushed back of spring and summer in Twente, and swimming in the mill pond at Oele, walking through the fields with Zien, riding his bicycle to the baronet's estate at Twickel. And nostalgia followed: "If I think about all those places I say to myself, 'what a difference!' There are beautiful places here, but they don't mean as much to me yet." He might have recalled Engels's tearful observation when he returned to the Rhineland after a long exile: "What a lovely land, if only one could live in it!"

Hendrik had sent his two younger sisters the money they needed to join him in America. "When my sisters are here," he promised Zien, "I will start saving for my trip back. One more year and then I hope to come back. Maybe I will get a raise soon and then, if I have that money together, and I were willing to spend another couple of years here in diecasting, then if I want to stay in the Netherlands I should be able to find a better job there than weaving. You learn to work here. A molder makes more here in one day than a weaver in Hengelo makes in two."

However, he could hardly have entertained thoughts of going back to the Netherlands for any reason other than to visit Zien. He liked his job and was paid a living wage to do it. And the Americans in the foundry were good people who knew what they were doing. "One American who worked in the other factory and talked a little Dutch laughed once and told me that in America it's like this," Hendrik wrote: " 'Be good, write everything down and don't forget a thing.' And the man is right. Now I know and I will make it. . . . My dad said to me yesterday that out of 100 weavers like me who come here, only 10 will make it. But now I work with pleasure every day, and come home in the same good mood as when I left in the morning." He was on the verge of gaining his long-sought independence. His father had found a job again, Hendrik said. "He and my sisters can make a good living here, so I don't have to worry about them. . . ."

In the spring of 1908, Tonia and Rika Meijer landed in Hoboken and followed the same route Hendrik had taken to

Holland, Michigan the year before. Hendrik and his father took the interurban tram to Grand Rapids to meet their train. For Zien, Hendrik described what must have been a familiar immigrant tale of waiting and worry. They had arrived at the Union Station in Grand Rapids early in the morning. "At 11 a.m. the train from Detroit was coming in and we thought they could be on it," Hendrik reported:

Many people were waiting already. One man was waiting for his bride-to-be, one for his wife. Three boys were waiting for their two sisters and mother and dad, and one boy from Zeeland was waiting for his mother and dad and their six other children. So we didn't have to be afraid that the girls wouldn't have company. The 11 o'clock train arrived in Grand Rapids two hours and forty minutes late, so we sat half asleep in the station until 2 p.m. If you looked around, lots of people were sleeping, and maybe dreaming about the small shoreline of the Netherlands. Then finally the train came, but no emigrants were aboard. Those [who were waiting] who lived in Grand Rapids could go home, but Dad and I, who had come from Holland, and that boy from Zeeland who was waiting for his family . . . could do nothing but go and look around Grand Rapids and wait for the 6:30 train to come in.

First we went into the city, but there you got sick, because it was no better than Amsterdam at night. Carriages with drunks, and prostitutes who make you want to throw up, and you start thinking about when it will all end. So we saw all we wanted to see and went back to the waiting room in the station. There were about ten people there—two black people too. So with talking and sleeping it was finally 6:30 p.m., time for the train to come in. There were two girls on it for the boys who were waiting for them, but no one from our family. I asked one of the ladies if they knew a Tonia, and she said, "Yes, she was in the same cabin with me." She said they were on the same train to Detroit, and then had to change trains and would be in Grand Rapids at 1 a.m. I also talked to a man who said Tonia had been with him to Detroit. He had told her that she had to change trains, but she stayed on the train, and the conductor let her out at the next stop so she could walk back. They finally arrived at 1 a.m., and they looked like they had just taken the train from Zutphen to Hengelo. They told us how nice the trip was. In Grand Rapids we had to wait until 5 a.m. before we could get a tram to Holland.

The boy who had been waiting with us at the station all this time had a nervous spell. In place of one of his brothers, who he could have used on the farm, came a sister with a baby. Tonia told us [the sister] had been working for a family in The Hague and the man of the house got her pregnant. . . . Dad almost cried with that poor boy. The girl was beautiful, about twenty years

old . . . just standing there with her hands in her pockets, looking sad, her child close to her, as if to say, "I'm the guilty
one. . . ."

In Holland a clutch of friends met the newcomers at the
station. The table was set at home; neighbors had baked a cake;
and the house quickly filled up with immigrants anxious for
news from the Old Country. Said Hendrik, "I let them talk
and fell asleep on the sofa."

A friend in New Jersey confided to Hendrik that he had
missed out on labor protests in the factory town of Paterson
because he did not understand English. To Hendrik that was
no excuse. "If I were there I would have found those
meetings," he told Zien.

His own experience, as he became more comfortable with
English, was considerably different. When he joined a new
radical group in Holland, he boasted to Zien, in confidential
if hyperbolic tones, "I am the only Dutch[-speaking] member
of the revolutionary organization in the whole USA. Everything
that is talked about in the meetings is a secret. They work
secretly too, because the detectives, the police dogs and the
police themselves are making it impossible; and they try to do
everything to make the revolutionaries unable to do anything,
just like in Russia." His attitude was common among activists
on the left. As Richard Hofstadter observed in *The Age of
Reform*, "There was something about the Populist imagination
that loved the secret plot and the conspiratorial meeting."

Holland, Michigan's radicals convened on Sunday afternoons. "Sometimes there is a speaker from Chicago or another
city," Hendrik wrote. This group may have been the Modern
Sons of Marx, which had rejoiced the previous summer when
defense attorney Clarence Darrow won an acquittal for union
organizer William "Big Bill" Haywood in the bomb murder
of former Idaho Governor Frank Steuenberg. The case became
a *cause célèbre* for American radicals. Because Steuenberg was
a prominent Dutch-American, the trial was also followed
closely in the Dutch-language press, which called it "Het
Groote Proces" (the Great Trial). According to the *Holland City
News*, the local chapter of the Modern Sons of Marx had sent
a telegram to Haywood with the message, "Wage slavery must
surely go. Congratulations on our victory."

Younger immigrants like Hendrik tended to be more
radical than the largely rural and small-town Hollanders of
previous generations. "We wanted to get some kind of

newspaper together here," Hendrik reported in the spring of 1908.

> We talked about this for a long time, and finally the English-speaking group told us they would help. But just as everything went fine at first, so it's going miserably now. . . . It's impossible to describe to you how it went and whose hands it fell into. The English-speaking ones are social democrats and first-class speculators. The organization named a committee with three people from each group [English-speaking and Dutch-speaking]. We decided on the name *De Volkstem* ["The Peoples' Voice"] for the paper, and each and every one of us was planning to get to work to get the socialist ideas to the people. Good idea, right? It was supposed to be a propaganda paper on a regular basis like *Recht door Zee*, but now it is in the hands of a couple of English [-speaking] socialists who do it on their own without keeping contact with the organization. First they said, "You give us the stories and the material to write from," and we liked that idea. And they told us we could write for them, but not use too much criticism or sharp language, because they would inspect the first edition. I told them that when I write, I can only be sharp and to the point. . . .

Hendrik suspected that the English-speaking leader of the local socialist organization envisioned a publication with commercial potential rather than the organ of party propaganda he had in mind.

"You Dutch people are anarchists," the American told him. "Whenever you put out a paper it goes under."

"Yes," Hendrik replied, "but we stand up again and start over under a different name."

"Nonsense," said the American, "we cannot work with you."

"You knew that before," Hendrik replied. "Only one Netherlander is working with you, and he never knew the battle that went on in the Netherlands."

But the young radicals never lived up to their rhetoric. They found themselves swept up in the tolerant tide of the Progressive Era. That first decade after the turn of the century was, according to Henry F. May, an era of reform in which "radicalism, like religious doubt, had been converted into progress." In Holland there was precious little religious doubt anyway, and radicalism proved to be an equally scarce commodity—not entirely unknown, but never a match for the American Dream. Hendrik too was caught up in the promise of the age. Anything seemed possible, even to a hotheaded young European.

It was hard to keep the flames of radicalism alive in a town like Holland, Michigan in 1908. And in Washington, D.C., a president with the Dutch name of Roosevelt advocated change and reform. The labor unrest which led to violent strikes in the Lake Superior iron range, the breweries of Dayton, or the Philadelphia transit system was unthinkable in De Kolonie. Of one disturbance the *City News* wrote, "There was a strike Saturday in the ranks of the men employed by the city to build a sewer on West Fifteenth Street. A number of Hollanders [i.e., more recent immigrants], claiming that they did not get their share in the American 'Square Deal,' refused to work and became so violent that it nearly came to blows. They were, however, soon appeased and sent to work."

Two of Hendrik's letters to Zien had been published, without his authorization, in *Recht door Zee*. Lightly edited, they turned up on the front page as part of a series on the experiences of American immigrants from Hengelo. Receiving a copy of the "article" from his older sister, Hendrik told Zien: "I started reading 'To the New World, by H. Meijer,' and I still did not get it, because that first sentence was yours, Zientje. But soon I noticed it was my own writing from a letter I had sent you. I was upset that you let others read my letters. I think a letter to you is very personal. . . . When you write your girlfriend, you sometimes write things that aren't suitable to put in a newspaper. And the style of writing is different in a newspaper than in a letter. . . . But then I thought, 'what's done is done.' "

The irritation was only momentary. Surprise turned to pride as he continued, "The by-line wasn't right either, because your name should have been on there too. You played a part in all this and now I get all the honors." Zien explained that her father had shown one of the letters to the publisher, "except the last page, because that was kind of personal." She had written the introductory paragraph herself.

Others were also reading the new correspondent's "article." At a practice of the community band, Hendrik was daydreaming when the director, who thought he had dozed off, tapped him on the shoulder. Hendrik looked up. "Pardon me," he said. "I'm not asleep."

"Well," the conductor replied, "it would be no wonder if you were—someone who writes for newspapers."

Hendrik quit the band to avoid the expense of buying a uniform. When the drummer left and his uniform fit Hendrik,

Naar de Nieuwe Wereld

DOOR

H. MEIJER.

»De Nieuw Amsterdam«, zoo heet het zee-
kasteel wat ons zou overzetten naar gene
zijde van den Oceaan, naar de »nieuwe we-
reld«.

Vanaf Rotterdam zou de reis worden aan-
vaard.

Toen we aan boord kwamen was het daar
een drukte en beweging van belang. Passa-
giers van verschillende naties Russchen, Po-
lakken, Hongaren, Turken, ja bijna alle rassen
waren vertegenwoordigd en stonden als vee
op de markt op één rij geplaatst, met de
scheepspapieren in de hand klaar om geïn-
specteerd te worden. Zoo hondsch als die men-
schen behandeld worden kan ik met de pen
niet duidelijk maken,-ze worden als vee op

"To the New World" was the title of the first of Hendrik Meijer's reports on his immigrant experience to be published in the radical newspaper Recht door Zee.

however, the molder was pressed into service with a new instrument, playing at a rally for Democratic presidential candidate William Jennings Bryan. "And so Saturday I marched with the band," he wrote. "And I really let those drums have it, Zientje; the ground shook under my feet."

In late spring Holland's tulips bloomed and the foundry-men went outside for lunch. Sliding his cap down over his eyes on a sunny day, Hendrik reclined on the grass. A breeze blew off Lake Macatawa, and there was a smell of hyacinths and the trill of birds in the air. "Friday I fell asleep on the grass," he reported to Zien. "I didn't hear the whistle blow or anything. The molders knew I was sleeping, and when I came in late they all yelled 'hooray'. . . and the boss laughed out loud. I like it so well here, Zientje, and I don't have to be afraid of being without work. . . . The times are getting better, so there is more need for workers."

Hendrik witnessed his first Memorial Day, when "they place flowers on the graves of all the soldiers who freed the slaves. . . . Everything is in bloom, and youth is all around us." With warm weather he swam in Lake Macatawa. He bought a violin and began taking lessons. During a slow period at the foundry, he worked as a farm hand. When work picked up again, an unemployed friend took his place on the farm, but the experience introduced him to another occupation and kindled his wanderlust. "I did it just for fun," he told Zien. "I would like to farm, but in the west, in states like Dakota or Montana or Washington. It is such a free life, separated from the world of immorality."

II

I'm like the man who is sentenced to death and gets one last wish. He says he wants to see Naples first. I want to see Chicago and the other big cities before I come back. With that thought, and my violin, I start work every day.

—Hendrik Meijer, 1908

After a year in his new country, Hendrik was acutely aware of his promise to return to Hengelo. "One more year, Zientje," he wrote in June 1908. "The time is going by like a shadow." For Zien, however, time passed more slowly. One can imagine her situation. She was twenty-two years old and had known Hendrik Meijer for three years. She loved him, but could she be certain of his intentions? Her friends were marrying. Neighbors asked her when Hendrik would propose, and she had no good answer.

But Zien kept busy. She directed the children's choir of the socialist organization and played Nora in a production of *A Doll's House*. There were dresses to make—often bridal gowns, of all things—anarchist debates, and meetings of the Malthusian Society, the temperance group, or even, when a communist gathering was canceled for lack of support, a meeting of Catholic workers. It was all very diverting in its way, but for Zien the rounds of lectures and debates and the speeches by the same people on the same subjects must have begun to sound like a broken record.

Hendrik had escaped his former life. For others there was no way out of the working class neighborhoods. "Tukkert's wife tried to kill herself," Zien wrote in one letter. "She slit her throat twice, but they say she will live and is doing pretty well. In a way it's too bad; she did it to get out of her misery, and those people don't want to live any more, no matter what.

That happens more often lately—people hanging themselves. I'm not surprised; it's no wonder in this crazy world."

Many desperate people looked to America for answers. If most Americans were not yet rich, they were assumed to be on their way. Zien relayed to Hendrik a question from her younger brother: "Frans asked me, do you have plenty of money?" Yet if America was the land of plenty, why should Hendrik not be making plans for Zien to join him? A tailor shop customer "could not understand how you could leave me when you were going steady with me," Zien reported. "She thought that was so cruel."

In contrast to Zien's routine, Hendrik's world fairly brimmed with variety. In Grand Rapids he saw a vaudeville show on the Fourth of July. "A group played a comedy about a colored houseboy and we laughed so loud," he wrote. "Then there was music and dancing and someone who was an impersonator. He imitated people like Dreyfus, Zola, Rothschild, Sousa, Bryan, Wilhelm III and more well-known figures." At an amusement park on Reeds Lake, hot-air balloons ascended, dangling gymnasts who performed stunts on a trapeze. The crowd gasped when the acrobats let go of the bar and then opened parachutes and landed in the lake. Wrote Hendrik, "I didn't like to watch them fall. What if the parachutes didn't work? They'd be dead before they hit the water." Performing in a tent were "real Indians—so they said." That night, fireworks exploded over the lake.

After a visit from friends who lived in Chicago, Hendrik determined that that would be his next destination. He saw the visitors off at the Macatawa dock and told Zien, "I would have liked to go with them." So on a Saturday night in the autumn of 1908 he sailed for Chicago. The boat left Holland with a handful of passengers, who paid $2.75 for round-trip tickets. "If you wanted to sleep in a bed both ways, you had to pay $1.50 more," Hendrik reported.

> I just lay down on the carpeted floor. I slept until about 4 a.m., and then I started to tidy up a little bit, got some fresh air and walked up and down. At about 5:45 we could see some buildings, but it was hazy yet. . . .
>
> I had sent a friend a postcard that I was coming, if he would be so good as to come after me. At 6 a.m. we got off the boat. I looked around for my friend, but didn't see him anywhere. One of the passengers wanted to help me, but I told him no thanks, because he was drunk. . . . I waited about 45 minutes, but no one came. So my patience was coming to an end. I asked

two or three people where I could take the train to Larabee Street, but no one could help me out. Then I asked a gentleman from Germany. He pointed to a big, tall building where he said I had to get on the tram. Finally this farmer (me) sat on the tram. I was on the tram for 45 minutes and after all that, the conductor let me off at the wrong place. But after some more asking and looking I found number 513 and I knew they lived upstairs in the back. So I went up the stairs and knocked on the door. They were still in bed and a lady yelled to me to go down the back way. They looked so surprised to see me. It was as if I had just fallen out of the sky.

Hendrik visited the Lincoln Park Zoo and the opera house and saw a play. He bought a postcard for Zien in a bookstore, where "the owner fell over in his chair he was so drunk. You can see real alcoholics here. At 7 a.m. they already walk slowly from one bar to another—women too—some of them have big cans or containers to get beer in."

The wide-eyed young immigrant discovered a city that hummed like a live tension wire. "I have never seen so many people together in one place," he told Zien. Engulfed by pedestrians at the intersection of State and Randolph, he felt quite like a farmer coming to the city for the first time: "In one street 65,000 people pass each other every day." Intent on their business were merchants and shop girls, laborers, junkmen, fruit peddlers, clerks rushing to the commodity and grain markets, newspaper vendors, and deliverymen. Hendrik added: "There are always policemen on the corners blowing their whistles to let people cross or let trams go by, or horses and buggies. One wagon was loaded with coal and it broke down right on the streetcar tracks. In no time at all twenty trams were waiting, filled with people in all their Sunday clothes. . . ." He lost his way and wandered through the stalls of the open market. At a foundry he told a foreman he was looking for work. "Not a chance here," was the reply.

After returning to Holland, he reported to Zien, "I have to go again sometime, because I've only seen a little bit of that big city so far. I want to see the statue of the martyrs [in Haymarket Square] and the meat and sausage company Upton Sinclair's always writing about [the setting for *The Jungle*]."

He had not forgotten, however, his more pressing obligation. He talked about accompanying friends who were planning a visit to the Old Country in 1909. "I will try to get good work in the Netherlands," he told Zien. "But if I have no success, are you still planning to come over here? Write me what your feelings are, okay?'' Their separation bred uncertainty, and he needed to be reassured of her feelings even as he tried to describe his own: ''Do you ever think back on the evenings when we walked to Driene, when all was still around us and at night we could see the lights of Hengelo?'' he asked Zien. ''It was so nice then that we forgot all the misery and sadness in life. But every day I believe I did the best thing for both of us. Because if I had stayed there, what future would I have had—or you either? Now I know more about the world. I've learned and seen different things—and not so much worldly as spiritually.''

In a fortune teller's tent at a Hengelo carnival Zien heard a prediction of her future. ''The fat lady came in behind a curtain,'' she told Hendrik. ''I was already stamping my feet with pleasure. . . . I was going to get *married* within eighteen months—two years at the most, a marriage out of *love*. There would always be *money*, and sickness in the family, although I would not be sick myself. Two children, a boy and a girl, and I would live in this city all the time. So now you know what the future holds, Meijer. . . . I will not leave Hengelo, according to her. She could see it in my face that I was corresponding with someone overseas. We had better break off now,'' she added, making her point with a laugh, ''because I am staying in Hengelo all my life anyway . . . ha . . . ha.''

Hendrik countered with predictions from a seer in Holland whose crystal ball revealed a more favorable future to him: ''First she told me, Zientje, that you would certainly cross the ocean. . . . You were terribly in love with me—is that true? . . . She said you were in financial need, so I sent you a dollar right away. . . .''

If Zien was anxious about emigrating, Hendrik's mother showed no reluctance at all. ''My dad wants it and we can't say anything about it,'' Hendrik explained to Zien. He had no patience with his mother's behavior; she infuriated and embarrassed him. ''Father always had a good stiff drink in Hengelo too,'' he wrote. ''But now he has not had any beer or liquor on his lips for a long time. And it's not because we don't want him to, Zientje, but he said himself he doesn't want to drink anymore. They don't have bars here [in the city of Holland, where an anti-saloon ordinance was in effect], so if you want beer you have to buy it at the brewery for at least a dollar at a time. And you can only buy whiskey at a drugstore after you give your name and address. So that's different than in Hengelo. We hope this and everything else will open her eyes. There's nothing else we can do.''

Hendrik worried about his mother's influence on his youngest sister, thirteen-year-old Rika. ''If all of us were of age it would be different,'' he wrote.

> But Rika would be worse off as a result [of their mother's presence]. If he wants to live with her again, he should go back to the Netherlands; I promised him I would take care of Rika. But that wouldn't work either, Zientje. So I planned to write Griet that dad would not let her [their mother] come over here. . . . But dad didn't like that idea at all. All week he has been so quiet. . . . But we can't do anything about this either; I don't want to make my whole life miserable because of her. We sent her three dollars, and now it's over and done with.

His mother's plans made Zien skeptical of Hendrik's intentions. ''You know what you told me when you left,'' she reminded him.

> If your mother and dad were over there in America with you you would not help them in any way. And I told you, ''You know better than that. . . .'' And you said, ''Zientje, you don't know what I went through with that woman.'' And I know I don't, even though I was brought up in a house where we went through a lot of misery too. The last day you were here you had such a fight with her—you were silent all day. You said that circumstances had made her like that. I believe it; but if your family has to suffer for it, then I think it's better to break up than to stay together. You [Hendrik, his father and sisters] have lived so happily together for a year and a half, and I think this will mean going back to the old ways again.
> You said you were afraid your dad would start drinking again—well, now they will do it together. You know that too. It would be one chance in a thousand that she could quit just like that. Griet said too, ''That lady cannot change.'' I know this for sure, she doesn't care. . . . She even told people that Tonia was not her daughter, just your dad's. . . . When a mother says things like that, then I couldn't live with her. I'm not writing this to hurt you in any way, but you should know what you're getting yourself into before it's too late. You'll probably say, ''I'm leaving again anyway, and if it gets too bad I'll leave right away.'' But can you bear to leave that little girl [Rika] alone? . . .

Zien's warnings changed nothing, however; in Hengelo, Maria Meijer was packing her belongings for the journey.

When Hendrik was not working, or writing letters at the kitchen table with the family's collie curled up at his feet, he practiced his musical instruments. He played clarinet at the wedding reception of a fellow radical who married an American girl. "First it was a real American wedding party," he told Zien, "but then it turned into more of an Old Country wedding with dancing and singing." When the groom brought out beer, Hendrik chided him. "I asked him if his brains needed more help. He said, 'I only had a glass and a half.' I said that made no difference: 'You are going around with it and setting a bad example.' He said he didn't see any harm in it. I said, 'You don't want to see it.'" These social democrats who drink, Hendrik told Zien, "are as dangerous as a bad priest."

* * * * *

While the smelting furnaces were being rebuilt during Christmas week, Hendrik rode back from Grand Rapids with his father one night on the interurban trolley. "It was a good thing we went together," he wrote to Zien, "because after 10 minutes in the tram we found out we were in the wrong one. We had the right line, but the wrong car. We got out in the middle of nowhere to get the right tram. The snow was coming down and the wind was blowing. . . . Dad kept saying, 'I'm so glad I'm not alone.' Then I saw the tram coming. I was waving my arms and he saw us standing there and stopped to pick us up. The people inside looked at us as though we were robbers, but I didn't have any weapons with me."

Hendrik had planned to travel back to Hengelo in the spring of 1909, but that winter he had to inform Zien of a change in plans. The friends with whom he had expected to travel decided instead to strike out for San Francisco. "All of a sudden they got it in their heads to go there, and came to say good-bye to me," he wrote. "One said, 'I'm a wanderer anyway and I'm not tired of it yet.'" Hendrik might have described himself the same way: his wanderlust also remained unsatisfied. He could no more stay in Holland than in Hengelo.

Indeed, sometimes the two cities no longer seemed so far apart. Ice skating out on Lake Macatawa, he met an old friend from the Dutch army. In the band he played clarinet with other Dutch immigrants. In fact, all the musicians were of Dutch descent, although Hendrik was among the few not yet fluent in English. "They call us the Green Dutch," he told Zien, "'Groene Hollanders.'" When the band entertained at the Holland post office, the performance began with a prayer. "It was all in English, and all of a sudden everyone had their eyes closed," he wrote with an air of condescension.

So I amused myself by looking out the window to see what was going on in the street. They're dumb people as far as that goes, Zientje. They are way behind compared to in the Netherlands. If you say, "I don't believe in anything," they just look at you. One man said, "I can see why you wouldn't go to church, but not to believe—that's awful." Of course, I told him why I didn't believe, but then they try to come up with all those Bible verses. . . . Always talking about Christianity and Christ, but they don't practice what they preach.

The concert made him bow out of a trip to Flint with friends who were looking for work in one of the new automobile factories. The friends were hired by Chevrolet; but Hendrik's father and sisters persuaded him not to follow them to the other side of the state. Hendrik had decided, however, that he needed to make more money. When his sister Griet and her husband wanted help to emigrate, his own trip back to Hengelo, once so definite, was further cast into doubt. But he promised Zien, "If I have a good summer, I will come to you."

In April 1909, surely to Zien's dismay, Hendrik quit his job at the furnace factory after arguing with his foreman. "I said to him, 'What do you think I am, a horse or a human?' I picked up my tools and left. . . . I could have done the work, but the boss was after me, I knew that." To heighten Zien's anxiety, Hendrik decided, with the advent of spring, to try his luck in Chicago. His friend there was surprised when Hendrik turned up on his doorstep, but his wife was not. She told her husband, "I thought that hothead would be here sooner or later."

At first Hendrik simply needed a job. He walked across the city in response to a newspaper want ad for "colored wagon washers"—assuming innocently that "colored" referred to the wagons, not the washers. He tried for a conductor's job on the trolley, then searched again for foundry work. Most skilled molders belonged to the Iron Molders Union. In Holland, Hendrik had worked only in nonunion shops, and since he did not have a union card, Chicago's foundries were closed to him. At a union office he was told he would have to be an apprentice molder for four years before he could become a full member of the union. Hendrik added a year onto his Michigan foundry experience and explained that he had worked in the same trade in the Netherlands.

Hired after a two-week wait, he used the interval to explore the metropolis that Carl Sandburg had recently proclaimed "the city of the big shoulders." "I walked miles and never got

tired of the roar of the street—'' the small-town poet wrote after
his first visit,

> . . . the trolley cars, the teamsters, the drays, buggies, surreys,
> and phaetons, the delivery wagons high with boxes, the brewery
> wagons piled with barrels . . . now and again a man in a saddle
> on horseback weaving his way through the traffic. . . . I walked
> around the block in the loop, watched the frameworks of the
> Elevated lines shake and tremble and half expected a train to tum-
> ble down to the street. . . .

Hendrik bought a street map,

> so I could keep track of where I was going. I spent one morning
> at the slaughterhouse that Upton Sinclair and all the others wrote
> about. . . . Every day—no, every hour—six hundred pigs, three
> hundred cows and one thousand sheep are slaughtered there.
> One man chains the legs in back, another kills the animal; the
> next one cleans it; someone else takes the insides out; another
> cuts the head off and drops it in a hole (I don't know where that
> goes). A little farther down they cut it in half. Then the animals
> go to a cooling room, where they are cut up into little pieces.
> Government inspectors are all over. . . .

To its detractors, Chicago was "Sodom on the Lake."
Hotels ran poker and crap games openly, and in the Loop alone
were fifty known gambling joints. Ethnic gangs roamed the
neighborhoods around Maxwell Street, and hoodlums of the
Black Hand shook down innocent Italian immigrants with
impunity. Murders went unsolved because no one dared
testify. No one helped the police, who were themselves often
entangled in a web of corruption.

Hendrik saw the dance halls and hock shops, the tintype
galleries and penny arcades. In the Levee, a notorious district
only a few blocks square, two hundred whorehouses
flourished. On Dearborn Street the Everleigh sisters ran the
world's most famous brothel in a voluptuously decorated man-
sion. Their clients included politicians and police chiefs and
the occasional prince.

From the slaughterhouse Hendrik had walked down Green
Street. "Women were tapping on the windows and calling,
'Come in, gentlemen, come in,' " he wrote. "I thought to
myself, no wonder these girls prefer this life to working in the
place we just came from." A world apart from the red light
district were the neighborhoods of elegant townhouses: "At
night the streets there are full of expensive cars," Hendrik
reported. "These are streets where Chicago's aristocrats have

their parties." Dance music spilled out of windows and doorways, and the avenues glittered with electric lights.

Returning to Holland one weekend to pick up some clothes, Hendrik arrived before dawn. "You should have seen my family's faces when I knocked on the door at 3 a.m.," he told Zien. "Dad couldn't sleep anymore after that. I was wearing a new hat—a brown hat—quite a dandy, Zientje. I will have a new suit made too, and I also have a pair of brown shoes, so now I can show off. We are in Chicago now, you know."

"Showing off" was anathema to Zien. "I cannot see you as a dandy yet," she told Hendrik. "I see you in corduroy pants and your wooden clogs, not with brown shoes and top hat, etc., etc. But as the saying goes, 'When the farmer goes to the city, he is lost.' "

A friend named Koopmans, another restless young mill hand and former Dutch soldier who had arrived in America almost simultaneously with Hendrik, was crossing the country and working at odd jobs. He periodically sent Hendrik postcards, each one bearing a different postmark. The two men regarded each other as kindred spirits, although neither was a particularly diligent correspondent, and Hendrik told Zien that he had asked Koopmans to be patient with him. He had been preoccupied with making his way in Chicago, and besides, he admitted, "writing gets so boring."

The complaint was not intended to reflect on his correspondence with Zien. But by midsummer, ten weeks—and Zien's twenty-third birthday—had passed, and she had received nothing but a card. She was anxious—and furious. Her birthday was hardly news, she wrote. "You don't have to tell me that; I know it already, and in those twenty-three years I've gotten a lot wiser. . . . I always thought I was going with a friend who would treat someone else as he wished to be treated himself. But I was really wrong. Now I understand that what you wrote me about Koopmans was not meant for Koopmans, *but for me.*"

> Is this the same person who, two years ago when he left, was standing with tears in his eyes after I told him I did not think it was a good idea then to stay together and yet be so far away from each other? I knew then that it would not work out. But as the saying goes, tears say more than words. Because you told me that if I didn't want to come over after a couple of years, *you* would come back. . . . But now I know what those tears meant. . . . When you did not feel at home there [in America] you needed me. But now she's too much to bother with. You

wrote me once that you were leading a lonely life. Don't you ever think about anyone else? I think you've had more fun these last two years than I have.

Two and a half months had elapsed since she had heard from him. She was not even certain where he was. Still in Chicago? Back in Holland? She sent her ultimatum in care of his father.

The extended lines of communication had produced a frightful misunderstanding. "My whole body was shaking when I read what you wrote," Hendrik replied. "I cannot understand how you could picture me as such a villain." His sisters had been sick, his father was hurt, and he had rushed from Chicago to Holland and forgotten to mail the letter he had written her. "I have proof of this," he said, in case Zien refused to believe him. He claimed he had come back to his old job at the furnace factory chiefly for her sake. "The cost of living is cheaper in Holland, and I can make the same wages here," he wrote, "and since I want to come back to you, I want to save money."

He defended the time and money he had spent to make life more comfortable for his father and sisters: "Put yourself in my place, Zientje. Could I have done it any differently?" He had not meant to imply, by the remark about Koopmans, that his letters to Zien were also a burden. "Would I do such a terrible thing?" he asked. "If I were that way I wouldn't want to live another minute. And now," he concluded optimistically,

> I hope to get a letter soon. If you want me to, I will come to Hengelo within three or four months. But don't think I would treat my girlfriend like that, Zientje. . . . I don't think I'm such a false person. Maybe I do things I shouldn't do, or should do differently, but I certainly don't do those things on purpose. You know as well as I do that I *love you* a lot, but I didn't know that the world was as black as you painted it, Zientje. . . . Let me know if you want me to come back, or if you believe you are dealing with someone not worth answering.

He told her that he had burned her angry letter, but he had really saved it. Zien was away when Hendrik's reply reached Hengelo, but her parents, aware of her anxiety, opened the letter and forwarded it with a postscript: "You will read that all is okay." Zien did, and she answered immediately with the letter Hendrik had been waiting for. The day it arrived, one of his sisters showed up at the factory with two letters. One, from the Dutch Ministry of War, notified him that his furlough had been extended (he was still on reserve status). The other letter came from Zien:

> I was thinking these past few days that if Meijer still cares for me he will tell me soon. . . . I know it hurt you when you got my letter, but I felt the same hurt. When someone who knew I was going around with you asked me what kind of a job Meijer had, where he was living, did he work for the streetcar line, etc., etc. and I had to say, "I don't know"—that doesn't feel very good. . . .
>
> My thought was that Meijer would like to put an end to our friendship and is afraid to write me about it, so I'll write myself and ask him. . . . If this would have been the case then I really would have been mad, because if you have the nerve to ask me [to wait for you], then you should have the nerve to call it quits. But thank heaven it's not true and I made a mistake thinking it might be.
>
> Maybe we can talk this whole thing out in person. I hate it like this, not knowing what's what. Because then it would be better to break up. You might have had a miserable time, but so did I.

Hendrik's pay was raised to $13.50 per week after he threatened to quit. To Zien he boasted, "When I started in this trade for $1.25 per day [$7.50 for a six-day week], Geels and Riphagen [two immigrants from Hengelo, both of whom worked in furniture factories] laughed at me; and now Geels works ten hours for $1.60. Riphagen . . . still has to pay back the $100 for his trip. . . . I can save money now, and then we know what we have to do. I always took care of other people," he wrote. "Now it's time to think about myself. . . . Not a day passes by that I don't think about you and what happened between us. I think it has brought us closer together. If I had plans to break up, I would have stayed in Chicago, but I never gave that a thought."

When he returned to Holland, Michigan, Hendrik discovered that his father and sisters had been planning for his mother's voyage. "I did not know about this at all," he explained to Zien. "But in a way, I'm glad I didn't know. I pay for my room and board, and if I don't like it anymore, then I'll find another place to live. She will have to live a whole different life here. Yet if she were not here, my dad would not feel right."

For Hendrik, every day seemed to confirm his wisdom in emigrating. Neighborhood youngsters threw a surprise party for Rika's fourteenth birthday. Her life seemed idyllic compared to Hendrik's childhood in Hengelo. As he told Zien, "I was working in the weaving mill [at her age]; and she still has three years to go in school." Even his mother's arrival in the fall of 1909 did nothing to dampen his enthusiasm for the New World. "She likes it real well here," he reported to Zien soon afterward. "And if it stays like this it will be better all the way around." The prediction proved true. The strict mores of a dry town and the discovery that she was diabetic may have helped Maria Meijer stop drinking. Reunited with her husband and children, she spent her remaining years in Holland, Michigan (she died in 1922, at the age of 62) on peaceful if not close terms with her only son.

Time and again, to Zien's distress, Hendrik had delayed his return to Hengelo. But when Zien began to receive money orders from Michigan that would go toward Hendrik's living expenses back in Hengelo he asked:

> Did you really believe I would toy with you? You can't always make yourself as clearly understood as you would like in a letter. I hope to come to the Netherlands as soon as possible—not because I like the Netherlands, but only because I know you are not planning to come over here. If I had not had to come with my family it would have been so different, Zientje. But as the saying goes, "What is, is; and what will be, will be." [He would use the same expression forty years later when his first grocery store burned to the ground.] Yet I can't say as I feel bad about it. I know I helped my dad and even my mother up from out of the mud they were sinking into. That cost me a few years of my life.

Hendrik went so far as to offer to look for a job in Hengelo—if that was truly what Zien wanted. He wished to make it clear in advance, however, that he might not find work there. In that case, his choice was easy: "Then we pack up again," he declared. "I'll tell you once more, I'm not coming back because I like the Netherlands; I have more sad than pleasant memories there. I have had to work every day here too, but now that I know my English better, it gets easier all the time."

Hendrik also anticipated trouble removing Zien from the obsessively cozy Mantel household. Neither of her older brothers had married; everyone still lived under the same roof. Mrs. Mantel made a fuss whenever Zien was away, and Zien wrestled with guilt at the thought of leaving—seemingly hoping that the day of decision would never come. Hendrik urged her to think hard about emigration. What would happen, he mused, if they moved into one of the Dutch neighborhoods on the south side of Chicago? "They call that the sunny side of the city," he wrote. "If you were here, Zientje, we could go there together—but your mother would be worried sick with Zientje so far away."

For her part, Zien hinted that Hendrik might want to consider returning for good. And in doing so she changed her tune about the working conditions her family had fought to improve. Hengelo's revolutionaries-in-waiting, she noted, "don't have to fight for anything anyway. They make good money in Stork's factory. So Meijer, if you want to come back, you can make *good* wages—and that's what you're after. Maybe then . . . you would like to weave again." When a friend found a job that paid nine guilders a day, she asked her boyfriend pointedly, "Can you do better?"

To Hendrik such a comparison meant nothing. The pay scale in the mills might have improved, but he had seen too much to go back. America promised opportunity, while the emotional pull of the old struggle in Hengelo was fading. When Hendrik Meijer walked down Michigan Avenue in a new suit he felt himself the equal of any man. In Hengelo, where rigid class distinctions still prevailed, that sense of self-esteem would have been impossible—even at nine guilders a day.

*   *   *   *   *

When the furnace factory closed down over the Christmas holiday in December 1909, Hendrik accepted a friend's invitation to ride along on a city snowplow. He arose at 4 a.m., "but we were disappointed," he told Zien. "There was not enough snow, so the plows did not go out today. We already have a couple of feet of snow, and now the wind is blowing so hard. . . . It is still snowing and we hope it will keep snowing, and that we'll have to go out tomorrow. I set my alarm for 4 a.m. again." He had fashioned a barbell at the foundry. "This afternoon I lifted it 100 times," he boasted, "my dad 32 and Tonia's boyfriend 34. . . . So don't fight with me, because I'm scared of myself. . . ."

He planned now to depart Michigan in mid-April 1910 and arrive in Hengelo by the first of May—"if I don't get lost in the middle of the ocean," he added. "I read in the newspaper that the *Prinz Wilhelm* got lost coming from the West Indies. And another ship caught fire in mid-ocean. But I'm not scared to go aboard. I have a nice pair of binoculars, and I'll be able to see the coast of the Netherlands from afar."

April stretched into May when he missed a week's work with the flu. Rika had been sick, and he helped pay her medical bills and finance the new furnace her doctor had prescribed to keep the house warmer. Then another sister needed a coat. Each new obligation set back his plans, and he also wanted to visit Chicago one last time. But he had promised Zien in March that by May he would have all the money he needed. "Really, Zientje, for sure," Hendrik insisted. "The letter I receive from you now will be the last one, and then I'll see you in person." He anticipated her frustration at the delay. "I hope to receive a nice, cheerful letter from you," he wrote. "And you won't blame me for putting you through this wait again. If I get the money back sooner, then I'll leave sooner. But it will only be a couple of weeks longer, and no more. . . . It hurts me to disappoint you again. When you receive this letter, some weeks will have passed by already."

When friends asked Zien about Hendrik's long-awaited visit she gave a stock reply: "I told them I will see him when he gets here, but just when . . . I don't know for sure yet." At news of further delays—and his side trip to Chicago—she exploded. "I won't play this game any longer," she wrote.

> I think that if I had known it would go on like this I would not have been crazy enough to wait for three years. . . . It's better that you stay there, until Tonia and Anna are married and your mother and dad and Rika are taken care of too. Then you'll have done real well for your family. But call it quits between us. . . . You keep writing, "This is the last time I have to postpone the trip," but I don't believe it anymore. . . . If you have to wait to save more money, like you wrote in August, that won't help you. If you don't have enough for a trip back after three years, I can't understand it. . . . I can take care of myself, Meijer, and thanks for the nice three years we had. I don't know if you call this a cheerful letter, like you asked me to write. . . . I received your postcard from Chicago. You were right, Meijer, take one more trip. . . . You can't leave Rome without seeing the Pope, right?

But in late April Hendrik booked passage out of Hoboken on the *Nieuw Rotterdam*. On May 20, 1910, he sent Zien a postcard showing Eighth Street in downtown Holland and the finish line of a Grand Rapids-to-Holland auto race. On the back was the message, "I'm leaving here tonight at 9 p.m."

3

Hobo
with a Collar

There is a lot to see here, Zientje, and a lot to learn.
—Hendrik Meijer, 1909

On their first night together Zien and Hendrik saw the sun come up—at least that was how they described it later. "We had hours of tender love and felt so dear to one another and so close," Hendrik wrote after he had returned to the United States. "I hope those days and those tender feelings return. They are always in my thoughts."

That summer he helped the Mantels preserve currants and strawberries. For a few weeks he rejoined the loose fraternity of idealists and rabble-rousers who convened their meetings around the Mantels' kitchen table. The kerosene lamp flickered as they talked into the early hours of the morning. Zien's days and nights were so hectic that for months afterward she attributed her chronic fatigue to a summer of overexertion.

The couple reached a compact that summer. Hendrik knew he could not stay on in Hengelo—and that Zien would have to wait once again while he crossed the ocean. But this time, when he found the right job in the right place—*when he got settled*—she would join him. (Being a progressive young couple, they also decided not to have children right away. "We will use our heads and do without that, so that we can have some fun first," Zien wrote.)

In September 1910, Hendrik returned to America. Aboard the *S.S. Ryndam,* he shared a cabin with a German seminary student who removed his $35 bankroll from the ship's safe as they approached New York. "He is keeping it under his shirt, near his heart," Hendrik noted. "I think he will be quite the minister." He met a woman with three children who was going to America to marry a man she had never met. A young man from Utrecht had noticed Hendrik bid farewell to Zien and assumed he was lonely. "He did not know what was going on between us," Hendrik told Zien, "so it was nice to talk." On Sunday passengers gathered on deck to read the Bible. The choppy crossing was understandably less momentous than Hendrik's first trip three years earlier. "Everything was new and different then," he wrote. "Now I know more and know where I'm going."

Although he disembarked at Hoboken carrying less than the required $25 in his pocket, a new green suit he had bought in Chicago gave him the appearance of a prosperous young man. As he approached customs, he reached confidently into his pocket as though to withdraw his wallet, and the official waved him through. In Bayonne, New Jersey, he looked for work at a Standard Oil refinery, and then made pipe for a few days in Somerville. But the landscape was grim, he grew bored, and moved on to Michigan for the winter. "In the spring I want to go back to Chicago," he told Zien, "and then in the summer I'll go after that conductor's job."

That summer the lovers had sealed their marriage plans. The moment had arrived for Zien to think seriously of emigration; and perhaps she could, finally, because being together had shown them how much they meant to each other. She found it hard to accept his absence. "When I heard someone coming, and he was whistling," she wrote, "without thinking, I thought it was you. . . . Every minute I have been thinking, 'Where would he be now?' "

Back in Holland, Michigan, Hendrik shifted jobs quickly. After stoking coal at the gas company for a while, he met the president of Holland Furnace on the street, and two days later he went back to work in the foundry. He began sending Zien a ten-dollar money order as often as he could—once and occasionally twice a month. "It's a Dutch custom that the husband give all his money to his wife and she is in charge . . . ," Zien wrote. "Slowly I'll teach you all the laws of marriage."

Zien's brother Ferdinand was enthusiastic about her plans to join Hendrik in America. He dreamed of following suit, and Hendrik encouraged his ambitions, thinking his support might smooth the way for Zien. "If he wants to come . . . we could work for a farmer in the western wilderness for $30 a month including room and board," wrote her fiancé. "After eight months the two of us could buy something and farm together. In America, everything is possible."

Zien worried about her mother's reaction to their plans but reassured her that "Meijer has it all figured out. If we have the money, he'll let us come back and visit you, or, better yet, have you come over to visit us."

"I'm too old for that," her mother replied.

"I can imagine that this will be a miserable time for her," Zien told Hendrik, "and that it will be harder for her than we think."

Her mother was hurt, in fact, that the couple had not discussed their plans with the family before Hendrik left. She fretted over her daughter's frequent colds and swollen neck. "If I don't start feeling better, mother won't let me go," Zien informed Hendrik. "She's afraid that the trip will be too much for me." Would not the uncertainty of Zien's health be an unfair burden for Hendrik? Her mother entertained a legion of doubts. Said Zien, "I think she's scared."

By December 1910, Hendrik had paid off the debts incurred on his trip to Hengelo. "That was fast," he boasted, "but it shows that if you work at it you can do it." He ventured to suggest that if he did not find work on the trolley lines in Chicago in the spring, he might keep moving west, perhaps to Seattle or Spokane in the state of Washington. "The climate is beautiful there, or so they say," he wrote. "I was thinking maybe Ferdinand would like to go with me; I would really like that."

In Holland, newspaper reports regularly extolled the virtues of the west. Kansas was calling for 20,000 hands to bring in the fall harvest. The *Holland City News* noted that two young men from neighboring Zeeland "have caught the 'wanderlust' and have left for the wild west. They will go to Colorado, with the intention of spending some time there and perhaps locate there if prospects seem good." Naturally, reports in Dutch-language newspapers held a special credibility for immigrants. One advertisement promised *Gezondheid, Welstand, Zonnenschijn* ("health, prosperity, and sunshine") in Fountain Valley, Colorado. Dutch settlers in Iowa, the Dakotas, Montana, and other points west provided a network of information about jobs and land—and no end of propaganda about the virtues of a particular locale. Railroads offered special rates and sold land along their lines. The Burlington Route boasted of fruitful valleys in the basin of the Big Horn and Yellowstone rivers. Another road offered a round trip from Chicago to Billings, Montana for $25. An advertisement for Texas proclaimed in Dutch, "This is the place where energetic young Hollanders can settle and in a short time become independent."

Hendrik told Zien about a foundry in Washington said to be surrounded by flowers—just like in the Netherlands, he might have added. Yet he wondered how Zien would react to another move, and this time to somewhere so remote, when it was only recently that she had even agreed to emigrate. "It is too much for you all at once," he wrote rather apologetically, "but that's what life is all about."

In late December, Zien told Hendrik that she hoped this, his twenty-seventh birthday, might be his last one alone. But she also noted the death of a woman who had recently emigrated with her husband: "They said her homesickness had a lot to do with it." And she worried lest her mother hear such gossip.

When Hendrik tried to find work on the trolleys in Chicago, his family predicted that he would run amok on the big city tram line. "But no, sir," Hendrik assured Zien. "I'll be real careful, just as careful as I am when I hold you. . . ." On a visit to Chicago after Christmas he figured that his prospects with the tram line looked favorable. The chief of the conductors' and motormen's union said they would be hiring more drivers in the spring. Buoyed by the news, Hendrik hoped Zien might join him the next summer. He reassured her: "I don't think you can die from being homesick. We have not been homesick here."

"Next year," Zien's father told his children when they sat down to dinner in Hengelo on New Year's Day, 1911, "there will only be three of you."

Zien ordered rugs with which to line her packing crate. The Michigan Central Railroad allowed each passenger 150 pounds of baggage. If Hendrik met her in New York, she could bring along up to 300 pounds—a rather significant hope chest. If he was not to be there when she landed (an eventuality she dreaded that grew more likely the further west he went) she would not have to worry, Hendrik told her. "When a woman travels alone, it all depends whose agent you get. You've never seen anything like it, Zientje. When the boat docks, all these agents from the different railroads are there waiting. They tell you, 'I'm from this or that company,' and they bring you to the station. You'll get there no matter what line you take."

But much to Zien's dismay, Hendrik was preoccupied with speculation about the West. Of Washington he wrote, "They say it is beautiful there. Here we have more humidity in the summer and it's colder in the winter. And don't go thinking I would be living in a no man's land. There are nice big cities like Seattle and Spokane. . . . And I know it would be too far for you to travel alone, Zientje, but if Ferdinand would still like to come, you could come to America together in the fall."

Lest she think he was making an impetuous decision to go west, Hendrik noted, "I've always wanted to go there, as long as I've been in America." He took pains to reassure her, however, that his future was not tied to a particular locale. He could be happy anywhere, he said, as long as she was with him. Yet he encouraged her to consider destinations other than the standard Dutch ones of Michigan and the Chicago area. "I don't want you to think I don't like it here or am not making good money," he wrote. "I can do the work, and do it with pleasure, but I would rather have a healthier job." He held to the conviction that whatever the job, he would give it his best, but he was tired of "the indoor life," and harbored a dream of farming his own land.

Although he did not mind the work, the foundry, like the cotton mill, was no place for dreams to stop. His comrades were a jovial crew, but not the sort of whom his fiancee would approve. "We had some variety yesterday," he wrote in January 1911. "Two molders were so drunk they couldn't stand up straight. . . . They had a keg of beer in the barn next to the factory, and they finally both fell to the floor."

Timid and uncertain about her upcoming trip, Zien wanted Hendrik to be there when her boat docked. "I think [you're] taking too much on again," she warned, "and it will go as it did when you were planning to come back over here, when you couldn't make it financially and were so miserable you didn't even want to write anymore. . . . I think it would be better if I stayed here a little longer. Then you'd be free to travel around, because if you don't get that job on the tram, you'll want to go on to Washington (let me know how much farther that is)." Then came the clincher:

> To tell you the truth, Meijer, I think it would be better for you to stay single, then you would not have me to worry about, and you could come and go as you please. I will tell you this much, with all your traveling you will stay poor. I believe that if Meijer has some money it burns a hole in his pocket, so he spends it. . . . And about Ferdinand and me going to Washington together, I don't think that will come true anyway. And I *won't go alone* to Washington. So I think maybe it's better for you to go alone. . . . Our ways are too different. . . .

Zien's words jarred Hendrik into a renewed sense of purpose. In February he announced suddenly that he would not change jobs after all; he would not embark on an adventure that would risk the savings he was setting aside for their future household. "I will take care of my Zientje first, and to hell with the rest," he vowed. Her trip would cost $62, and he planned to send $150 so that she would have enough to buy whatever she wanted to bring along. "If your family will bring you to Rotterdam, then I'll pick you up in Hoboken," he added. He advised her to bring along as many home furnishings as she could, as well as a new blue suit that her brothers could make for him, and he enclosed a sample of American grocery prices.

Hendrik was saying the right things, but his heart was not in it. His resolution to stay in Holland proved to be short-lived, and the symptoms of wanderlust quickly reappeared. "If I were you, I'd go to Washington," a doctor told Hendrik, offering him the help of a relative who lived in Yakima. From the firsthand report of a reliable countryman, a small city in the remote Northwest might shine as radiantly as El Dorado. "They have only two months of light winter, Zientje," Hendrik wrote afterward, "beautiful weather almost all the time. . . . [The doctor's] nephew told him there was plenty of work. I don't plan to throw my money away, but I want to better myself, and it won't make any difference what state we're in—it's all strange to us anyway. . . ."

The argument was a familiar enough one for him to anticipate Zien's reaction: "Now you probably think, 'Yes, but in Holland [Michigan] there are people we know, friends.' But I tell you, I'd rather have no friends than the ones I have here. . . . In September a family from here is going to Washington too, and they promised me they would take you along with them if I go. If they left sooner, I could always come and pick you up [in Holland] myself. . . . There are many women who come to America—and to Washington—all by themselves," he added, playing on her pride, "but I don't expect you to do that." Indeed, he expected a tirade at this latest reversal. If there was a common characteristic of the Mantels, he had observed, it was their tendency to become overwrought, whether the issue was politics or a domestic problem. Hendrik cautioned Zien against undue anxiety: "Don't make yourself nervous about anything now, because when something happens at your house everyone gets upset and all the Mantel family muscles are set in motion. Don't think

I'm going into the wilderness, Zientje. [Yakima] is the same size as [Holland]. I can make the same money, and in the fresh air.

"We would not be the only Hollanders there," he continued. Nor, in the home country of the militant Industrial Workers of the World—the Wobblies—would they be isolated politically: "I read in a socialist newspaper that there are many social democrats there, so as far as discussions go, you don't have to feel left out." (In fact, in the election of 1912 the Socialist party received a higher percentage of the vote in Washington than in any other state.) Although the Wobblies disturbed many Americans with their glib references to "direct action" and its implied threat of violence, they too, like the Mantels, found the idea of revolution gloriously romantic.

Hendrik wasted no time mounting a campaign to justify his adventure. Zien received a plea from his recently married sister Tonia, whose husband John Ver Schure shared Hendrik's wanderlust. Tonia was plainly worried that her husband might follow her brother to Yakima. As her son Len recalled, Hendrik "was always trying to get John away from 'those damn Dutchmen' " in Holland, Michigan. But if Zien were to accompany Hendrik, he would be less likely to encourage Tonia's husband to go. "You see, Zientje," she wrote, "we are married and have a good life together."

> It would be hard for me if we were separated for a while like that. . . . You have to understand that we have been married for ten months now. We have a nice new house, beautiful furniture, and John makes good money. So I said, "What if we don't like it in Washington? Then I've lost everything." Then he [her husband] said, "He who doesn't dare gets nowhere." But Zientje, I hope you won't break up with Henk if he goes to Washington. He really means well and is crazy about you, and you know he's not a guy who plays around. And it wouldn't be so bad for you to go to Washington, because you're coming from the Netherlands anyway, so it should make no difference whether you go to Holland or Washington, because it is all new for you anyway. . . .
>
> I know it's hard to say good-bye to your parents and brothers, but you see, Zientje, you cannot always live with your parents. You'll want to get married someday. . . . If you love Hendrik, it would be hard for you to break up with him, and I know for sure, that he loves you very, very much and it would be good for him if you were over here. . . . You should know that it's healthy to live [in Yakima], and you should also know that foundry work is dangerous. You get burned so easily. Last

week Saturday . . . he burned his heel; then he gets a spot on his neck; then here, then there. . . .

Hendrik had told his sister—as she related it to Zien—that he also had been scared at the prospect of coming to America, and was no less apprehensive about setting out for the Pacific Northwest. "I'm doing it as much for Zientje as for myself," he had said. "And I would not fool her."

As evidence of his commitment to Zien, he bought a thousand-dollar life insurance policy which named her as beneficiary: "So in case you come over here and I should die you'd have enough to go back to your home." The note from the doctor's nephew in Yakima further emboldened him. "I can't be certain you'll get a job here," the man had written, "but they are almost always looking for good people who like to work. . . . They are kind of scared of hiring bums who work for one day and then start to drink again. . . ." The government was hiring laborers for public works projects, such as the construction of irrigation canals and reservoirs and the paving of streets. "I know this," he had concluded, "the living is good here and everyone makes good money. But you have to see that for yourself. The weather is beautiful. Even if you have an outdoor job you can work year-round." Added Hendrik in a postscript, "This person is my doctor's nephew, so I can trust this information."

But Zien's health cast a shadow over Hendrik's plans. A severe and chronic swelling in her neck was diagnosed as an enlargement of her thyroid gland, a goiter. Hendrik adroitly added concern for her ailment to his argument for moving west, emphasizing the benefits of a dry climate and higher elevations. "[In Holland] the climate is such that even strong people suffer from it," he wrote. "The doctors here recommend those western states and say they're the healthiest to live in."

Hendrik had planned to go west by himself—just as he had planned four years earlier to come to America alone. But at the last minute two younger friends, Scholten and Huizinga, decided to go along. "We had some hard times there," he told Zien later. "Sometimes we didn't have a penny to our name. When I hear that song that goes, 'It's raining outside and I don't have any money and I don't know where to go,' I think about my companions and myself in the west."

After waiting in line at an employment office, he got a job as a farm hand. One of his cohorts was not so lucky. "When I turned around I saw Huizinga standing there with tears in his eyes," Hendrik recalled. "When I saw that, I gave the job to him, and then he said to me, 'What are you going to do?' I said, 'Don't worry about me, I can take care of myself.' So he went out to the farm and Scholten and I were left." For several days they subsisted on little more than apples—a Washington variety Hendrik would never eat again. "When the money was gone and we didn't know what to do anymore, I was lucky to get a job at a foundry," he continued. "I asked the boss for a $5 loan, and afterward he forgot to deduct it from my paycheck."

The job paid $2.75 per day. "I melt the iron and then when that's done I mold it," he explained to Zien in April 1911 in the first letter she received from Yakima. "As far as foundries go, I'm in the wrong city, so I'm lucky to get work here, because every day someone comes in asking for a job." Hendrik and Scholten rented a second-story room with a bath and a sink for two dollars a week. "Then we bought a small oil burner and a teapot so we could make breakfast in the morning and lunch at night," he told Zien. "In the afternoon we eat dinner in a Chinese restaurant for 25 cents." With wages of $16.50 a week, and his food and rent costing little more than $5, he could save money once again.

Yakima proved to be all that its boosters promised. Hendrik sent Zien a postcard showing two children surrounded by an abundance of fresh fruit. If life in Holland or Chicago had suggested that America was the land of opportunity, what Hendrik saw in Yakima confirmed it. As recently as the turn of the century, the slopes of the Yakima Valley had been barren hills covered with sagebrush. A decade later the valley was an oasis: water had been diverted from the Yakima River to irrigate the surrounding slopes, and farmers tilled rich topsoil on land where cattle had starved to death a few years before. Opportunities for farmers, wrote Washington historian Norman H. Clark,

> were positively lyrical: twenty dollars would clear an acre of sagebrush and provide it with ditches, and for the man who would cultivate it diligently, it could in two months yield a cash crop of vegetables or alfalfa; in a season a bounty of hops, wheat or grapes; in two years, peaches like the nation had never seen; in three years, apples and pears that would have brought distinction to orchards anywhere in the world.

The Cascade Mountains, with the snowcapped peaks of Mount Adams and Mount Rainier, rose up to the west, protecting the valley from damp coastal winds. Yakima was a frontier town just growing up, large enough to support a modest red light district, but chiefly a place of shaded lawns and bustling stores. Irrigation ditches along the streets enabled residents to cultivate fruit-laden gardens. An electric trolley ran up Yakima Avenue, though buckboards still were the primary mode of transportation. The Hotel Washington and the Yakima Valley Bank occupied corners on the main intersection. Down the street an elderly Indian squaw named Yakima Susie begged for pennies, and a thirteen-year-old boy named William O. Douglas peddled papers for the *Daily Republic*.

Yakima struck more than one newcomer as an enchanted land. The Douglas family had arrived by train late on a spring evening a few years before Hendrik had. "The houses of Yakima were dark. The streets were pitch black. Only the flickering streetlights marked the way," wrote the future justice of the Supreme Court in his autobiography. "A soft, warm southwest wind was blowing over the ridges of the Cascade Mountains. Spring was coming to the Yakima Valley. I felt it in the air."

Orchards climbed the foothills around the city. For many immigrants the American Dream still meant a farm of one's own, and farmers were drawn to the valley. If agriculture was what Hendrik had in mind, however, Zien was not enthusiastic. "What's your idea for work there?" she asked impatiently. "Farm work? You didn't like that when you helped Engbert [his brother-in-law in the Netherlands, with whom he had labored the previous summer], and my sewing hands are no good for it either."

Hendrik sensed Zien's reluctance to leave her familiar surroundings. "From the Netherlands the trip always looks worse than it really is," he wrote. "Ladies who are traveling alone always get lots of help from the conductors. But you don't have to worry about traveling alone, Zientje, I'll see to that." He assured her that either a friend or his sister Tonia's husband would meet the boat in Hoboken and bring her as far as Michigan.

Just as quickly as he had gone to Yakima, however, he talked of moving on. If work slowed down in the fall, he said, he might have to try his luck in Spokane, or even back in Chicago. Zien was not surprised at such speculation: "You are a traveler, I tell you. . . . You wrote that there are so many people who walk with their beds on their backs, so to speak, as they travel from one city to another! That would be something for you too, right? And then me in the woolen blanket on your back . . . (I'm not so heavy). Then you would have everything you needed with you. . . . We could go from city to city."

By May, when Zien had received $40 of the $150 Hendrik had promised for her trip, her fiancé was growing anxious about his future at the foundry. "Last winter they didn't work because the boss left with $5,000," he noted. "But now the factory belongs to some bank." Scholten, his roommate, could not find a job and returned to Michigan.

Few men stayed long at the foundry. As Wally George, biographer of Muskegon foundryman George W. Cannon, observed of Hendrik's fellow molders, "Job movement within their craft was as inevitable as darkness following the day." Hendrik worked alongside four different molders in his first eight weeks. "The first one was Spanish and had come up from Mexico," he wrote to Zien.

> He was almost always drunk, so the boss paid him one after-noon and told him not to come back any more. After that came an Englishman who barely had a shirt on his back. The boss gave him a job, but almost every night he asked for his money, so he was fired too. After that came a nice, clean young man. We worked together and had a lot of fun. He wanted to stay all sum-mer, he said, and then go home to New York. His name was Mike Webb. . . . He worked all week and then the day after pay-day he came in an hour late. And the next day it was close to 9:30 when he came in—drunk. I said to him, "Mike, what are you doing? You started to save some money so you could go home." And after we had a good talk he said, "You're right, but a person is so weak . . ." I told him he should be strong, but he said, "I'll leave with the first train, and I promise you, Henry, I'll be a good man from now on." I don't know if he will, but I know he left on the first train. I was sad when he left. We'd known each other only a short time, but we were good friends.

Unlike Holland, Michigan, with its nearly homogeneous Dutch population, Yakima embodied the American melting pot. William O. Douglas recalled that "class distinctions were nonexistent in our eyes: we went to the same schools as the elite; we competed for grades with them and usually won. We went to the same church." For Hendrik, who was struck by the contrast between the grime of the foundry and the tennis whites of well-to-do children at play down the street, the melting pot meant washing up in the same bucket with a Swede, a Russian, an Englishman, and even some Americans. "I learn all kinds of languages here," Hendrik told Zien. "Two Swedes are in the room next to me . . . and the people I rent my room from are French."

On a day off, Hendrik went "rattlesnake hunting" with friends and swam in the cool Yakima River. He volunteered himself as a guinea pig in a medicine show to get corns treated, and once, strolling down Yakima Avenue, encountered a street-corner evangelist.

"You are all strong people, most of you are working, and who gives you that strength? God!" shouted the preacher to a group of onlookers. "So you should give him something in return."

"I turned and walked away," Hendrik wrote to Zien. "Last week a man was reading from a Bible on a street corner. He was mad at the government. It looked to me like he was a Christian anarchist. After he was done talking, I asked him some questions. I said, 'Isn't it God who makes all this misery?' "

"No," the Christian replied, "God made the people free, and they did all this to themselves."

Replied Hendrik: "Yes, but God is almighty and knows everything; he should have known all this would happen."

"He wanted to leave it up to the people, and he trusted them to be good," answered the Christian.

"Well, that's nice," Hendrik said. "Say you see a blind person and there is a danger that he might walk into a river or something, and I could save him but I don't? Who's at fault then?"

"You are," said the Christian.

"It's the same with God then," Hendrik retorted. "He is at fault, and not the people. If he came to us and said, 'I am here to help you,' then that would be love and I could believe it."

As Hendrik observed to Zien, "Those people are trying to win over your soul, but they don't know anything about what goes on in the world."

Yakima was like Holland in that respect. In its churches, Douglas wrote, "everyone was being prepared for the After Life. The Here and Now of existence was up to the individual." A "social democrat" who had chimed in on Hendrik's side of the argument invited him to a party meeting, but Hendrik told Zien, "I did not feel at home."

The foundry closed temporarily the day former President Theodore Roosevelt came through town on a speaking tour. Hendrik did not idolize him the way many Hollanders did. "The factories were closed until his train departed," he wrote Zien. "There were mothers and little children in the crowd, and those were the ones he talked about the most. He said [to the mothers], 'Give us the children, and give them the future.' Then the people laughed and applauded. After he left, the slaves went back in their holes."

William O. Douglas, then a teenager, had eagerly awaited the former president's arrival. "But when the train pulled in, it was an anticlimax," he wrote many years later. "The charisma which we had expected was missing. There was no loudspeaker and only those in the front rows could hear what he said from the rear platform of the Pullman car. Voiceless, Roosevelt was no magnet, no charmer, and we went away disillusioned."

*   *   *   *   *

In Michigan one of Hendrik's friends had become a barber. "I was thinking, Zientje, that maybe I should try that too," Hendrik ventured. "In Spokane and other big cities they have barber schools, and they say you can learn the trade in six weeks. That doesn't seem possible to me, but I know a guy who learned it and now he works in Chicago for $12 a week plus tips. That's not too much, but you can always start something for yourself." Realizing that any new scheme would only strike Zien as another breach of trust, Hendrik argued that the barbering business would be advantageous not just for him but for *them:* "If you came over here and didn't like it, I could always start up in the Netherlands."

Again Hendrik was stricken by the familiar restlessness. He saw no real opportunity in the Yakima foundry. He wanted something—perhaps not a farm, but at least a trade—that offered the hope of striking out on his own, an expression not so much of an entrepreneurial spirit as of a simple desire for independence. He preferred to be neither capitalist nor wage earner, and he had neither the money nor the background to be a farmer. But a barber—to a man of his background, such an occupation had the ring of a profession. Hendrik's friend was an enthusiastic role model. "I would like to open my own barber shop, because there is nothing better than being your own boss," he told Hendrik, adding, "I was thinking that it would be a good job for you, because you can make good money after a while." Not only that, but "being your own boss" sounded nearly as compelling as the train whistle that once blew outside the Hengelo mill.

However, Zien was in no position to appreciate that impulse. "You wrote that you were planning to learn another trade," she replied.

> I don't know what to think about you sometimes. Have me come over, get married, and go to school to learn another trade? Don't you think you're taking too much hay on your fork? Would it be better if I stayed here this winter to see what you want to do, and at the same time save more money . . . ? How about the job on the tram? I think it would have been better if you had gone to Chicago instead. . . . I want to tell you this too: It won't be as easy to travel all around when we're together as it is when you're alone. Think about that real hard, Henk, before you let me come over. . . .

Before Hendrik could respond, however, events in Hengelo provided him with ample time to contemplate the future. A specialist advised surgery to remove the massive goiter in Zien's neck. Unless she would be thoroughly recovered, there was no question of her making the trip until the following year—1912. Her mother, particularly, was anxious about Zien's health—to the point, one suspects, of using the illness as a means of delaying the trip. Hendrik offered to help pay for the surgery and urged that Zien have it performed in the Netherlands by a doctor she trusted and near her parents, who could tend her. The prospect of another delay did not appear to upset him; it would give him time for barber school in the fall: "Then I can work for half a year in a barbershop and I'll have a good start."

He told the story of a young couple living in his boardinghouse in Yakima. They worked in a store all day and came home to a spartan two-room flat. "This life would not be good for you and me," he said. "Let's not be in too much of a hurry. . . . I might take things lightly sometimes, but there are also moments when I'm real serious, just like anyone else. You wouldn't like it if I did like Karel Keuzekamp, who told his wife how beautiful everything was here, and then when she came over she didn't have a chair to sit on. . . ."

Yakima became a lonelier place after Hendrik's companions departed, and Zien knew the inevitable result: Hendrik would be brooding over his future and hatching new plans. "So now you have more time to think about different things again, and your head is filled with ideas," she observed.

If he planned on barber school later that summer, then she would not even think about coming over in the fall, regardless of how quickly she recovered from her surgery.

On June 2, 1911, the anniversary of his return to Hengelo the year before, Hendrik sent Zien a postcard showing a boy kissing a girl. He asked her, "Do you have the same thought I do—to watch the sun come up with me like we did last year?"

He threatened to quit the foundry unless he got a raise, prompting his supervisor to grumble that they had too many molders to begin with. But at the end of the day the boss called him in and asked, "If I pay you $3 per day will that make you stay?" It did. Hendrik wrote Zien: "You can tell me not to travel and try things, but now you can see that if you never try anything, then you don't get anywhere either. I know that if I had stayed in one place maybe I would have saved more money than I have, but look how much I've learned—all the things you see, they mean something too. Ask most men my age if they have more than me. They don't, and they stayed in one place all the time."

Hendrik held out the possibility that if Zien waited until March—"one winter more"—he could meet her in Hoboken himself. "Wouldn't that be a lot nicer? This isn't just a promise or sweet talk, Zientje, I really mean it."

On June 7, 1911, doctors removed a large growth from Zien's throat. She was placed under local anesthetic only. "They worked on her for two and a half hours without putting her to sleep," Zien's mother informed Hendrik. "That was really something, but it had to be done that way because of her vocal chords. When I saw her that afternoon I got so scared, because she looked more dead than alive." Her brother Wilhelm wrote: "You know Zientje; when something has to be done she is strong and takes it real well." Three days later, Zien described her surgery in a letter so graphic that Hendrik joked about converting to vegetarianism.

"You really went through a lot, girl," he wrote as soon as he heard about the operation. "Many people would have said, 'forget it,' and been too scared. I hope it did you good, and that all the misery is over for you now; then at least you'll know it was for a good reason." She was about to turn twenty-five, and for her twenty-sixth birthday Hendrik promised, "We'll have some cocoa together." As he wrote the letter, someone in the next room was singing "Meet me in dreamland tonight. . . ." "That's such a nice song, Zientje," he added. "I hope it will come true for us."

Recuperating under an umbrella in the Mantel's yard, Zien feigned surprise at receiving a money order from Yakima. "It looks," she observed, "as though I still have a man who keeps his word." But Hendrik was worrying about losing his job, and he advised Zien, "The best thing for you to do is to send letters to my dad's address, because when you receive this letter I don't think I'll be here any more. It is still summertime, and that's the best time to look for work. . . ."

The temperature climbed above one hundred degrees one day while he broke up pig iron with a sledgehammer. "And still in the distance," he mused, "you can see snow on the mountaintops."

The mountaintops receded later that summer as Hendrik came east again by train. At every stop railroad police checked for men riding the rails. "Yakima Bill" was among the most notorious of the railroad "bulls" who chased tramps and vagrants from the yards. "I saw so many hoboes," Hendrik told Zien.

> In Billings, Montana the police got two of them off the train. When we arrived in Spokane a neatly dressed young man asked me if he could use my suitcase. I said, "No, I use it myself for a pillow." Then he asked someone else; I couldn't understand what he wanted with a suitcase. Another man gave him one and he crawled under the seat and put the suitcase in front of him. He sat like that the whole night. In the morning we got a different conductor who saw him sitting there and told him to come out. He got up, combed his hair, brushed off his clothes, and the conductor said, "Your ticket, please." He said, "I have no ticket." The conductor said, "Well then, you have to pay me now." He said, "No money." So the conductor stopped the train in the middle of nowhere and told him to get off.

As the train gathered speed, Hendrik saw his fellow passenger standing by the side of the tracks, "still brushing off his clothes—that's what you call a gentleman hobo."

By late July Hendrik was back in Holland. He may have had to swallow a little pride to return so soon from his vaunted western adventure, for he wrote Zien, "As you can see, I am back in the old city again, and my pen can still write it." He immediately visited the friend who had studied barbering and was making a good living in his own shop. "I have plans to become a barber," Hendrik announced to Zien a week later. "When I came back from the west, I went through the school [in Chicago] and it looked real good to me. . . . I don't want to be in a factory all the time, and if I ever don't like it any more in this country, then I can do that work in the Netherlands as well."

The following week Zien received a postcard from Chicago. "Today I was a barber for the first time," Hendrik wrote. "What a person can do or become, eh?"

II

You are never too old to learn the barber trade, and better your chances for success in life. . . . The industrious, ambitious man should never be satisfied until he is working for himself and is his own master.

—from a brochure of the New Method Barber School, ca. 1911

The first thing a student learned at the New Method Barber School was how to properly hone and strop a razor. "It requires a very short time, however," the school assured prospective students, "and he immediately takes his chair and begins shaving and haircutting."

"The first day all I did was sharpen razor blades," Hendrik informed Zien. "The second day the teacher showed me how to shave the first customer, and then I had to do the second one myself. I did all right. The people were satisfied when I was done with them. The student next to me cut someone on the lip and had a hard time stopping the bleeding."

The school, an unprepossessing storefront on Chicago's West Madison Street, promised the "quickest and most approved methods of teaching." Quick it was. But a barber's first few shaves sometimes brought to mind the trade of his medieval counterpart—the bloodletter. The results were sometimes grim, sometimes hysterical, and sometimes a little of both. "There's one student here we call 'The Butcher,' " Hendrik reported. "When he cuts someone, he wipes it clean with his fingers, and then on his white coat, so by the end of the day he looks like a butcher."

Beginners started in the school's "free department," where there were no mirrors. If the student barbers' efforts were frequently clumsy, however, their clientele seldom complained. The school served westside neighborhoods described by a journalist of the day as a "vast wilderness of shabby houses

. . . mostly wooden, begrimed with soot, rotting, falling to pieces. . . . The streets are quagmires of black mud, and no attempt is made to repair them." Jane Addams had established the Hull House settlement project in this immigrant slum twenty years earlier. Here were neighborhoods where, as the barber school brochure brightly described it, "there is an abundance of free material. The poorer classes, necessarily large in a city of over two million inhabitants, have learned to avail themselves of the gratuitous treatment afforded by this institution, and are glad to present themselves for practice in the free department."

The customers lived up to their billing. "The men who came in were not the best of people," Hendrik wrote to Zien. "If you could hear the stories they tell about their lives as hoboes—some of them are just tramps. If you were a writer you couldn't find any better material."

Tuition for the course was $35 or $40, depending upon the variety of tools a student chose for his first kit. The total cost of the schooling, including Hendrik's room and board with an Irish landlady named Mrs. Gillespie, was about $60—not too much for mastering a new trade.

Once a student learned the basics and could give a shave good enough to justify his charging for it, he advanced to the graduate department, where he took up "shampoos, seafoam, hairsinge, facial massage and all other branches of the trade. . . ." Here customers paid for services rendered—a nickel for a shave, a dime for a haircut. Students kept half of what they took in, which, the school noted, "is often a great help to those whose means are limited, or who wish to economize."

But the New Method Barber School promised much more than a quick course in cutting hair; it offered a young immigrant with an uncertain future nothing less than the American Dream itself. For where else were the twin lures of wanderlust and security more in harmony? "A barber always enjoys the privilege of traveling," the school told prospective students. "He may go around the world if he chooses, and find employment anywhere fancy might induce him to stop; for good, honest, industrious, reliable barbers are needed everywhere. Or, if he prefers to settle down, he may enter business for himself at any time and be his own boss."

What more could a man ask? On the one hand, Hendrik felt the tug of adventure and the urge to explore the continent. On the other, after the years of travel and uncertainty, he needed a job that would allow him to support a wife and some-day raise a family. And he still dared aspire to be his own boss.

"Generally speaking," the barber school's brochure explained, "one takes up barbering with the single idea of making a living from his knowledge. This knowledge can be obtained at less cost and in a shorter time than any other trade, art or profession. . . . That it is fascinating as well as profitable is proven by the fact that so few people ever drop it to take up any other means of getting a livelihood." (In Hendrik's case that claim was both true and false. He certainly did find another means of getting a livelihood, but he cut hair literally until the day he died.) It was secure employment too—a vital concern for the young Hollander at that time. Read the newspapers' "situations wanted" columns, the brochure advised. "Now think. Did you ever see in one of these columns an advertisement from a barber seeking a position?"

After four years in America, Hendrik had a good command of English, but many of his "customers" at the school were also immigrants. The vague way men described their tonsorial preferences was not always easy to translate. Gestures were often required. "People come in wanting different hairstyles," Hendrik noted, "but after you work in the same shop for a while you get to know people, and you know what they like." Students also practiced on each other. When Hendrik took his turn in the chair he received a haircut first, then a shave, then a shampoo complete with finger massage. Finally there was a facial rub from an electric massager and some sweet-smelling lotion for his hair.

Six weeks after the course began, Hendrik returned to Holland, Michigan. He worked nights in his friend's barber-shop, and looked for a daytime job that would tide him over until he found a full-time opening as a barber. But finding another job was not easy. "I cannot do rough work," he explained to Zien, "because then my hands won't be smooth enough to be a barber." He tried working as a painter with his brother-in-law John Ver Schure, but that was no job for a barber. "I got such dirty hands," he said, "and I couldn't get them clean at night." Instead, he found himself bending over a loom again, weaving carpets in nearby Zeeland. Zien had ample reason to wonder whether Hendrik's new trade was a lasting occupation or just another job in an endless series. But she did not want to discourage him from a course that might finally enable her to join him. She sent European razor blades wrapped inside radical newspapers.

This card must be placed in front of your chair, where all can see it, as designated by law.

No. **2020**

Chicago, *Aug 16th* 191 *1*

This Permit Expires *Aug 1st* 191 *4*

This is to Certify, That *Hendrick Meijer*

has been duly registered under Section 8 of the Barbers' State Law regulating the training of apprentices or students in such trade, and has made affidavit that it is his intention to serve his apprenticeship under

Name *New Method Barber School*

Address *612 W Madison St.*

Barber's STUDENT

•In case of any change in employer, instructor, school or shop, this permit **must be returned**, and a new one will be issued.

After a term of three years' practice under a qualified barber, the said applicant shall return this permit and will be notified where to appear for examination.

Any violation of the above rules shall be considered a misdemeanor and shall be punishable under the law governing the Barbers' State Board of Examiners of Illinois.

Barbers' State Board of Examiners of Illinois
Room 410, 30 North Clark St., Chicago

On August 16, 1911, Hendrik Meijer received his student barber's license—to be "placed in front of your chair, where all can see it"—from the State of Illinois.

Hendrik's barber friend longed to return to the Old Country and wanted the younger man to take over his shop— an idea Zien readily encouraged. But Hendrik was not prepared, so soon after learning the trade, to buy his own shop. And he knew the other barber's situation at first hand. "He had it pretty good at home [in the Netherlands]," Hendrik observed. "Personally, I look at things from a different point of view. I was never sorry I came over here. I've seen a lot and been through a lot and have a whole different view of things."

Although he was interested neither in buying the shop in Holland nor in returning to the Netherlands, Hendrik consoled Zien with the promise of his newly acquired skill. If he ever *had* to return to the Netherlands, he could open a shop of his own in Hengelo or Enschede. He hoped someday to have a shop in America; but first he needed the experience that came with a full-time job. He told Zien that once he found something reasonably secure, she could join him. He did not tell her that he preferred not to stay in Holland, where she might take years to learn English, and where their neighbors were some of the same Calvinist countrymen they had rebelled against in Hengelo.

Searching unsuccessfully through the want ads, Hendrik thought again of Chicago. But living there would make it harder to save money for Zien's trip. Nonetheless, he was determined to get out of Holland. As he wrote to Zien:

> I heard two Germans sing from an opera this week: "I'm only a wanderer and nobody knows me," and I thought how true that was. Once you're used to that kind of life, it's hard to abandon it, and you like nothing better than to be here today and there tomorrow. Sometimes I think maybe I should start on my way to New York already, and then stop in Buffalo to see if I could find something there [Zien had a friend there]. . . . It never hurts if you know a little about different things or different places.

His search for work in the new trade continued into Michigan's coldest winter in years. He nearly found a job in Zeeland, but then the shop burned down. "It's a good thing I didn't [get the job]," he reflected. "Otherwise I would have lost $20 worth of tools." He studied want ads, cut his family's hair ("Barbers are good for everything"), and read news of strikes by textile workers in Massachusetts. Hearing of tens of thousands unemployed in Chicago, the one-time follower of Domela Nieuwenhuis mused, "You would think it would lead to something. If all these people would organize, like they did in Amsterdam, then they would have to listen to them. But most of them go to church on Sunday—to thank the Lord for all the good things they received that week."

Presidential politics in 1912 presented the newcomer with an unusually colorful spectacle. Theodore Roosevelt split with the Republican establishment of President William Howard Taft to launch his Bull Moose campaign. Hendrik could not fathom the public's general indifference to the swirl of political activity. Only 40 percent of Holland's voters were registered, he told Zien. "In the Netherlands they want everybody to have the right to vote. Yet when they have the right, as they do here, they couldn't care less. Who will make the laws?" It was enough to inspire a measure of cynicism in a young radical who had identified with the struggle of the masses—and to challenge the assumption of nineteenth-century radicals that giving everyone the vote was a first step toward utopia.

Hendrik despaired of weaving carpets. He complained to a co-worker that if he had to do that kind of work for the rest of his life he would hang himself. The other man was unsympathetic: ''He said to me, without blinking an eye, 'I hope you put the rope around your stomach.' '' When Hendrik admitted a twinge of envy of another man whose wife had joined him in Holland, Zien said, ''Too bad, but that's what you can expect when you want to do all sorts of other things. . . . You are just like my dad: twelve trades, and after the thirteenth, still no job. You'd better keep on weaving your carpets.''

As for barbering, Hendrik told Zien: ''I'd like to find a daytime job, and then, when you come over in the spring, start for myself. I can do the work, but like I said, we have to wait. Time will tell.'' In colder weather men were letting their hair grow out a little and waiting longer between shaves. The barber trade slowed down. ''It is so cold here,'' Hendrik reported. ''They say it hasn't been this cold in years and years. Some people have frostbitten fingers. They say then that you can't feel any pain, but you don't have any feeling left at all. A train was snowed in near here, and the passengers had to be transported away by sled, and when they got to the depot, it was on fire.''

* * * * *

Finally, in March 1912, Hendrik found a full-time job in the little college town of Big Rapids, Michigan, sixty miles north of Grand Rapids. ''I told them there that I had been a barber for three years already,'' he wrote after his first day. ''It went real well today, and if it keeps going like this, then I won't have any complaints. . . . I work in a nice clean barbershop with three chairs and three barbers. One boy keeps everything clean and shines the customers' shoes. He also takes care of the baths; you get seven baths for a dollar.'' Sometimes, with a good tip, Hendrik made a dollar on a single customer. But the days were long. He had to be at the shop, and usually on his feet, from seven a.m. to eight p.m.

The Michigan winter was even harsher that much farther north. Spring came late, and Hendrik's room in a boarding-house felt like a refrigerator. Only days after starting work he told Zien, ''As soon as the sun shines on the other side of the fence . . . I'll go find work in a barbershop in Grand Rapids.'' He also wrote to friends in Buffalo to ask about work there, thinking, as he told Zien, that ''in the big cities maybe it would be easier to find something.'' After four weeks he was ready to leave Big Rapids. ''I am getting sick of this dump,'' he wrote, ''so I'll be going pretty soon.'' Even in April, winter clung to the north woods: "We've had snow for five months now, so I hope summer will be at our doorstep."

His brightest moment in Big Rapids came when he struck up a friendship with a professor of Dutch descent who taught at the local college, Ferris Institute. The professor was the only Netherlander Hendrik met there, and the only man in town with whom he could speak Dutch. "He sat in my chair and we talked," Hendrik told Zien. "He smiled at how much I had already traveled in America. The other barbers said, 'Talk English, you guys.' " But the professor cut short their sarcasm. "You people are laughing because he once wore wooden shoes," he told them, "but he has seen more of America already than you Yankees ever have. He is a hobo with a collar. . . ." The other barbers laughed again.

The professor advised the young barber to get more education. Zien may have sensed seeds of guilt being planted when Hendrik assured her, "But I won't do that; you have been waiting long enough." Still, if things *had* been different, he said, he might have taken the professor's advice. "This is a school where you can learn all kinds of different things. I wish I had known ten years ago what I know now—but that's water under the bridge."

Hendrik lived in a boardinghouse and took his meals in restaurants. "Not a day passes that I don't think of you," he told Zien. "We belong together, so if all goes well, maybe soon we can start our lives together." He made friends with an IWW organizer who had a vaudeville act, but he hardly seemed to miss the petty squabbles and overblown rhetoric of "the struggle."

At the barbershop he earned ten dollars per week, plus half of everything he took in after the first sixteen dollars. But the handsomely appointed shop was not always busy. Farmers with mud on their boots sometimes appeared ill at ease in the fancy surroundings. In his best week Hendrik made only seventeen dollars; and to top it off, he found his boss insufferable.

"I could not get along with this man," he told Zien.

He was so dumb. When I heard him talk sometimes I just wanted to say, "Oh man, I wish you would keep your mouth shut." Not that I had any arguments with him—the barbershop isn't the place for that, or I could never have kept my job. I learned that a long time ago—when and where you can talk. . . .

I got into a fight with him about a simple thing that was missing. He said that I had had it last, and I said he was lying. And it turned into such a fight. I asked for my wages, but he said he didn't want me to leave. So I gave him one week's notice so he could find another barber, though he thought I would stay and promised me more money, etc. But after that week was over I left, because I couldn't stand that man any more.

The following week Hendrik stumbled onto a temporary job in a shop in Greenville, a farming community thirty-five miles northeast of Grand Rapids. He started on a Saturday and made $4.50. Within days the proprietor offered him a permanent position, informing him that his three predecessors—all drunks—had been fired.

The first postcard Zien received from Greenville showed Baldwin Lake, a picturesque setting within the limits of the town. In 1912 the bustling "City of Maples," as boosters hoped it would become known, boasted a population of five thousand. Greenville's largest employer, the Ranney Refrigerator Company, manufactured wooden ice boxes and kitchen cabinets, and the town's potato market once had been the largest in the world.

The fire brigade was still horse-drawn, but change was evident along Lafayette Street, the main thoroughfare. "Ten years ago we would run a block to see an automobile," the *Greenville Independent* reported the week Hendrik arrived. "Now we can hardly miss one purposely when we cross the street." Greenville was largely a Danish settlement, with few Hollanders to be found, and that suited Hendrik just fine. "It's too bad you have to learn English yet, Zientje," he wrote. "I would rather go around with English-speakers than with people from my own country."

The shop on Lafayette Street where Hendrik worked was on the ground floor of a small hotel, the Phelps. Guaranteed $12 per week, plus everything he took in over $18, Hendrik was soon averaging $19.50, plus 70 cents in tips. His chair, in the middle of a line of three, faced a mirror and a countertop filled with bottles of tonic. A spittoon stood at the foot of each chair, and in the middle of the shop was a large porcelain sink for shampoos. On the back wall a shelf held the shaving mugs of regular customers.

Hendrik's luck seemed to change with the seasons, and Zien sensed a new confidence in his letters. She started making her plans as though this might be the time and place they had been waiting for. On a postcard of the hotel and barbershop, Hendrik marked an X with the note, "You can see the lazy barber sit by the window." He had taken a room in a boardinghouse and struck up a warm relationship with his boss, who invited him to dinner one Sunday night. Later they went mushroom hunting. When a barber from Holland called with a job offer, Hendrik declined.

He was amused at the portrait of America painted by another Dutchman in *Recht door Zee*. That immigrant had seen only Holland, Michigan. "He doesn't look any farther than the end of his nose . . . ," wrote Hendrik. "If he had my long nose he would have seen a little more."

Taken with his new surroundings, Hendrik was ready at long last to invite Zien to join him. But now he gave vent to another worry: "I wrote you in my last letter that I planned on staying here," he said in late May 1912. "And the boss would like me here too; he told me that himself. But I'm afraid that when you come over here, there will be no one for you to talk to. There are no Hollanders here, and I work during the week until 8 p.m., and Saturdays until 10 or 11 p.m.—sometimes even until midnight. So now I am afraid you might get lonesome here."

He need not have worried so much about Zien. She was more concerned with how his job went than whether there were other Dutch immigrants living nearby. Of his late hours she said,

> Tell the boss, "When my *wife* is here I can't work that late." But now, all kidding aside, you said that if I could speak English things would be better there and you would stay there. Well, I can learn, if you would see to it that as soon as I get there I can get lessons. I will have the time for it, so maybe it won't take too long. And then we'll find friends to go around with. . . . If you get along so well with the boss, then I could come over to the barbershop in the afternoon to talk and keep you from your work, like you did with me two years ago, remember? And if you don't have any customers, then we can study English together. So I leave it up to you. I'm afraid that if you change [jobs] again, it will cost you money again for sure, and maybe you won't find such a good job.

Her message was plain: sit tight, because this time I am almost on my way. Zien admitted that her letters lacked the tender expressions her fiancé used: "I was not born to do that, Henk. And you have more time for it in the barbershop. I can do it better talking to you in person, and you know that too, right?'' Hendrik was anxious to hear about her preparations. ''I hope in the next letter you can tell me how things are coming along,'' he wrote. ''Otherwise I'll take a Yankee girl; I'm so sick of writing letters all the time.'' By mid-June he had been in Greenville more than two months, and he spoke only English, as he had in Yakima, Chicago, and Big Rapids: ''. . . English all the time,'' he wrote. ''I will always speak with an accent—you keep that. But I can understand it [English] just as well as Dutch.''

Hendrik's boss, Arvin Albro, had a single vice—the ponies. ''And if I guess right,'' Hendrik wrote, ''he loses more often than he wins. He knows I don't approve, so he doesn't say much to me about it. He told me once, 'You know how I gamble, but keep it to yourself, because my wife doesn't know about it.' They have a whole group, and they do it secretly; but when he gets that special paper [the racing form] in the morning I can see in his face whether he won or lost. Sometimes when he wins he tells me about it—he's so happy that he has to tell someone. Lots of things happen in this world, Zientje, and the people who go into the factories day in and day out never find this out.''

Fresh from his experience in Big Rapids, he professed no patience with men who were afraid of losing their jobs or fearful of talking back to their bosses. Now, with Albro, he enjoyed a rapport with an employer such as he had never had before. When he asked how long his job would last, Albro replied, ''You can work for me as long as you want to.'' Hendrik was delighted. ''So that shows that he likes me as much as I like him,'' he told Zien. ''It has been two months since I started working here, so he knows me by now.''

When Zien tried to mask her anxiety about emigrating in cynical remarks about the capitalist ''land of the free,'' Hendrik responded, ''It seems to me that you cannot say good-bye to your Netherlands yet. Well, enjoy it while you can. When you are over here you will think a lot about it. More than once I've thought, 'I love your land, your rivers, your windmills and the wonder of your dikes'—and who wouldn't? That's the way the Netherlands is: too small to feed all of its children. And if there weren't so many people who wanted so much from this earth, then it would be better; but that's the way it is and that's the way it will always be.''

As far as he was concerned, he was in Greenville to stay, and he only awaited news of Zien's plans. ''I think it's time you came over here," he wrote, adding again a threat that she probably took too seriously: "Otherwise, I'll have to find someone here. . . ."

Zien seemed surprised at Hendrik's haste after the months and years of doubt and delay. "Are you in such a hurry all of a sudden, or is it because you're at your third boardinghouse in nine weeks?" she asked. "It seems that you are a difficult person to please as a boarder. I'm glad I know that beforehand. You had better wait now until I come over and take you in as a boarder, although if you're too hard to get along with, then I'll show you the door and take in someone else, just as you were planning to. . . ."

She worried that Hendrik had not saved enough money to buy furniture—or was it that she was now the one trying to buy a little time? Suddenly the roles were reversed. Hendrik appeared more anxious, and Zien was holding back: "Now that I've waited this long, I don't want to be worried about the first bad day we have." So she passed back to him the burden of setting a date: "You write me what time is best for you. . . . You should know that better than I do."

*   *   *   *   *

By August 1912, when Hendrik had been a barber for a year, Zien finally determined her travel plans. She would leave Hengelo in late September or early October, after completing a pattern-making course in Amsterdam. (The course would be useful if she wished to work as a seamstress. She then could make her own clothes in America; and she told Hendrik, "otherwise I won't have anything to do there.") With a departure date of October 12 or October 19, she would sail on either the *S.S. Potsdam* or the *S.S. Nieuw Amsterdam*. "When I get my ticket I'll let you know," she wrote. "What should I put on my trunk, Henk? My address as well as yours? Do you want me to get a ticket to Greenville, or just to New York?" In the midst of her anxiety over preparations, she was relieved when Hendrik promised to meet her in New York.

By mid-September Zien had returned from Amsterdam, and her parents were preparing to see her off. Her father said something about grandchildren, but Zien downplayed the idea. "I told him they are too expensive to have so soon," she wrote. "I can bring along my own baby doll . . . that's cheaper, and that's good enough for me; I'm such a thrifty person anyhow." Finally, she was able to write, "This will be one of the last letters you receive from me, Henk, and then, thank Heaven, the letter-writing is over for you." In the next letter she enclosed a passport photo of herself, adding, for her fiancé's benefit, ". . . and next month, in person."

The week Zien wrote that message, Hendrik sat down one night at the little table in his sparely furnished room. His hand quivered as he picked up a pen; alarm seized him as he began to write, and his letter revealed a man whose world seemed on the verge of crumbling. His boss's father, also a barber, had lately lost his job in Grand Rapids. When a friend of the father stopped by Albro's shop to secure a job for him, Hendrik jumped to a horrified—even paranoid—conclusion: that he should start looking for a job himself, for he would soon be replaced. With Zien scheduled to sail in a matter of days, he panicked. "I have always been on the go," he wrote now, "but it was never my plan to take you away from a good home and bring you over here to take you from city to city." At his wit's end, he imagined that if he lost this job, all his planning was for naught. He had no home to offer Zien. Under the circumstances maybe it would be best, though he could hardly bring himself to suggest it, if she stayed in Hengelo—at least a little while longer.

Zien reacted to the suggestion with the fury of five years' frustration and the terror of a lover whose fondest hopes had been dashed on the brink of realization. She hardly knew where to begin. After "Dear Hendrik," she paused.

> As you can see, I started this letter the same as always. But as soon as I wrote it down I had to put a line through "Dear Hendrik"—and that is done quickly enough. My hand is trembling and I have tears in my eyes as I write you this letter. I received your letter this morning. . . . I am finally told the truth in your own handwriting. I can't bring myself to believe that you would do such a thing. But now I realize that you have used me like a toy all this time. I can't take it any other way: all these years I waited here for you, and then, in a single day, I am told to forget everything. Why didn't you do this sooner . . . ? For a while you planned to change jobs anyway, and now you are all depressed and don't know what to do anymore. I thought you got along with the boss so well. There must be another job for you somewhere. . . . Just think if one of your sisters had been treated this way—how would you have liked that?
>
> The boys have been so busy with your suits and coat to have them all done before I left. [Hendrik had placed an order with the tailorshop for Zien to bring along.] My suitcases are standing here all packed and ready to go, and then I get this letter. It's enough to drive me crazy.

Was there another woman? Was that the real reason why he was suddenly telling her to forget their relationship, after more than five years of waiting? Was it truly the threat of losing his job that had upset him so much? "I thought you were so strong and that it didn't matter what kind of work you did," she continued. "But if this is what you want, then you could never have felt very strongly about me, Meijer, and so it might be better this way."

Then, worried that she might be overstating her case, she tried to look at the situation from his viewpoint:

> Are you so depressed, Henk, that you would throw away everything we had, just like that? There will be work for you again some day, I'm sure of that. And if you cannot be in New York at the dock, then I can write those people from Zaandam whose son is living in Paterson [New Jersey]. They promised me he would see to it that I got to the right train, etc. And I would get there, too, just like Tonia did, if you could just come to Grand Rapids. . . . And the two of us can make it better than you can by yourself. Together we have four hands—can't we make a living for ourselves? That is, if you still love me. . . . I was mistaken when there was trouble between us three years ago, so I hope you are making a mistake now. . . .

To her everlasting relief, her hope was justified. The day after Hendrik mailed his letter of woe, he followed it up with another. He hoped that somehow the second might reach Zien first, for he had made a ghastly error. Albro noticed him moping about and asked if something was wrong. Hendrik confessed his fears to his boss. He recounted the barber's reaction in his second letter to Zien: "He said I didn't have to worry for a moment that he had something against me, and he wanted to do everything for me that was possible. His dad had only asked if he could work for him during the week when the fair was here in Greenville. I misunderstood the whole thing. So this is my explanation for that letter, and I hope you will reconsider."

He urged her to write soon, adding that of course he *would* be waiting in Hoboken when she docked. He gave her a forwarding address at the Amstel Hotel:

> Write me right away, Zientje, and I will be in New York when you arrive. I hope you'll be on board then, because I have to be back to work that next Saturday. You can stay in Holland, Michigan then for a week, with my parents or Tonia, while I get things ready here. I thought it would be silly to buy things when we didn't know yet if we would be staying in Greenville. But

you find something wrong everywhere you go, and as far as my boss is concerned, I never worked for a better one. So it's not my plan to travel any more, especially not now that you'll be here—I would have to be sure that we would be much better off.

He urged her, in a final stab at reassurance, not to worry about him; he would be in Hoboken to meet her. Just remember to bring peppermints (to combat seasickness) and clean clothes in the suitcase she kept with her in her cabin, he said. Now he waited anxiously for Zien's reply.

It was not long in coming. "I am trying to hold onto my pen, that's how shaky I am," she wrote in a surge of relief. "I just received your letter, and I was waiting for it all day yesterday. . . . I am happy that everything is good again. I could not understand how there could be such a change in you in a single day. . . . I lived through two days [between the letters] in such sorrow. . . . I did nothing but cry and write letters. Father did not cancel my trip for the 19th of October, so everything will stay the same." She even said she would understand if he could not make it to Hoboken, although she certainly hoped he would. Her response when she heard, a week before her departure, that he would meet her after all, brought a surge of jublilation and relief and a one-word reply: "Fantastic!"

In Greenville the fair drew more than ten thousand visitors for motorcycle races, a parachute drop, and Buckskin Bill's Wild West Show. Nor was that the only news. The week before, "anti-saloonists" had persuaded the Montcalm County Sheriff to raid the county's blind pigs, and the *Independent* reported that authorities seized "quantities of 'soft' drinks said to contain large percentages of alcohol." In the barbershop, Hendrik, assured of employment, could breathe freely once again.

* * * * *

Mother and daughter cried as the Mantels saw Zien off in Rotterdam. After the ship slipped out of the harbor, her parents and brothers repaired to a vegetarian restaurant for soup, peas, endive, and potatoes. In a letter timed to arrive when her daughter reached Michigan, Mrs. Mantel appended a note to her future son-in-law:

> When you receive this letter, a whole new way of life will have begun for you. You don't have just yourself to take care of anymore. . . . Your wishes to be together have come true, and I hope you will be good to her. . . . I know she will be good to

you. You wrote that you could not take care of her as a mother would, but try to be as good to her as you possibly can. . . . I don't doubt for one minute that you will take care of her. Not only that she will have food to eat, but also that you won't give her the worries of a big family, because it is not good for a woman to have too many children. Now you probably think I'm getting ahead of myself, but it doesn't take long to get that way. I know Zientje is well informed about all those things, and I hope you will agree with her on this, because it would be better if husband and wife were in agreement.

She signed her letter "Mother," adding the postscript, "If this is OK with you, I'll refer to myself that way with you. Tell Zientje to eat well; she has to take care of herself now."

Hendrik rode the train from Detroit to New York with a Greenville haberdasher who was running for Congress. The merchant, a Republican, tried to encourage the barber's interest in American politics, but Hendrik's mind was on other things. He reached Hoboken on the morning of Tuesday, October 28. Zien's ship was scheduled to dock at 6 p.m.

When Zien came down the gangplank and picked her way through the crowd beyond customs, Hendrik was waiting. He drew her into his arms, and the hours and days, months and years, were over. Neither one could believe it. They sent a telegram to Hengelo. Frans, Zien's younger brother, expressed the thoughts of the household: "Maybe Zientje is in New York right now, walking on Meijer's arm."

Arm in arm they did walk, but only briefly. At Niagara the next day, they walked to the falls in a cold rain. (Their daughter later delighted in telling classmates that *her* parents had honeymooned at Niagara Falls *before* they were married.) Hendrik was anxious about being away from his new job; so when they arrived in Grand Rapids on November 1, Zien went on to Holland to stay with Hendrik's family, while he went back to Greenville to find a place for them to live.

Albro helped him hunt for suitable lodging. "We looked at an upstairs apartment," Hendrik told Zien. It was across the street from the shop, "so at lunchtime and at night I won't have to walk very far." But that prospect fell through, and he spent a week searching without success. In the meantime, he wrote to Zien to suggest that his brother-in-law in Holland find out what papers they would need to get married there, or at the county seat in Grand Haven. "I have never done this before," he quipped to Zien, "so I don't know how it works." He asked if she would mind staying with him in the boardinghouse until they found a place to live, but she discouraged that. Meals were a problem for a vegetarian. "It's not as bad for you as it is for me," she told Hendrik.

As to where they got married, that did not much matter. "I don't care about those papers," Zien wrote blithely. "We can make October 28 our wedding day; that's the day I came here on the boat. I like that better, don't you Henk? The day we came together as *friend* and *lover*."

They planned an official wedding date of November 11, 1912—quite coincidentally the anniversary of the Haymarket executions. Hendrik's sister Tonia and her husband accompanied them to the Ottawa County Courthouse in Grand Haven, where a justice of the peace performed the ceremony. Zien's father did not know it was their wedding day when he wrote to them on November 11: "If I were over there I would go to Chicago. We mailed some leaflets out to mark this day. You can read about it in *Recht door Zee;* it was on the front page." The day after their wedding Hendrik left Zien in Holland and returned to Greenville. "Dear wife . . ." he began his first letter to her, adding, "I thought, 'let me see how that looks when I write it.' "

GRAND HAVEN, MICH.

— Huwelijkspapieren werden uitgereikt aan:

Harry E. Nienhus, 28, Olive
Jennie D. Arens, 28, Olive.

— Henry Meyer en Gezina Mantel, beiden van Holland werden Maandag in het huwelijk verbonden door Vrederechter Dickinson. De bruid is nog slechts twee weken in dit land.

Hendrik had anglicized his name when this wedding announcement appeared in De Grondwet, *the Dutch-language newspaper in Holland, Michigan. The account noted that the bride had arrived in the United States barely two weeks before the ceremony.*

Within a week of the wedding, Hendrik had found a place for them to live, a wood-frame duplex near the railroad depot with a "nice living room and kitchen downstairs, a bedroom upstairs that includes a bed we can use, and *electric light*. . . . So this will be just fine for us, and I have the key already.'' The landlord and his wife lived in the other half of the house. ''I've known him for a long time already, and you'll like them too,'' Hendrik told Zien. ''It's about four blocks from the street where I work, so now you can start packing and send me a letter to let me know when you're coming. If you come with the same train I did then you'll have to change trains in Grand Rapids. . . . You'll only have five or ten minutes to do that. But Tonia is coming with you anyway, so she can help. . . .''

Their rent was five dollars per month. Albro gave Hendrik a kitchen table, and there were already some chairs in the house. Now, after all the tension and uncertainty created by one man's decision five years before to escape one life and carve out another, the writing—and the waiting—was over.

''Don't forget to bring my overshoes with you,'' Hendrik reminded Zien in late November 1912. A week later she came to Greenville.

Part II

The Entrepreneur

The world hates change, yet it is the only thing that has brought progress.

—HENDRIK MEIJER

4

The Case of the
Unlucky Landlord

*Everywhere is an atmosphere of hard work. Everyone takes work
seriously and as a matter of course.*

—From a description of Greenville in the City
Directory of Greenville, Michigan, 1917

For virtually all of the next twenty-two years—from 1912 to
1934—Hendrik Meijer made his living as a barber. He was
twenty-eight when he started, and he had just turned fifty
when he took the precarious step in 1934 of selling his barbershop to open a grocery store.

Invariably dapper, tall and broad-shouldered, Hendrik had
a professional appreciation of the importance of appearances.
And life in the barbershop suited him. In a freshly pressed cotton jacket, wool trousers, and ankle-high black shoes, he held
court for a colorful assortment of characters, entertaining them
with stories about life in the Old Country and the West. The
shop, like a general store, was a center of talk. With the banker
Hendrik would debate the merits of American intervention in
the Great War. In the next chair his apprentice might smear
lampblack into a railroad fireman's scalp, then convince him
that he needed a shampoo. Hendrik was ready on a whim to
spring a practical joke on an unwitting patron.

At no time, however, did he accept the idea that he would
be a barber for the rest of his life. For a long time he thought—
naively, it seems in retrospect—that his future lay in farming.
It took the cold splash of the Depression to concentrate his
energies on a more practical venture. Until then, he pursued
one ambition after another. Before his marriage, a restless urge
to explore had led him to Chicago and then west to Washington. Later, in Greenville, he tried to make a living in half a

dozen different ways. But he kept coming back to the barber-shop, because one after another of his schemes failed. In middle age he must have felt as though he were treading water. He approached the age of fifty less secure financially than he had been twenty years before. In 1914, when he opened a barbershop of his own, he and Zien managed to save half his earnings, and the shop prospered. Twenty years later, with a family to support, he faced the Great Depression in a quicksand of debt.

Shyness kept Zien from becoming at ease overnight in her new surroundings, but she was determined to learn English as quickly as possible. In the meantime she did what she could to furnish their home. For cupboards she used orange crates hung with fabric, and she stored potatoes in the cool Michigan cellar. The first few weeks she slept late and occupied herself with baking bread, cooking applesauce, and writing letters. Hendrik bought her a box camera, thinking it might help her become acclimated to her new environment. She learned to develop her own photographs and would include them in a stream of letters to the Netherlands.

In the spring of 1913 Zien sent away for seeds and planted a garden. "You must be proud of those beans you grew, Zientje," wrote Frans, her youngest brother, when the Mantels received a photograph of Zien in her garden. "You look just like a little farmer." Her parents questioned the cooking arrangements. "What about Hendrik?" they asked. "Can he get used to it, or does he still eat meat? You can easily be a vegetarian there in the land of milk and honey. . . ." But Hendrik never became a convert. Spare ribs and sauerkraut remained his favorite dish, and he was known to indulge in a beefsteak.

After Zien arrived, Hendrik's correspondence with the Old Country suffered. The radical newspaper went months without a report. "What's happened to our correspondent in Greenville?" Zien's father asked. "We don't hear much any more for *Recht door Zee*." Indeed, Hendrik had neither the time nor the inclination to dwell on the interminable squabbles in the Netherlands. Nor did he involve himself with Greenville's socialists, who met in a little hall over the Family Theater. With Eugene Debs running for president, the American socialist movement reached its peak in 1912. In predominantly Republican Greenville, for example, Debs's party was second only to the GOP in party registration. As the *Greenville Independent* observed in the winter of 1912, "The socialists seemed to have gulped down the democrats."

Not only was Hendrik preoccupied with Zien and his prospects in Greenville, but as he matured he became less dogmatic, and he increasingly found his radical bias tempered by all that he had experienced in the New World. And, conscious of his immigrant status in a conservative Midwestern town, he grew more reticent about condemning the status quo.

In April 1914, two years after he had been hired as a temporary barber, he left Albro to open a shop of his own in a small building on Greenville's north side. At the age of thirty he had become his own boss.

He rented his new shop from an eccentric Dane, who would not speak with him after Hendrik refused to shave off the man's syphilis sores. The entire shop measured little more than ten feet wide. Two cast-iron chairs with brown leather upholstery and elaborate wrought footrests faced a long mirror. Along the opposite wall stood a row of wooden chairs and a sink for shampoos. Two bare light bulbs hung from the ceiling. A screen door opened onto North Lafayette Street, where a nine-foot wooden barber pole rose from the sidewalk. Standing with his arms crossed, wearing his customary white jacket and bow tie, Hendrik posed by the pole for one of Zien's snapshots.

Zien sewed the shop's linens and laundered the towels, at first by hand, then with a small washing machine. She handled all the money Hendrik took in. "So long as there were only two of us," she said later, "I put half of what we made in the bank." Her tenacious thrift helped Hendrik establish a relationship with the bank that would prove crucial in the Depression years, when he became desperate for credit.

At noon Zien sometimes walked up Lafayette Street, over the Flat River bridge, and past the glove factory, carrying a wicker basket with the lunch she and Hendrik shared at the shop. Around the corner stood the Ranney Refrigerator Company, whose president, Ellis Ranney, was a director of the Commercial State Savings Bank and a regular customer in Hendrik's shop. Reclining in his usual chair, his face lathered for his morning shave, Ranney was a willing sparring partner when the talk turned to politics. "My dad was a very liberal thinker, and you just couldn't get any more conservative than Mr. Ranney," Hendrik's son, Fred, recalled sixty years later. Yet there grew a powerful rapport between the two men. When

Ranney, who was ten years older than his friend, occasionally fell asleep in the barber chair, Hendrik took care of incoming customers in the other chair so Ranney could sleep undisturbed.

*   *   *   *   *

War came to Europe in the summer of 1914, and the Dutch army was mobilized to protect the country's fragile neutrality. In Hengelo, the Mantels received a card ordering Hendrik to report for military service. The Dutch consul in Michigan urged immigrants to return to the defense of the homeland, and in New York a boatload of young men set sail for Rotterdam. "Those Dutch boys who left that poor land to find a better life in this country are going back now to give their lives . . . ," Hendrik wrote to Gerhard Mantel, "and when it's over and done with and they ask for a job, they'll show them the door and tell them it was nice of them to come over and fight for their country. . . . Even married men are going back, so that land must be dear to their hearts."

Hendrik's barbershop patrons wondered whether he had thought of returning to the Old Country—especially since the Dutch government threatened men who did not report for duty with never being allowed to return to the Netherlands. To such questions Hendrik replied, "I'll do as *I* please, and if they find me, then they can do with me what *they* please."

Nationalist passions akin to those that had erupted in Sarajevo with the assassination of the Austrian archduke, Franz Ferdinand, also struck down European radicals and the ideals they revered. French socialist Jean Jaurès was shot in the back in a cafe on the Rue Montmartre by a young nationalist who denounced him as a pacifist and traitor. In the barbershop Hendrik appealed to more conservative patrons with an argument that Jaurès would have appreciated: "I tell them that if an anarchist . . . wants to get rid of someone with a crown on his head, the whole world wants to see him dead. But when that monster with the crown gets it into his head to kill thousands and thousands of people, then you are supposed to agree with him, because your country is telling you to. Is it any wonder that when a son is killed or a father loses his life, those people turn against the government?"

Social Democrats in the German Reichstag supported appropriations for the buildup of Germany's army, overruling socialist leader Karl Liebknecht, who was later killed in the trenches. "Over here they say that Germany wanted to get more territory so it can sell more of the things it makes," Hendrik observed in a letter to the Mantels. "Karl Liebknecht said last year that the Krupp Company spent money in France to start the war, because it would give the company more business. . . . What a rotten world this is. . . . The strong and healthy [young men] go [to war]; the cripples are left home to multiply."

After several Dutch opponents of the war became conscientious objectors, Hendrik wrote to the editor of *Recht door Zee*, "That's the only way out, and all we can do is praise those boys for standing up for their rights. . . ." He was skeptical of the pro-British propaganda in American newspapers that depicted Germans as barbarian "Huns" committing savage atrocities against women and children. But the barbershop provided a good barometer of public opinion. Hendrik observed the American tilt toward England and France and finally toward American intervention—an achievement in part of the press, he concluded cynically. "The *Chicago American, New York American* and the Hearst magazines only print what that millionaire Hearst tells them to," Hendrik wrote. "The real friends of the people are behind bars."

That was strong talk, but he had a point. The jailing of Eugene Debs for his opposition to American involvement in the war reminded Hendrik of things he had seen in Yakima. There, as elsewhere in the West, police were cracking down on the IWW. After cataloguing recent injustices for his friends in Hengelo, Hendrik concluded, "And then you think we live in a free country here . . . ? When you come into New York on the boat the Statue of Liberty looks impressive, but the truth . . ." He left the sentence unfinished. William O. Douglas wrote in his memoirs of the time during his boyhood in Yakima when he watched police round up IWW members. These American workingmen of Hendrik's generation were radicals to be sure; yet often, as in Hendrik's case, only their rhetoric was remotely subversive.

In Hengelo, barely a dozen kilometers from the German border, factories closed so that conscripts could stand in line for their uniforms. Zien's oldest brother, Wilhelm, was called up. As the Germans pushed through Belgium, tension mounted in the border areas. After one particularly anxious weekend, Zien's father wrote, "That whole Saturday you had the feeling that the Germans would come any minute now. Wilhelm was at the tunnel on the Anninksweg. . . . On Sunday . . . the alarm sounded and they had to start digging trenches.'' Roads were barricaded with barbed wire. Rumors flew of the Germans invading from one direction or the British from another. ''Maybe the army wanted to get the military atmosphere going,'' Mantel added. ''Nobody knows for sure what is going on. . . . Hendrik, if I were you, I would take it easy and stay over there. And if your country should need you . . . I can always take your place.''

With the German border closed, the Dutch lost their chief trading partner. Unemployment spurted upward, and the Mantels' tailoring bills went unpaid. An apprentice in Mantel's shop crossed the border to make uniforms for the Germans. The public mood was gloomy, but Mantel was not surprised. ''We have been telling this to the workers for years, and now they can see for themselves what a capitalistic society can do to us,'' he wrote. ''If they don't learn anything from this, they never will.'' Mantel was demoralized by the response of his comrades at a weavers' union meeting. Patriotic zeal—not proletarian disgust—was the prevailing emotion. The capitalist-inspired conflagration in which workers of the world should unite was at hand, and Mantel reported sadly, ''The workers are not interested anymore.'' Domela Nieuwenhuis stopped by the house on the Anninksweg on his way to Enschede, where the town's military commandant barred him from speaking.

On the occasion of Zien's twenty-ninth birthday, her youngest brother, Frans, sent her a copy of Nieuwenhuis's short biographies of four radical heroes: English reformer Robert Owen, Russian anarchists Bakunin and Kropotkin, and Reformation martyr Michael Servetus, who escaped from an Inquisition prison only to be burned at the stake by Calvinist Protestants in Geneva after he was discovered attending a church service in their midst. The three yellow pansies Zien pressed inside the front cover are still there today.

Working alone and entirely dependent on his income from the barbershop, Hendrik was loathe to close the shop—even for a day. Getting away meant finding a substitute to keep the shop open. ''You take what wages you want, or we'll settle that when I hear from you,'' he told a barber from a neighboring town in the spring of 1915, when he and Zien planned a visit to Holland, Michigan.

For Zien, clubs and volunteerism provided ample opportunities for a newcomer to become involved in community life.

She sewed Red Cross bandages for war casualties—"Belly Bands for Belgians," as they were called. And after America entered the war, Hendrik posted a sign in the shop window that showed him to be a Third Liberty Loan subscriber.

The couple had reached the point where they were ready to start a family. On April 3, 1916, Zien gave birth to a daughter, Johanna. The new mother promptly sent a snapshot to Hengelo, where her father observed, "Zientje holds on to little Jo like she used to hold her doll."

*   *   *   *   *

In May 1917 Hendrik sold the barbershop to pursue what he hoped would be a more lucrative opportunity. At the urging of friends at the Holland Furnace Company, he had gone to Holland to talk with his old employers. Holland Furnace, introducing its patented heating systems across the country, offered Hendrik the position of sales manager for the state of Iowa—to be assumed after a short training period in Michigan. He knew how to make the furnaces; now he had to learn sales and installation.

Hendrik was assigned to work with the company's representative in the nearby town of Ionia. Departing Greenville early every Monday morning, he returned home late on Saturday night, leaving only Sunday to spend with his wife and year-old daughter. But the rigors of the work week were hardly the worst of it. Apparently—Hendrik was never certain—the man he was assigned to work with thought that by training Hendrik the company was grooming his replacement. His reaction was to work the young barber absurdly long hours in the heat of summer.

At first Hendrik ascribed the grueling schedule to the other man's incompetence. "I don't think he's opened a store before," he wrote to Zien. But then he began to suspect more serious shortcomings. The Ionia man sometimes failed to report all his sales to the company on time. When Hendrik grew disillusioned with the long hours and suspicious bookkeeping maneuvers, Zien begged him to complain to the company president. But he would not hear of it. He blew up at her, in fact, and said he was not a squealer—that he would quit first.

And quit he did. In August 1917, he left Zien and Jo with his family in Holland, joined the barbers' union, and found a job with a shop in Muskegon. For twenty-five dollars a month he rented an upstairs flat that included a bath but had only an inadequate stove for heat. "It looks clean and we could rent out the front rooms; it would not be so expensive then," he wrote to Zien soon afterward. "I have a job in a shop for $20 per week . . . so you see I did not sit still. . . . If we rent four rooms out, we will have three rooms in the back and the back porch for the baby. If we don't like it and we find something better, then we'll move again." After the United States declared war on the Central Powers, Zien watched soldiers march to the depot on their way to Europe. As she wrote to Hendrik, "You can understand how that makes you feel inside."

The experience with the furnace company had been frustrating. Hendrik remained restless—and not at all certain that his future lay in the barbershop. A friend in Chicago who sold used furniture inspired Hendrik to think about starting such a business in Muskegon. Cutting hair could provide him with a reliable income even as a new venture got underway. So he entered into an agreement with a judge to buy a lot on which to construct a building with space for both a barbershop and a secondhand furniture store. When the judge demanded a kickback on building materials, however, Hendrik balked, and the judge threatened the barber with forfeiture of his down payment. By this time Hendrik's wife and daughter had joined him in Muskegon, and he sent Zien, pushing Jo in the wicker baby carriage, to ask the judge to return their money. The ploy worked; but Hendrik abandoned his Muskegon adventure. Zien remembered the season there as a time of doubt and hardship, and the flat near the waterfront was always cold.

Within the span of several months, Hendrik had shifted his ambitions from barbering to the furnace company to the furniture business, as though waiting for lightning to strike—or not waiting, exactly, because again and again he tried to carve out a different course. But nothing worked. He left Muskegon when the opportunity arose to buy into a barbershop back in Greenville, a downtown operation with three chairs and a cigar counter. And he invested the last of his savings in a dilapidated farmhouse which stood on sixteen acres a mile north of his original barbershop. Quickly he replaced one dream with another: he had begun to fancy himself a farmer.

In the Old Country the odds favored a man's practicing the same trade all his life—and spending his life, as Hendrik had written, in "one and the same place." It need not be so in America, where in 1918 in Greenville, Michigan a new citizen tucked his naturalization papers inside a book by Nieuwenhuis. The Mantels were alternately amused and bewildered by their son-in-law's zigzagging path. Zien's father had stayed in Hengelo, but circumstances had forced him to ply different trades, and he had a sense of Hendrik's restlessness. "The barber and the seamstress on the farm—that's something special," he mused. But the barber was serious. He threw himself into chores and projects, from rebuilding the barn to digging ditches. In the spring of 1919 he bought his first cow, and Zien quickly learned how to milk it.

That spring, Zien became pregnant for the second time, although she did not mention the news to her parents. She wished the pregnancy to be a surprise in the event that her mother could make the transatlantic trip she had long dreamed of. Zien's mother understood as much when the letter arrived in mid-December with news that Zien had given birth to a boy they named Frederik Gerhard Hendrik, after the baby's grand-fathers and father. Was the pregnancy kept secret, Zien's mother asked, "in the event that I would have been there for this happy event?"

Fred Meijer was born in the farmhouse in Eureka Township on December 7, 1919. Ellis Ranney, the icebox manufacturer, sent the only flowers Zien received for the occasion. In the Netherlands Zien's brothers anticipated Hen-drik's reaction to the event. "The boss must be so proud of his son," Frans wrote. "He can be a big help on the farm some day. I can see little Fred. Ger. Henry become a big farmer over there in America. But who knows ahead of time what will become of such a little boy?"

More restrictive immigration laws, Frans Mantel's marriage plans, and a freak accident in the tailorshop, in which a heavy sewing machine fell on Mrs. Mantel's foot, conspired to under-mine her plans to visit America. Mrs. Mantel's injury appar-ently aggravated a case of rheumatism in her leg. "I always have to have something go wrong with me," she said. When she began vomiting and suffered severe pain in her stomach, Zien's father wrote to Hendrik, "If mother doesn't get any bet-ter, don't you think it would be good for Zientje to come over here in case her sickness takes a turn for the worse? . . . Maybe Zientje could come over with little Frederik. . . ." Mantel enclosed a few lines from his wife, noting, "She is so weak she could not finish the letter."

Gerhard Mantel's suggestion came at an awkward time. Hendrik's savings had been nearly exhausted by the episode in Muskegon and buying the barbershop partnership and farmhouse in Greenville. He was reluctant simply to pack his wife off, yet Zien was the only surviving Mantel daughter, and closest of all the children to her mother. Now, by all indications, her mother might be dying.

In August 1920, with Johanna four years old and Fred barely eight months, the family left the farm vacant and departed for Hengelo. This visit contrasted sharply with the carefree summer Hendrik had spent with Zien and her family ten years earlier. Now he and Zien were married, with children and a mortgage and business commitments in Greenville. The trip jeopardized the security Hendrik had struggled for and had only begun to achieve, but he thought it important—and Zien never forgot his decision.

In the Old Country surprisingly little had changed. Hendrik and Zien walked through the woods on the estate at Twickel, and Hendrik carved their initials in the trunk of an oak tree. By the time the family returned to America several weeks later, Mrs. Mantel's spirits revived and her health appeared much improved. (Indeed, she lived three years longer, dying at the age of sixty-three in August 1923.)

While in the Netherlands, Hendrik placed advertisements in Twente newspapers offering to represent Dutch manufacturers in the United States. A mill in Zwolle arranged for him to sell its lace and linens, and upon his return Hendrik tried without success to peddle the lines in Chicago. At his suggestion, the mill dropped its prices. He was urged to try the big city again. "You should be able to do some business now," they advised him when the price reduction came through. But no orders were forthcoming. Perhaps Hendrik was not born to be a salesman; he chose the week of Pentecost to make a spring trip to Chicago. From the Netherlands, the textile manufacturer inquired sarcastically, "Don't you understand that most of the business people are traveling [on holidays] or not in a mood to buy?"

Hendrik moved from one enterprise to another as readily as the wind shifted. He thought of selling linen tablecloths, then turned to barber's blades, hoping to sell to American barbers, with the Mantels buying the product directly from the factory. "I will send you $200," he wrote to Gerhard Mantel. "Then you can see how many you can buy with that. . . . If they are cheaper by the five hundred, then I'll let you make the decision." Nearing middle age, with a family to support, he was trying to go in several directions at once.

KANTFABRIEK TWENTHE
BORNE, HOLLAND

H. MEYER, REPRESENTATIVE

Hendrik used this business card on sales trips for a Dutch textile mill.

During the summer of 1921, Hendrik ventured into the lace trade once again. At the urging of his Dutch suppliers, he went to New York. "Now is the season for selling," they told him. When he complained about the cost of traveling, they offered to pay some of his expenses, observing impatiently, "We hope this satisfies you." Hendrik had yet to make a sale.

"Because you're a complete stranger to New York," the textile house noted, "please be advised that you should take along on commission a traveling salesman who is used to visiting New York." The company offered to throw in an extra 2 percent commission if he took their advice, adding, "As you can see, we are always trying to bend over backwards, trusting that you will do the same for us in New York by taking care of it to the best of your ability. . . . We are very eager to hear from you and would like you to send us a telegram 'left today' as soon as you leave for New York. . . . We'll pay for the cost of the telegram."

Heedless of their advice, Hendrik set out by himself on a sweltering day—a Jewish holiday, of all things, so that many of his contacts were not available—possessing neither the skills nor the tenacity a good salesman required. After one unsuccessful appointment, he walked from 36th Street to the Metropolitan Museum. "There were beautiful paintings by Rembrandt, Potter, and Israels, but not half as many as in Amsterdam," he wrote to Zien. "Then I went to the park and sat down, dreaming away. Once in a while I would fall asleep. All of a sudden a man sat down next to me and told me his hard-luck story. He said he was a diamond polisher. . . ." Learning that Hendrik was a Mason, he called him "brother" and showed him his Masonic pin.

The supplier had sent a list of thirty potential customers in Manhattan. Hendrik called on several and noted their responses alongside their names: "genoeg aan hand" (enough on hand), "te hoog" (prices too high), and so forth. He fanned himself with his hat as he trudged along with the big sample case. "I haven't sweated so much since I left the foundry," he told Zien. And when the day was over, he had nothing to show for his efforts.

That fall the lacemaker, despite—or perhaps because of—its grand aspirations for an export market in the United States, went out of business. When the value of the Deutschmark began to collapse under the Weimar Republic, competitors from Germany undercut the prices of Dutch manufacturers, and Hendrik's talents were no longer required. "So Meijer won't become a great salesman for that company," Zien's father observed.

In Greenville, however, the barberhop where Hendrik had resumed his partnership was actually flourishing. He bought his first car, a used Model T, then traded it for a Chevrolet. He took the family on weekend excursions to Holland. (Detroit was still a grueling seven-hour journey by automobile.) By 1922 he was buying white leghorn chicks for the farm, but he had also held onto the blueprint for the commercial building he had once envisioned in Muskegon.

In 1923 he bought the corner lot south of his original barbershop on Lafayette and Charles streets in North Greenville. "We don't have a good barber on the north side," Ellis Ranney had told him, and Hendrik planned a new shop that would fill that need. The property, 22 feet wide by 82½ feet deep, cost $1,500. Ranney helped get the bank to approve the mortgage. Later that year Hendrik bought a boiler out of war surplus stock and began work on the building he had been thinking about for a half dozen years. Just below the roof at the top of the two-story, shale tile facade he affixed a stone plaque. Ranney persuaded him to have his name—the anglicized *Meyer* Hendrik used in those years—and the date—1923—etched on the plaque—because, as Ranney told him while they watched the construction, "You may never build another one."

After selling his partnership interest in the barbershop downtown, Hendrik installed his new shop in the basement of the North Greenville building. Beneath a barber pole, an outside stairwell led down off the sidewalk to the shop below.

Having discarded the idea of a used furniture business, Hendrik looked for another tenant, a store or a restaurant, for the main floor, and added rental apartments upstairs. He had no trouble finding a family to run a cafe on the ground level, or transient tenants to rent the second-floor rooms. His shop in the basement, open from seven a.m. to seven p.m. or later, and closed only on Thursday afternoons and Sundays, built up a steady trade. Ranney came in every morning for a shave, and once a week he received a shampoo, a twenty-cent haircut, and a witch hazel steam massage. On Sundays Hendrik sometimes visited Greenville Hospital patients in need of shaves or haircuts, and he performed similar chores on the dead for Greenville's undertakers. Railroad men and farm hands frequented the shower stalls at the rear of the shop, where a shower with soap and a towel cost twenty-five cents.

The prosperity of the 1920s meant that people had more money for discretionary expenditures like haircuts. Hendrik hired an apprentice to handle the increase in trade. As his shop thrived, Zien made sure that much of what he earned was deposited at the bank. "Zien was the boss," said Hendrik's niece Jeanette Oudman. Middle-class comforts were evident in a family portrait taken in the Meijer dining room in 1924. Hendrik and Zien are seated at the table in their best clothes, with Hendrik holding a newspaper. In the foreground, flanked by china cabinets, are Johanna and Fred. Johanna holds a doll; Fred, wearing a sailor suit, sits behind the wheel of a wagon-size tractor. Gifts one Christmas included a bantam hen for Jo and a bantam rooster for Fred. In those years, a friend who needed a loan could usually count on Hendrik for help.

Business boomed during the summer, particularly when a highway department crew widened the main county road outside Greenville. "Those men would come in from working with that cement and they would take a bath and you would shave them, and every second or third stroke you would have to sharpen the razor from all the cement in their whiskers," Hendrik's apprentice recalled. "They would shampoo their hair in the shower and you would reshampoo it, and that went on from spring until fall. We opened the barbershop at 7 a.m., and you went in there at 6:30 in the morning and got the fire going in the hot water heater, and a lot of times we would get done at 1 a.m. or 1:30 on a Saturday night."

Hendrik was buoyed sufficiently by his prospects to sign another mortgage the following year. He outlined for Ranney his plan to buy the ramshackle structure immediately to the north, which had once housed his original barbershop. He wanted to replace the older structure with two narrow storefronts that he could lease out. Greenville was growing, and he was confident of finding tenants.

In the fall of 1924, with Ranney's guarantee on the mortgage, Hendrik paid two thousand dollars for the lot and the building on it. Characteristically, he was distracted by other schemes at the same time. For some months he had scoured the county looking at dairy farms, because cows had replaced chickens in his agrarian fantasy. At first Zien scoffed at the idea of milking cows: she was a city girl; she had not come to America to be a farmer. But when Hendrik worked late at the shop, *someone* had to milk the animals. When he bought a horse, Zien proved at ease with that animal too, remembering lessons her father had taught her from his days in the Dutch cavalry. When Fred was seven, Hendrik bought him a pony, only to sell it a year later after it kicked a neighbor girl.

Zien took snapshots of family outings—picnics at Baldwin Lake, children's birthday parties in the yard. In one photo of their daughter, Johanna is dressed as a Dutch farm maid, balancing a yoke with two milk pails on her shoulders. In the summer Hendrik's sister Anna's children, Fred and Jeanette, visited the farm. With Johanna and Fred they rode horses and hoed beans and watched Hendrik and Zien milk the cows.

The Meijer household reflected Hendrik and Zien's puritan values, and they *were* thoroughly puritanical, whatever some of their political views—and even free-love rhetoric—might have suggested to the contrary. Indeed, one warm summer day they were napping on a sofa on their front porch when a visitor made a wisecrack about their sleeping together. Hendrik scolded the man furiously, revealing an intensely Victorian apprehension about the subject of sex.

Although Hendrik shied away from political activity, ideological convictions were much in evidence in the Meijer household. On the living room walls hung green felt plaques with portraits and quotations of revolutionary heroes. And Hendrik's was the only barbershop in town where a black man could get a haircut.

Hendrik's mother had died in 1922 at the age of sixty-two. His sister Tonia, stricken with tuberculosis, died in 1925. Some time afterward his father, by then retired, came to Greenville for a short stay. Frederik Meyer—he too had anglicized his name—had thoughts of staying on with his son and daughter-in-law, but Hendrik refused his offer of money for room and

Gerhard Mantel

Hendrik Meijer (right) and father
Frederik Meijer, c. 1907

Gezina (Zien) Mantel (right) and mother Johanna Mantel, c. 1910

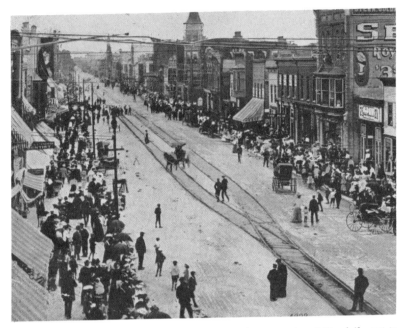

Eighth Street, Holland, Michigan as it appeared on a postcard Hendrik sent to Gezina in 1907

Hendrik (left) and co-workers in the foundry of the Holland Furnace Company, c. 1909

Hendrik at age twenty-eight in Greenville, 1912

Zien took this picture of her husband in front of his first barbershop, c. 1914

Hendrik and Zien, c. 1913

Hendrik in his barbershop, May 5, 1915

Hendrik, Zien, Fred, and Johanna   Hendrik, Fred, and Johanna, c. 1928
in 1924

The prosperity of the 1920s is evident in this family portrait in the Meijers'
Greenville farmhouse.

Fred paints weekly specials in the front window of the North Side Grocery, 1934

(Right) Hendrik, Johanna, Zien, and Fred, c. 1932

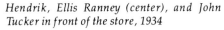
Hendrik (left) and cafe proprietor Pat McCann in a doorway dynamited in the basement wall of the Thrift Market in 1937

Hendrik, Ellis Ranney (center), and John Tucker in front of the store, 1934

Johanna with a young cus-
tomer in an early shopping
cart, c. 1940

Hendrik built this building at the corner of Lafayette and Charles in Greenville in 1923. He
installed his barbershop in the basement and
rented out the upper floors. In 1940 the ground
floor became part of the Thrift Super Market.

The Thrift Market began to take on the appearance of a supermarket in 1937
when it was expanded to span two storefronts.

The Greenville store had been expanded nine times before it was destroyed by fire in 1946

A new Greenville store occupied this Quonset building in 1946.

In 1946 this vacant potato warehouse became the company's first office.

Inside the new Greenville supermarket: Hendrik and family are at rear

Fred and Lena Meijer lay out newspaper ads in their living room, c. 1948

Checkout lines stretch far down the aisles at the opening of a Meijer Supermarket at Michigan and Fuller Avenue in Grand Rapids, February 1952

Hendrik gives a haircut to grandson Elbert Magoon as Johanna looks on, c. 1950

Laying brick during supermarket construction in Grand Rapids in 1951

A customer wins a basketload of groceries at the grand opening of the first Grand Rapids supermarket in 1949.

Hendrik with the author, 1952

Hendrik with grandchildren Louise and Elbert Magoon, c. 1953

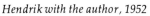

Christmas, 1951: Hendrik and Zien joined by Fred, Don Magoon, Johanna, and Lena at a company party

Hendrik and Zien visit Hendrik's sisters (from left) Anna, Rika, and Griet in Holland, Michigan in 1958. At lower left are Johanna and daughter Carol Magoon. (Right) Aboard ship, c. 1950

Riding a tandem motorbike in Hengelo

Hendrik and Zien with the initials Hendrik carved in a tree near Hengelo during their courtship in 1910

Hendrik and Fred drive Isettas through the aisles of the Michigan and Fuller store in an advertising promotion, c. 1955

Grand opening, 1959. With associates and family looking on, Hendrik cuts the ribbon for a new supermarket on Plainfield Avenue in Grand Rapids. At Hendrik's left is grandson Elbert Magoon, wearing the traditional "Thrifty" Dutch boy costume.

On the site of the first Thrifty Acres store, 1962. (Right) Miss Michigan of 1958, Margaret Pierce, joins the family for the opening of a supermarket at 28th Street and Kalamazoo Avenue in Grand Rapids. From left: Hendrik, Zien, Miss Pierce, Lena Meijer, Doug Meijer, Mark Meijer, and Fred Meijer.

Grand opening of the original Thrifty Acres store, June 1962

Hendrik (in suit) rides a penny pony shortly before the first Thrifty Acres opens in 1962. Other riders include Fred Welling (left), later the company's senior vice-president of properties, and Harold Hans (far right), senior vice-president of merchandising.

In 1984 a Meijer store opened in Cascade Township, Michigan, down 28th Street from the original Thrifty Acres. Below: Fred (seated), store director Dan Stephens (in suit, standing), and associates in the parking lot before the opening. (Photos by Paul Boice)

Returning to the Netherlands for the last time in 1963

board. In retrospect, the son's pride probably interfered with his judgment. His father wished not to be dependent on him, and chose instead to stay with Hendrik's sister Griet in Holland, where the four Meyer sisters and their families lived within blocks of one another. Father and son continued on good terms, however. Frederik Meyer visited Greenville periodically—his grandson Fred remembers fetching pipe tobacco for the old man. In 1931, at the age of eighty, Frederik was struck by a car while crossing a street in Holland, and died of the injuries several days later.

In his early forties, with the shop thriving, Hendrik began to think about his long-term financial security. Rent from tenants offset his obligations on the corner building. To be sure, he had not given up his ambition of making a living off the farm. Indeed, he had added to his holdings by buying eighty acres a few miles north of his original property. He added a hay barn and silo and refurbished the old farmhouse for rental property, thinking that some day the family might move there. The climate for commercial investment also appeared promising. Hendrik calculated that the additional rent generated by the new building on Lafayette Street would enable him to devote more energy to the farm.

A two-horse team began hauling dirt away from the Lafayette Street lot in the summer of 1925. Hendrik did much of the work himself, and by the end of June the excavation was nearly finished. During the first week of July, however, heavy rains further eroded the excavated area and threatened to collapse his two-story building next door. While Zien and the children picnicked, Hendrik worked frantically through the Fourth of July to keep the foundation of his barbershop building from giving way. He poured concrete for the new foundation and braced the existing wall with timbers. Later he put support rods through the weakened foundation of the original building. When he complained to the contractor about the shoddy foundations, however, the latter replied, "You wanted a cheap building, didn't you?" Not everyone made the important distinction—later so crucial for a discount merchant— between cheap and inexpensive.

Apprentice barber Leo Swartz never forgot another occasion, when he heard an explosion and then saw Hendrik running down the street from his shop, shouting in his heavy Dutch accent, "Mine boiler blew up; mine boiler blew up." But not all his setbacks were as serious. One day when Hendrik went home for lunch, men from the lumberyard across the street moved all his furniture out to the curb and put a ''for sale'' sign on one of the barber chairs.

"Oh, they used to pull that stuff on Henry," Swartz recalled. But the jokes worked both ways: "When you worked for Henry Meijer you got a lot of it, because the people who came into the shop were all great kidders and storytellers." And no one was exempt. Hendrik had a rubber coat hook on the wall along with the conventional metal ones. When Ellis Ranney came in, it seemed as though the metal ones were always taken. Ranney would hang his coat on the rubber hook, take his place in the chair, and watch his coat slip to the floor. The industrialist turned the tables one morning while Hendrik was in the backroom firing up the furnace. He slipped the barber's razor strop inside his shirt and took it with him when he left. When the next customer came in for a shave, Hendrik reached for the strop and it wasn't there. "Just a minute," he said. He walked out the door and down the street to Ranney's office, picked up the strop that lay on the secretary's desk, and walked back to his shop without saying a word.

When business was slow and an amenable customer occupied the chair, Hendrik or his apprentice would put a little lampblack on their hands and run their fingers through the customer's scalp, observing soberly, "Your hair really needs washing." The customer would usually catch on and respond with a start and a smile, sighing, "Well, I needed a shampoo anyway."

Then there was the time a one-eyed fireman from the Pere Marquette Railroad offered to pick up the tab if Hendrik cut off all the hair of a friend of his, an engineer who would be coming in for a haircut. The fireman disappeared, and a few minutes later the engineer strolled in. He settled innocently into the chair as the barber wrapped the cloth around him. Hendrik started in with his scissors, then paused. He scratched the man's scalp, made a show of inspecting it closely, and shook his head. "Your hair's getting awfully thin," he informed the engineer. "If we massage it and cut it back it will grow in stronger." The engineer gave a grunt of approval, and Hendrik ran his fingers over the scalp, then turned the chair away from the mirror. After a little more clipping, he tipped the chair back and shaved his unwitting customer bald. When Hendrik turned the chair back toward the mirror, the engineer groaned, "Oh my God, what will my wife say?"

The fireman, who had returned in the middle of the haircut to discover that Hendrik had taken up his offer, could barely contain himself. When the engineer reached for his wallet, Hendrik said, "That's all right." Then he nodded at the fireman, who sat doubled up, tears of laughter streaming down his cheeks. "He'll pay for it," Hendrik said quietly, as the hapless engineer howled with rage.

When patrons asked how he had come to America, Hendrik had a standard reply: "Well, it wasn't easy. We didn't have much money, you know, but my feet are about a size fourteen, so I had some wooden shoes made a little bit bigger, and I just opened my coat and sailed across with the wind."

*   *   *   *   *

Hendrik's investment in the new building had reached $7,000 (a $5,000 mortgage loan, a $1,500 credit from the lumber company for materials, and $500 of his own money) before he decided he could not yet afford to finish it as he had originally planned. Instead of completing the two storefronts, he finished off the basement they shared and put a roof over it that slanted from front to back, allowing a six-foot clearance in front for a door that led downstairs. At the back, the roof sloped nearly to the ground. He put a door on the corner nearest his other building, and had to install his toilet at the top of the stairway, because Greenville's sanitary sewer ran through a pipe that was well above the basement floor. (Fred was a small boy when a hard rain backed up the sewer, and the entire family went down into the basement with pails and cans to bail out the overflow of raw sewage.)

By the late 1920s, however, Hendrik not only had the first and second floors over his barbershop rented, but was producing income from the new basement space next door, where he opened a pool room complete with sawdust on the floor and a lunch counter that sold hot beef sandwiches. Hendrik, Leo Swartz, and their customers would shoot pool when the barbershop was quiet. Of course, the tables attracted other penny-ante games, and the police kept an eye on the place.

"You'd be surprised at the fellows that hung out there at night," Swartz said later. The old man Hendrik had hired to run the pool room was given to dozing off on quiet afternoons. One day while the tables were vacant and the old man slept, Hendrik told one of his cronies to remove the cash register from the pool room cigar counter. The deed accomplished, Hendrik went downstairs to ask the old man for a cigar. The old man roused himself and went over to the counter where the cash register should have been located. It was gone. Stolen! The old man looked around in alarm before Hendrik burst out laughing.

The shop and the pool hall were popular gathering spots. If Hendrik needed help with a chore or a building project, there was always a crony available. Added Swartz, years later, "Henry had a lot of henchmen. . . . Maybe they would do something for their haircuts or their baths or maybe [after 1934] a few groceries."

Hendrik, meanwhile, was juggling a dozen different schemes. At one point he even applied for work as a postman. But his greatest enthusiasm was reserved for dairy farming. And in 1928, the year he turned forty-five, he made a commitment in that direction when he bought three registered Guernsey cows for $125 each. They were to be the basis of his dairy herd. On his birthday, his father-in-law wrote from Hengelo, "You are getting close to the fiftieth now too. . . . Your hair will get gray and you'll slow down a little, but when you become a *farmer* yet at this age, then you should be in good shape. . . . From barber to farmer, that's quite a switch."

Indeed, the Mantels followed his progress closely. Zien's youngest brother Frans and his wife hoped to immigrate, but with more restrictive immigration laws they anticipated a five-year wait. In the meantime Frans took a job with a bank in Amsterdam—and in the end remained a banker there until his retirement. Wilhelm and Ferdinand stayed with their father in the tailor shop, although the brothers quarreled over business strategy. Ferdinand turned to Hendrik for help when his father and older brother opposed expanding the shop to sell increasingly popular ready-to-wear garments. "Hendrik," Ferdinand wrote, "would you do me a favor and write Wilhelm sometime that he shouldn't be so scared about starting something new? People like bigger and better stores, so you have to do something about it, otherwise you will lose your customers." Hendrik responded with a letter to Wilhelm Mantel, and when Gerhard turned the store over to the sons two years later, Wilhelm had agreed "to make the store bigger and more modern so that we can keep up with the demands of our customers."

In Greenville Zien and the children played a part in Hendrik's plans at every turn. Zien made all of the children's clothes. Fred cut newspapers into strips for his father's shaving papers. He was eight years old and Johanna was eleven—both old enough to help with the multitude of chores Hendrik's succession of ventures created. It fell to Zien, however, to tend the cows when Hendrik embarked on his most ambitious endeavor to date—the Model Dairy. He borrowed the name from a huge dairy in Illinois, renowned for its modern facilities, which was owned by utilities magnate Samuel Insull. Hendrik's milk bottles bore the imprint of the name, along with *H. Meyer* in raised letters.

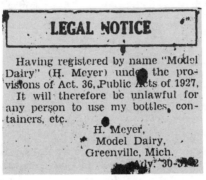

Hendrik registered the name of his newest venture in 1928.

Zien not only milked the cows, she also ran the milkhouse Hendrik had built next to the barn. The milk was dumped into a hopper and poured over cold water pipes to cool. Zien washed the bottles by the tedious routine of shoving them one at a time onto a whirling brush over the sink. Inspectors complimented her on the unusually low bacteria count in Model Dairy milk—evidence of a highly scrubbed cleanliness that was both an ethnic obsession and a source of pride. Before washing, the bottles had the lingering stench of old cream, an odor often nauseating to the uninitiated.

The Model Dairy soon had more customers than Fred alone could service on foot or with his pony. As the route grew, Fred, with Johanna or a friend like Dusty McFarland, delivered milk after school with a horse-drawn wagon. Later Hendrik switched to morning deliveries, before school and before the barbershop opened, and covered the route by car. Winter was the worst time for deliveries. One day when the Model T would not start Hendrik pulled a sled loaded with milk bottles. It was still dark on a bitterly cold morning, the only light a kerosene lantern strapped to the sled. Fred trailed behind, taking a couple of quarts up to each customer's doorstep. That morning he was in tears, cold and beleaguered as he shuffled up to each stoop with his mittens around a milk bottle. The sight of the little boy struggling in the cold was so pathetic that Hendrik also nearly cried. "I know it's cold, Fred," he said softly, "but we've got to get this milk peddled, and then we can go home."

But Fred recalled another morning, after Christmas, probably in 1929, when Hendrik went out with him in the horse-drawn sleigh. Fred walked alongside, running quarts of milk up to the porch of each customer. That morning his father was teasing him, urging the horse on just fast enough so that Fred could not keep up. The boy got angry and ran home, leaving his father to finish the route by himself. When Hendrik returned, he was so upset that he threatened to destroy his son's new Christmas skis.

Fred was not yet a teenager the day he took one of the horses over to the blacksmith's shop, where Hendrik was having a wagon made. The boy had just hitched up the horse to the new wagon and climbed aboard when the animal bolted. Horse, terrified boy, and new wagon thundered down the back streets of Greenville. The wagon careened out of control for several blocks until the horse crashed it into a clothesline pole, ripping off the harness and splintering the new wagon. The horse ran home. Fred climbed down off the wagon, still shaken, and ran after it. "Near the house," he recalled, "I met my dad and I thought, 'Oh, he's going to be mad.' The wagon was smashed, and the harness was all messed up. But my dad was so happy to see me alive and well that he didn't care about the harness or anything. I couldn't understand why he wasn't mad, but he was happy to see me unhurt."

Late in 1929, Hendrik finally roughed in the storefronts above the basement pool hall. He left the interiors unfinished while he began to look for tenants. It was not long before the cafe on the corner, Snyder's Restaurant, rented one of the new spaces. (It took Hendrik some time to catch on to the cafe owner's traffic in moonshine. Snyder kept it down by the furnace in the basement. His best customers were the railroad men, who took their jugs upstairs to Hendrik's rented rooms.) When the cafe moved into the new building, Hendrik rented the corner location to a druggist. That left him with one vacant storefront. If he could only find one more tenant and keep the barbershop going full steam while he built up the dairy herd, he would be doing all right. The rent from the buildings on Lafayette Street would assure him of an annuity for his old age.

II

When there is no vision the people perish.

—Franklin D. Roosevelt,
First Inaugural Address, 1933

Even as Hendrik was completing his second building, there were ominous signs that the stock market crash of 1929 would produce a serious depression. In Greenville, as elsewhere, it took a year or two for the news to alter the rhythms of daily life. There was no mistaking the situation, however, when the refrigerator factories began to eliminate shifts and lay off workers. Montcalm County's farmers watched the value of their crops plummet. The number of bankruptcies rose. Banks collapsed or trembled on the brink as farmers, businessmen, and homeowners defaulted.

Many farmers and factory workers now could not afford the haircuts that for ten years had brought them to Hendrik Meijer's shop after payday or before the show. Hendrik dropped his price for a haircut from a quarter to fifteen cents, but business still dwindled. In 1929 the shop had taken in as much as fifty dollars in a busy week; two years later, Hendrik might come home with three or four dollars. Because his assistant, Lester Lutz, also had to live off the shop, Hendrik cut back his own hours and spent more time with the farm.

One day another barber drove out to the house and invited Hendrik to ride downtown to a meeting of Greenville's barbers. Hendrik went along in his overalls, having just come in from the barn. The other barbers asked him to raise his prices to match theirs—some of the downtown shops were still charging twenty-five cents. Hendrik refused. He had little enough business now, he told them, and he would do nothing to discourage what was left. If he was cutting Fred's hair and a customer came in, the boy went off to school with an unfinished haircut.

One downtown barber leased his shop from a doctor whose rent came from a percentage of the shop's income. With business so slow, the rent had evaporated, and the doctor blamed Hendrik for depressing his revenues. "You'll do just as much business with higher prices as you will with those low ones, and you'll make more money," he told Hendrik. "We just raised our office calls from fifty cents to a dollar and our business hasn't dropped off one bit."

Hendrik saw a considerable difference between medicine and barbering. "When you have a stomach ache and go to the doctor," he replied, "you'll pay a dollar to get better. But you're not in the same position with a haircut." When he refused to raise his prices, the doctor vowed, "If you don't, we're going to put you out of business"—a threat he should have known would never work.

"I wouldn't have you SOBs for pallbearers," Hendrik shouted as he stalked out of the meeting. He walked home.

In hard times, wives cut their husbands' hair and parents cut their children's. By lowering prices Hendrik merely slowed down the loss of trade. Meanwhile, he removed the bathtub from the farmhouse and installed it above the drugstore so that some of the rooms could be rented out together as an apartment. But even then the tenants soon moved out and the apartment was empty. At home, the family washed in the sink.

The druggist on the corner also felt the pinch of the Depression. He wanted repairs which Hendrik could not afford. In August 1932, he sent the barber an ultimatum: "After witnessing [the] effect of [the] storm this morning, I am thoroughly disgusted and at the end of my endurance. I am sorry that I find it necessary to talk plain to you." According to the druggist, Hendrik had neglected to seal the windows, stalled on installation of a new stove, and failed to provide proper drainage in the basement. "I can't see what you gain by makeshift repairing," he wrote. "I don't wish to be unreasonable, but feel you haven't been fair with me and that you don't appreciate the fact that I have endeavored to hand you a check on the date, although it hasn't always been so easy. In conclusion, in the next thirty days if you don't do the fair thing I will have to take steps to jump the contract."

The "fair thing" was not spelled out, but Hendrik could no more afford to lose a tenant than to charge more money for fewer haircuts. Instead, he lowered the druggist's rent to forty dollars a month. Another complaint dropped it to thirty-five dollars, and even then the druggist fell behind on his payments. Finally, he paid only a percentage of his meager sales, enclosing this note with a payment in 1933: "Last month's earned proportion—maximum rent—was $20.07. This month going no better. This is all I can possibly spare this month."

There was no love lost between the druggist and the barber's other tenants. After an illegal slot machine was confiscated from the back of the drugstore, the druggist, upset that he had been turned in, informed the constable that Hendrik's assistant also kept one—down in the basement. Confiscating that machine meant that the farmers and railroad men no longer could draw the curtains or sneak next door on a quiet afternoon to play the one-armed bandit after their haircuts.

Despite Hendrik's growing desperation, his family never actually went hungry. Zien raised vegetables, and the dairy herd provided fresh milk. All too apparent, however, was the realization that any serious setback could push them over the edge. Hendrik could not possibly meet mortgage payments on the two new storefronts without finding a tenant for the one that stood vacant. He asked the bank to take over the buildings and release him from the mortgages. The bankers declined. They preferred any payment at all on a pre-Depression mortgage to what they could sell the buildings for in the shattered real estate market of 1933. After one intimidating visit to the bank, Fred asked his father how he could take so much abuse. "Fred, I can't pay them," Hendrik answered. "I'm behind— they're talking tough, but they're not foreclosing."

Hendrik hoped somehow to unload his burden. He offered to sell the corner building to a wealthy potato dealer for the remainder of the mortgage value, but the potato dealer told him, "Hell no. I'll buy it [later] for half that price."

The Greenville business establishment, Republican to the core, distrusted Roosevelt. Men like Ranney were afraid he would bankrupt the country or turn it socialist. But Hendrik supported the New Deal. He sent a dollar to Father Charles Coughlin at the Shrine of the Little Flower in Royal Oak after one of the radio priest's addresses in 1932 posed the choice of "Roosevelt or Ruin."

During the Depression years frugality reigned. At Christmas each of the children might receive a new pair of mittens, for delivering milk on icy winter mornings. Young Fred and his schoolmates, picking through leather scraps behind the glove factory on Lafayette Street, used the remnants to repair those Christmas mittens.

Much of the responsibility for the milk route belonged to Johanna and Fred. Johanna, now in high school, kept the books and collected from customers who were slow to pay. After Hendrik converted an old Dodge sedan into a pickup truck, his teenage daughter drove the route in pre-dawn darkness while Fred delivered the bottles door to door.

Hendrik developed a keen rapport with his adolescent son. He was quick to include Fred in every adventure, writing to Zien and Jo when those two visited Chicago for the 1933 World's Fair, "We were through bottling and [back] in the milkhouse at 7:10 [a.m.] and went uptown and got a watermelon. Brother [the family nickname for Fred] had an appetite for one. . . . We are getting along just fine. Take our advice and stay over Sunday. . . ." Fred scribbled X's (for kisses) at the bottom of the page, about which Hendrik added: "I am not responsible. . . ." He signed the letter, "Your brother and the big shot."

At the peak of the Model Dairy's production, Zien worked from dawn to dusk in the sour-smelling milkhouse. She milked two dozen cows and bottled up to two hundred quarts a day for more than seventy customers. Making claims for its creamier quality, Hendrik tried to promote his raw, unpasteurized milk as more desirable than the milk from Blanding's, the largest dairy in town and the Model Dairy's chief competitor. Yet he knew that in the long run pasteurized milk would triumph.

Much more slowly did he realize that he was fighting a losing battle as a dairy farmer. As with other farm products, milk was seldom a paying proposition in the Depression years. In 1932 Iowa farmers poured out their milk in roadside protests rather than sell it at a loss. In Greenville the price of a quart of milk dropped from twelve cents in 1929 to a nickel in 1932. With milk at twelve cents a quart, Hendrik's dairy had not been a paying proposition. Now the bottles cost as much as the milk did, and he was running out of bottles.

Along with supplying milk to many of Greenville's grocery stores, Blanding's Dairy also dominated home delivery. Hendrik encouraged his competitors to charge a deposit for their bottles—so that he could too. But Blanding's declined; with their wide door-to-door distribution, they were getting back most of their bottles anyway, including the ones sold through stores. When Hendrik sold milk to a grocer, his bottles often ended up on the porch of a Blanding's customer. Selling bottles of milk without a deposit was like giving the milk away; yet no grocer would charge a deposit for Model Dairy bottles when other stores sold Blanding's with no strings attached.

And not only had the price of milk dropped, so had the value of Hendrik's dairy herd. In fact, his luck with livestock proved to be notoriously bad. Of his three original registered Guernseys, bought before the Depression for $125 each, one bloated and died, one came in three-teated, and the third was dry. He sold the two survivors for five dollars each.

Hendrik's best hope lay in finding a tenant for the vacant storefront. Someone suggested a grocery store. Even in a depression, people bought food. As a matter of fact, fewer grocers had failed in the first years after the Crash than had in 1928 or 1929. Although sales had sagged somewhat, some of the large grocery chains continued to expand. Hendrik hoped one of them might be interested in renting a vacant storefront next to a drugstore in North Greenville, Michigan.

At one point the Great Atlantic & Pacific Tea Company—the A&P—had operated two stores a block apart in downtown Greenville. The Kroger Company had a single store in town, also south of the Flat River. But no chain stores served the sizable neighborhood across the river in North Greenville. Hendrik invited both companies to look at his twenty-one foot storefront. One chain's representative asked the druggist next door how business was, and the druggist, always a pessimist, replied characteristically, "No good." The agent probably would have reached the same conclusion on his own. In any case, neither grocery chain was interested. A local lawyer knew the owner of a smaller chain in Grand Rapids and thought he could help Hendrik persuade that grocer to put a store in North Greenville. When Hendrik and the lawyer went to see him, however, the man barely looked up from his desk. He too was uninterested.

Finally, Hendrik called on the firm of Lee & Cady, wholesale grocers in Grand Rapids who supplied the "Red & White" stores. Hendrik was more than a little surprised when an executive explained patiently that the firm operated no stores of its own. It was strictly a wholesale house that supplied individual proprietors with merchandise. These grocers joined together under the Red & White banner to share volume buying and advertising advantages that helped them compete with the chain stores. Therefore Lee & Cady had no interest in Hendrik's building—unless, the executive suggested, the barber himself wished to set up a store there. In that case, provided he had the credit, Lee & Cady would be only too happy to supply him with groceries.

Thus it was not vision as much as naivete and chance—tinged with desperation—that turned Hendrik Meijer's thoughts in a new and completely unexpected direction. Late in 1933 he decided that only fear of the unknown stood in the way of taking up Lee & Cady's challenge. Fear of the unknown had never been a compelling reason for him not to act before, and if the timing was not exactly propitious, well, there was not much he could do about it. He was a barber with a dwindling business, a dairyman with no prospect of profit, and a landlord with a vacant building. He had to do something.

*   *   *   *   *

The idea of selling groceries had long been attractive to working men who wanted to go into business for themselves. In fact, when independent merchants began to complain that chain stores made it hard for them to survive, industry observers noted that failure came not so much from unfair competition as from the fact that many individual grocers set up shop with little more than a dash of credit and a pinch of ambition. As a result, towns were saturated with small stores whose owners, whether they had been mechanics or bricklayers or barbers earlier in life, generally lacked experience in merchandising or operating a retail establishment.

The Depression had only exacerbated that situation. Men who had once turned to the grocery business chiefly because it was an easy way to become their own bosses were now turning to it out of desperation. By 1933 Greenville had nearly two dozen grocery stores, ranging from the A&P and Kroger markets, where customers paid for their groceries in cash, to the traditional neighborhood store, where most transactions depended on credit and a clerk frequently delivered the order to the customer's home. Some of these rudimentary establishments had their start in the proprietor's living room, where an unemployed worker would start by selling canned goods to his neighbors. "Parlor grocers," along with miniature golf courses and home beauty parlors, offered desperate people with a glimmer of entrepreneurial ambition the prospect of a livelihood.

Hendrik Meijer—he had reverted to the original spelling of his surname when he painted it on a new milk truck—was slightly more fortunate. As long as the bank hoped that someday he would meet his obligation, choosing not to foreclose on a building it would have to sell at a loss, he had a good place for a store. Never mind that one long-established grocer operated across the street, and another a block away. This was no time to be timid about competition.

Howard Kipp, who with his brother owned North Greenville's busiest grocery store—the one across the street—had patronized Hendrik's barbershop for years. So had many of the salesmen and delivery people who called on Kipp and other Greenville grocers. Hendrik knew Big George, who drove the bread truck for Michigan Bakeries, and Little George, who delivered Butternut Bread. Having divined few mysteries in the selling of groceries, Hendrik had developed opinions of his own about the retail business. He wondered why so many Greenville people drove to Grand Rapids to shop in a new self-service store. Why were the A&P stores so successful on a cash-and-carry basis? Hendrik had pressed Kipp with some of these questions, and added some suggestions on increasing a store's sales volume. (That became one of Hendrik's favorite words—volume.) But Kipp replied, "Henry, you take care of your little barbershop, and I'll run my grocery store."

Farther north on Lafayette Street, another grocer had been the only retail customer of the Model Dairy. When Hendrik found himself forced to sell milk to the grocer at cost, and then lost money when customers did not return their bottles, he decided he might at least lose less money if he sold his own milk at retail.

Behind on his mortgage and behind on his taxes, he hardly possessed the finest credit. But he had a friend. And he was not the first aspiring entrepreneur to benefit at a crucial moment from an older man's sponsorship. From flowers when Fred was born to his signature on several mortgages, Ellis Ranney had been a source of support all along. When Hendrik confided his plans for a grocery store, however, the older man's backing was hardly automatic. Ranney predicted failure; he told the barber that he might as well spare himself the agony of bankruptcy and take a job at one of Ranney's factories or farms. "Meijer," he said, "there are twenty-two grocery stores in Greenville that are hanging on by the skin of their teeth and you want to go into the grocery business too—you're crazy!"

Ranney was equally frank when the wholesaler asked for a credit reference, repeating his opposition to the new venture and warning that Hendrik would probably fail. "That's for pretty sure," he concluded. Then he paused, and added a qualification that effectively nullified all his other comments: "He *is* a man who pays his bills. He'll find a way to pay you back, and someday you'll get your money. You won't lose it." It was a backhanded reference to be sure, but as unimpeachable as anything Lee & Cady could expect to hear about a new account in the waning weeks of 1933.

Hendrik had said to another friend, George Smith, "George, I'm going to try another business. I'm going to have a grocery store."

"A grocery store?" Smith asked incredulously. "We've got too many grocery stores around here now." Years later he recalled Hendrik's ambitions: "He said he had a future; he sure fooled me." As Smith told Ranney, when the two men shook their heads over their friend's impetuousness, "I believe he's crazy."

Once Lee & Cady agreed to provide a beginning inventory, it remained for Hendrik to finish off the interior of the vacant building that was to become his store. On January 9, 1934, he sold the barbershop business to his former apprentice, Leo Swartz, for $350. Swartz agreed to lease the shop for five years, beginning at twenty-five dollars a month, and to hire his former employer for part-time work Fridays and Saturdays and whenever else business warranted. For Hendrik, that would keep a little money coming in.

The barber set aside $150 from the sale of the shop to pay for finishing the interior of the future store. Most of what was left went for a down payment on $1,000 worth of used shelf fixtures. (The fixture dealer was delighted with any kind of payment plan. By 1933 he had accumulated more repossessed equipment than he could ever hope to sell.) Hendrik bartered a violin for the ten-dollar plaster job—plastering walls to which Fred had nailed used wood lath.

Johanna had graduated from high school in June 1933 as valedictorian of her class, and she hoped for a college scholarship. In the meantime she was available to help run the store while her father cut hair or worked on the farm. Fred, who was just starting high school, peddled milk every morning. After school and on weekends he would work in the store too. For Zien there remained the routine of the milkhouse.

The wholesaler provided Hendrik with a list compiled in 1929 by *Progressive Grocer* magazine of suggested markups in a grocery store's various categories of merchandise. Margins ranged from a slender 10 percent on hotly competitive items such as eggs and milk (for which Hendrik had his own source of supply) to a suggested 33 percent on certain produce items, "fancy groceries," and insecticides. The goal was an overall gross margin of 20 percent.

By the spring of 1934, the economy was offering a glimmer of hope, and all but the most diehard Republicans were willing to concede that some of the experiments of the New

Deal might be working. As the *Greenville Daily News* noted, "Michigan, which one year ago saw nothing but gloom, is looking ahead to a brighter future. We battled the storm and survived. It was a rough sea, but we held on. Our hope, our faith, and our courage will be rewarded." In Lansing, state officials proposed a spectacular suspension bridge to span the Straits of Mackinac—to be built with federal public works money. Despite the resurgence of optimism, however, the Depression was far from over. A real estate agent advertised a hundred farms for sale, "at the lowest prices in years."

On June 20, 1934, a truck from Lee & Cady delivered the first load of groceries to the little store that Hendrik named the North Side Grocery. Zien saved the invoice; it was for $338.76. Hendrik had fifteen days to pay that first bill, but subsequent shipments would arrive COD. The Kipp brothers stood in the doorway as Hendrik unloaded his opening inventory and made a prediction: the new store would not last six weeks.

Ten days later, on June 30, 1934, unaccompanied by advertising or any other promotional effort save the word of mouth that went out through the barbershop and along the milk route, the North Side Grocery opened its door. The first morning, a Saturday, went slowly; only a handful of customers, friends, and curiosity seekers stopped in. Fred waited behind the counter in a white shirt and tie, filled with anticipation, when Ellis Ranney walked in. Ranney stepped up to the counter with a pack of gum and told Fred, "I want to be your first customer." Ranney had always been accorded a special deference in the Meijer household. He liked the grand gesture, and he took pride in sharing the Meijers' big day. He was the only customer in the store at the time, but Fred had checked out a couple of others already and was too attentive to the truth to let the banker's remark go uncorrected. "I'm sorry, Mr. Ranney," he began earnestly, "but we already sold—" He felt a tap on his shoulder. His father, in a low voice Ranney no doubt overheard anyway, growled, "If Mr. Ranney wants to be our first customer, Fred, Mr. Ranney is our first customer." That day they rang up total sales of seven dollars—cash *and* credit.

The layout of Hendrik's new store differed little from thousands of others. Produce, bread, and packaged goods such as potato chips were displayed on tables and in bins for customers to help themselves. There was little fresh fruit (Hendrik relied on local farmers), and dry produce such as potatoes,

INVOICE

LEE & CADY

WHOLESALERS
Grand Rapids :-: Michigan
Phone 4244

DATE SOLD

REGISTERED NO. ....

DATE SHIPPED ... JUN 28 193..
SALESMAN

VIA SHIPPED TO

SOLD TO *North Side Grocery*
Henry Meijer
Greenville, Mich

DELIVERY REQUESTED ....

TERMS 15 DAYS   Cash Discount   NET

Item No.	Shipper's Check	Quantity	DESCRIPTION	Weight	Price	Extension	√
1		1	Carton 48/5 Diamond Tooth Picks	1	1.57	1 57	
2		1	Box 18's Yeast Foam	1	1.33	1 33	
3		1	Case Tall Quaker Milk	1	2.75	2 75	
4		1	Case Baby Quaker Milk		1.40		
5		1	Case 12's Shredded Wheat	1	1.43	1 43	
6		1	Dozen Wheaties	1	1.40	1 40	
7		1	Dozen Kelloggs Pep ov rl	1	1.10	1 10	
8		1	Case 48's Phillips Tomato Soup	1	2.37	2 37	
9		1	Dozen Certo	1	2.90	2 90	
10		1/4	Gross Palmolive Soap	1	3.10	3 10	
11		1	Case 12's Lge Gold Dust	1	1.76	1 76	
12							
13						33 8.99	
14			Less value 1/2 Dz.			23	
15			1/2 Cent Stp			338 76	
16			Pd. July 17, '34			10 00	
17						Bal. $328 76	
18							
19							
20							

Claims for Shortage or Damage Must be Reported at Once

Shredded Wheat, toothpicks, and Palmolive soap are among the items listed on the invoice that accompanied Hendrik's first order of groceries in June 1934.

onions, and turnips predominated. Along the back wall stood a refrigerated display case for dairy products. In one corner, near the door to the back room, was a wood-burning, potbelly stove. With the help of his twelve-year-old cousin, Fred Veltman, Fred built a cereal display in the front window. On the windows themselves he painted signs that advertised the weekly specials. Johanna or Fred assembled the balance of a customer's order from behind a green linoleum counter, where a tall shelf extended nearly the length of the wall. Orders were rung up on the cash register or an adding machine and purchases "on account" recorded in a ledger book. Unlike A&P and Kroger, Hendrik started out selling groceries the same way he had obtained his beginning inventory from Lee & Cady—on credit.

As the summer wore on, business picked up only slowly. While Hendrik worked half the week in the barbershop downstairs, Johanna ran the store. When it was hot and there were no customers she might come out and sit on the front stoop, where she could hear baseball games on the druggist's radio. When a salesman came to call, Hendrik would come up from the barbershop.

In the store window Hendrik posted the blue eagle of the National Industrial Recovery Act. After the NRA, as it was known, was declared unconstitutional, the consensus among Greenville merchants was that the Supreme Court would strike down the new Social Security Act as well. When it did not, and the inspector came around, Hendrik owed him back payments. Times were still tough. Smoke seldom poured forth from the stacks of the refrigerator plants that were bellwethers of the local economy. It would be all of five years before Greenville's labor force was fully employed—and then chiefly because the refrigerator plants built gliders for the War Department.

COD grocery orders from Lee & Cady arrived with *cash* scrawled in chalk across each cardboard case. On occasion Hendrik turned to friends for a quick loan when the truck was on its way and the contents of the cash box would not cover the invoice.

To insulate the store's unfinished back room, Hendrik flattened out the cardboard grocery boxes and nailed them to the ceiling. That first winter the word *cash*, repeated in blue chalk almost everywhere one looked, stood as a pointed reminder to the barber and his family of just how precarious the times could be.

5

A Supermarket
Is Born

I

In that comparatively peaceful neighborhood of yours, though you may not know it, there is war. It is the struggle being waged on the corners of our towns and cities between those once amiable burghers who for so many years have been set down with tailors as the keepers of the public peace—our grocery merchants.

—Collier's, 1928

Hendrik Meijer's little food store was as thoroughly conventional in every respect as the red and white striped awning that shaded its front window from the morning sun. But he opened his store at a time of great upheaval in the grocery business. The decade before 1934 had been a worrisome period for many small merchants, fighting for their survival as they often were in the face of a twentieth-century phenomenon, the chain store.

World War I production efforts had accelerated a trend toward standardization in manufacturing and efficiency in distribution. Automobiles were not the only commodity that could be produced on an assembly line. The mass production of merchandise, coupled with the demands of prosperous postwar consumers whose appetites had been whetted by increasingly sophisticated advertising, inaugurated an age of mass consumption that placed unprecedented demands on the distribution system—wholesalers and retailers. A correspondent for *Collier's* magazine likened the situation to the output of a huge pump being forced through a leaky old faucet. Linking expanded output and eager consumers was the retailer; he would have to change his general-store approach if the flow of goods was to become as swift as possible.

Chain stores offered a rapid turnover of inventory that kept pace with the cranked-up capacity of American industry in the boom years after World War I. In food retailing, chains that sold groceries on a cash basis and encouraged customers to fill their own orders pumped more volume through their stores. They passed along the production of both farmers and food processors quickly and efficiently, employing newly developed principles of "scientific management" and efficiency experts whose ideas lent themselves more readily to a large corporation than to a single proprietorship. Chain food stores achieved greater efficiency in advertising and wholesale buying, and they pioneered the combination of meat and produce with dry groceries in a single store.

After World War I, chain store operations expanded dramatically. The chains' share of American grocery sales surged from one-fifth to nearly one-third as they spread from the big cities to smaller towns like Greenville. In shaving 10 percent off a typical grocery bill, chain stores offered consumers a clear advantage over the old-fashioned grocery store, which was described by Collier's as "the most unscientific thing in the world. . . . For the merchant himself it was, and in many cases still is, a sort of easy-going slavery with its interminable hours. It was without order or design."

Embattled local merchants, of course, recited a litany of chain store evils. They claimed that they were more in tune with the needs of local customers than a chain store could be, particularly when chain operations were bent on standardizing everything. They said chains brought with them the threat of monopoly, and they charged that chains were guilty of fraud and trickery with their practice of selling certain highly visible items below their wholesale cost.

A&P became the target of the most scathing criticism—not all of it undeserved. Customers complained of being short-changed by the cashier and shortweighted by the butcher. Managers were accused of "selling the broom"—propping a broom next to the cash register and having the cashier "accidentally" ring it up along with the customer's order.

Even so, consumers were casting a decisive vote for the chains with their pocketbooks. As a writer for The Nation noted, "Generally condemned by word of mouth, the chain stores are supremely honored by their patronage." Expectations were changing—and growing. Money saved at the food store became spendable income. In the explosive prosperity of the 1920s, a multitude of new spending alternatives tempted consumers, from automobiles and radios to stocks and Florida real estate. "This is an age of money," wrote Collier's in 1928. "It is like

a swift, rushing stream flowing through commercial America.''
The chain store had become a symbol of the new age.

Among small businessmen, however, the response to this
current was to build dams. With the arrival of chain stores in
small towns, particularly as they spread west and south from
the eastern seaboard, a furious battle was joined. Entire communities mobilized as independent merchants pressed for
government action and blamed the chains every time one of
their number went out of business.

But the case against the chain store was long on emotion
and short on sense. As Hendrik Meijer's experience had
demonstrated, entering the grocery business in the United
States never had been a particularly difficult process. When
a skeptical wholesaler asked him what he knew about selling
groceries, Hendrik replied, ''Nothing. I cut hair.'' Wholesalers
often gave credit freely to build up new retailer accounts. The
business was so easy to enter, in fact, that it attracted more
than its share of people who did not have a clue about what
they were doing. Yet once these fledgling merchants donned
aprons and stocked their shelves, they often insisted on pro-
tection from unexpected competition.

The grocery business had always been characterized by a
high rate of failure. A survey of the trade in Louisville, Kentucky in 1925 showed about 1,000 grocery stores in the city—
including 800 independent operators. During the next three
years—at the height of prosperity in the 1920s—more than 1,000
grocery stores went out of business, a turnover rate of more
than 100 percent. The vast majority of the victims were independents. Chains succeeded not merely because they could
command lower wholesale prices, but because they knew what
they were doing in hiring, stocking, advertising, and a range
of other retail skills. Among independent grocers, *Collier's*
declared, there existed a ''state of unbelievable chaos.''
Although many independents preferred to believe otherwise,
a *Collier's* reporter summed up the ultimate truth of the
marketplace: ''A man has no God-given right to be in the
grocery business.''

Around the country, however, small merchants and their
sympathizers—invariably including a representation of local
politicians—gathered for mass meetings and noisy rallies to
protest the unimpeded spread of chain stores. Local retailers
found their greatest support in the South, Northwest, and
Midwest, regions where populist prejudice against Wall Street

and big business was strongest. By 1930, retailers had established anti-chain organizations with 260 chapters across the
country. More than nine million people—7 percent of the entire
population—became associated with the anti-chain movement.
Their leaders encouraged boycotts and similar consumer
measures, but their greatest hope for success lay with the politicians. In one state after another, legislators introduced bills to
limit the growth of chains.

In Greenville, Hendrik and Zien received a reprint of a
radio address by the attorney general of Alabama, Charlie
McCall. In the demagogic tradition of Huey Long, McCall condemned the "Foreign Chain Store Menace" as a satanic threat
to the American Way: "My friends," he began,

> allow me to direct your attention to the simple truth that the
> onward march of unregulated foreign chain stores is endanger-
> ing your homes, your firesides, your business, the prosperity
> of yourselves and your communities—that gradually, like the fire
> drawing nigher, there is creeping upon your independence,
> individualism, and liberty, a monopolistic conflagration in the
> form of an absolute monarchy in the business world. . . .
>
> Whenever fair competition is strangled, then the government
> should protect the people by adequate laws and not leave it
> unregulated and subject to the kindheartedness of Wall Street
> chairmen—they don't even know the people. If a wave of sym-
> pathy arose in one of that bunch, it would gag him to death.
> Their interest is in protecting their pocketbooks and making them
> fatter by bleeding towns of all liquid assets and driving
> hometown merchants into bankruptcy.
>
> Wouldn't it be funny if fifty years from now you could drop
> in on the old hometown again and find all your old friends all
> gone out of business, independence and initiative crushed,
> college-trained children all clerking for the Bohunk Corp. of
> America chain [a play on the name of a New Jersey-based chain,
> Bohack], whose stores under the different names of its sub-
> sidiaries have taken the place of all your friends—chain grocer,
> chain clothes, chain drug, chain hardware, chain flowers, chain
> milk, chain bread, chain meat, chain fish, chain fruit, chain
> hospitals, hotels, boarding houses, hot dogs, chain babies, chain
> adults, chain cradles for the infants and chain coffins for the dead
> and chain graveyards in which to push up little daisies! . . . until
> Judgment Day, when instead of there being Gabriel with his own
> horn, there'll be a rattling of chains.

History reveals that every innovation in methods of retail
distribution has been opposed by those fearful of its impact
on the existing order. (When discount stores appeared in the
1960s, their department store and specialty store competitors

would echo some of the anti-chain sentiments.) Cooler heads questioned the logic of suppressing a patently more efficient method of retail distribution. ''The chain is here to stay, and we must accept it,'' trade journalist M. M. Zimmerman had written in 1931. ''The independent merchant can best meet this competition by using fair and legitimate methods.'' It was high time merchants quit complaining about change, he went on, and began to change themselves. There was no reason why independent retailers could not avail themselves of low prices, clean stores, good advertising, and new methods of promotion and display. The techniques of thousands of small merchants were hopelessly archaic, their operations little changed from the frontier general stores of fifty years before. Few had any accurate idea of their cost of doing business.

The family was the primary labor force, and the independent often survived only because his family worked long hours for little or no wages. So it was with Hendrik Meijer's grocery store. Had Johanna and Fred not been available to help, it would have been impossible for Hendrik to divide his efforts between the barbershop and the grocery store.

An early advertisement for the new North Side Grocery appeared in 1935 in a Greenville publication called the *Buyers' Guide*. Coincidentally, the same issue carried a report on a chain-store tax bill debate in California, which soon became the twenty-second state to pass a law to regulate chains. California ''progressives'' introduced a bill calling for a tax of one dollar for one store, two dollars for the second, four dollars for the third, and so on in a geometrical progression up to five hundred dollars for the tenth store and each one thereafter. Service stations, beauty parlors, and other special interests were granted exemptions, because the bill was aimed primarily at Safeway and the other big food chains. In Sacramento, independent merchants packed the California Assembly chamber. A progressive Republican assemblyman called for passage of the bill to stop the centralization of wealth, prevent the destruction of independent retailers, save the state from wage slavery, and keep the road to opportunity open for posterity. It was the Charlie McCall speech all over again.

Of course, the chains fought the bill, as did California's major newspaper chain, the Hearst papers. A Hearst spokesman warned of a 10 percent boost in food prices if the bill passed, and called it a tax on the efficiency of distribution. ''We have all lived long enough to know that the men run-

ning these chain stores have not got horns," the newspaper-
man told the Assembly. "They are not people who chew up
little babies." Although the bill did pass, Californians over-
whelmingly rejected it in a subsequent referendum.

Hendrik took his son to an anti-chain rally at a stadium
in Grand Rapids. They heard the harangues and observed the
enthusiasm with which fellow merchants demanded laws to
restrict the chains. But Hendrik was not impressed, and he
reacted much as another Dutchman, Erasmus, had when his
proposal for a simplified liturgy (a more efficient method of
distributing religious feeling?) had caused a storm of controversy in the sixteenth century. "I heard a camel preaching at
Louvain that we should have nothing to do with anything that
is new," Erasmus had one of his characters observe.

To Hendrik the anti-chain furor smacked of demagoguery.
He left the rally with a conviction few of his colleagues shared:
"Chains have something the public wants—" he told Fred,
"lower prices." He had saved a clipping from a 1923 column
by Arthur Brisbane in the *Detroit Times* regarding Henry Ford's
extraordinary success in selling inexpensive, mass-produced
automobiles. "The moral is," Brisbane wrote, "to beat your
competitors, give value."

Stripped of the sentiments it preyed on, the anti-chain
movement was a delaying tactic of a special interest group. "In
the struggle to survive," wrote Raymond Moley, an advisor
to President Roosevelt, "the independent looks for some sort
of relief and chooses his most active competitor as the chief
culprit." But the current of change would not be diverted by
man-made obstacles. Most Americans welcomed lower food
prices wherever they could find them.

Although anti-chain campaigns continued for a half dozen
years, the movement had peaked by the time Hendrik Meijer
opened his store. More enlightened independents countered
the chains by joining together in "voluntary chains" of their
own. They pooled their buying power with cooperative warehouses that substantially lowered the cost of products coming
into their stores. Through cooperative advertising, stores such
as those operating under the Red & White banner developed
a strong "group" identity. They marketed "store" brands
priced to compete with A&P's Jane Parker and the other chain
labels that were recognized as price leaders.

So strong was the identity of the Red & White stores when
Hendrik had searched for a tenant for his building in 1933 that

he assumed they actually comprised a chain. Instead, Lee & Cady, the Red & White wholesaler, provided the groceries that made Hendrik's venture possible. Such voluntary groups— the IGA (Independent Grocers Alliance) was the largest— helped to restore a competitive balance with the chains and set the stage for the second great change in food distribution— the supermarket.

*　　*　　*　　*　　*

From June 1934 to August 1935 Johanna ran the store while Hendrik worked as much as possible in the barbershop. Fred painted weekly specials on butcher paper signs that hung in the front window. (Because the store sold beer and wine, Zien worried that her teenage son might develop a taste for liquor; she also expressed reservations about selling meat.) When business was slow, as it often was in the first few months, Fred played Old Maid with Iva Bradley, the clerk who was the only non–family member working at the store. (Her pay was five cents per hour at the start.) Their modest trade depended in part on the vitality of the refrigerator factories. "We used to just sit and wait then for payday," Johanna recalled.

Late in 1934 the North Side Grocery joined Lee & Cady's group to become one of three new Red & White stores in Greenville. The day the Red & White sign went up, a Lee & Cady salesman set up a coffee urn so that Hendrik could offer his customers a taste of the wholesaler's private brand. The salesman left Fred in charge of serving sample cups and brewing a fresh pot. But the boy got confused, and when he gave out cups from the new pot, customers were strangely noncommittal about the quality—although no one was frank enough to reject free coffee. Finally Hendrik poured a cup for himself. "My God, what kind of slop have you got there?" he asked Fred anxiously. "Dump it out; dump it out." As he wrote to Jo later, when he fixed up an old pot to brew his own in the back of the store, "There's nothing more disagreeable than poor coffee."

Hendrik burned pine stumps from the farm to heat the store. In the back room, the family cat took care of rodent problems. "She sleeps nearly all day and works nights," Hendrik told Johanna. "The mice are gradually disappearing." When an older customer stopped by after Christmas and lamented that the grocer had not given him a present, Hendrik told Johanna, "I gave him a small bottle of port wine, and he was tickled like a little kid with a sack of candy."

In 1935 came news of Gerhard Mantel's death in Hengelo at the age of seventy-four, three weeks after hernia surgery. He had attended a conference of Dutch vegetarians only a few weeks before that. His sons had finally opened a larger tailor shop, but now, in the face of the Depression, they feuded with one another and struggled to avert bankruptcy. Wrote Wilhelm Mantel, "Our business is down to half of what we did before, and the upkeep is twice as high."

In August 1935, Johanna enrolled in the University of Michigan. It was something she had dreamed of since high school, but of course there had been no money. Finally, Roy Ranney, Ellis Ranney's brother, helped her win the scholarship which made her trip to Ann Arbor possible. (Ellis was an alumnus and vigorous booster of arch-rival Michigan State University.)

When Ellis Ranney learned of Johanna's plans he asked Hendrik to join him on a short drive in the country. The icebox manufacturer asked the grocer: "How can you afford to send her, Henry?" "We've got twenty-five dollars from the till, and she's got two jobs plus the scholarship," Hendrik replied. Ranney wanted to help; he reached for his wallet and counted out seventy-five dollars—a considerable sum in 1935. But Hendrik stubbornly rejected the suggestion of charity. So Ranney drove down to the store, where Johanna stood behind the counter, and he laid the cash in front of her. "Your dad wouldn't take it, so you take it," he said. Johanna, slightly bewildered, went next door to ask her father what to do. "Take it," he told her. Ranney's feelings had been hurt enough.

The day after Johanna left for Ann Arbor, Zien came down to the store, put on an apron, and went to work behind the counter. And soon after that, Hendrik gave up his job in the barbershop to devote all his time to the store. He came to know all the salesmen who called on Greenville's grocers. Traveling men of the old school tried to load up retailers with all the product their shelves would hold, and then some. The only justification they needed was the assumption that if their products did not fill those shelves, someone else's would. As the man from Lee & Cady warned him, "Watch out for specialty men."

To buy competitively, however, Hendrik listened carefully to the "specialty men"—or to anyone else who offered a good deal. As Maurie DeFouw, a salesman for Borden products, recalled, "Anytime we had a special, we would always cut it down to rock bottom for [Hendrik] to buy a whole mess."

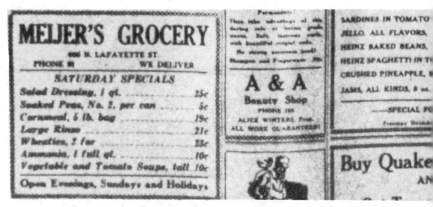

The earliest known Meijer's Grocery advertisement, dated August 2, 1935, appeared in the Greenville Buyers' Guide. *Hendrik's ad, nearly indistinguishable from those of his competitors, made the standard offer of traditional grocers: We Deliver.*

Other grocers noticed their new competitor's aggressiveness. ''That was the reason why after I started selling to him in Greenville he was about all the business I had there,'' DeFouw continued. ''Everybody else was mad at me. Kipp kicked me out of his store.''

The salesmen recognized where their best opportunities lay, however, and which grocers had the zeal and creativity to respond to the deals they offered. In fact, once Hendrik became a grocer full time, changes came quickly. As one wholesaler said, ''He was a good listener; that's why he was successful.'' First, he discontinued home delivery of Model Dairy milk. He never had made any money on the milk route anyway, and the Depression, coupled with the competition for bottles, had long ago turned a marginal business into a steady loser.

Late in August 1935, Hendrik notified his remaining route customers of the impending change. ''Sunday, September first, we shall be around to collect all of our bottles,'' he announced in a letter. ''However, we shall sell milk at the store, 605 N. Lafayette St. at the price of two quarts for 15 cents or 8 cents per quart, staying open nights, Sundays, and holidays for your convenience.''

By offering the lowest milk prices in Greenville, he set off a reaction among his competitors that ultimately cost him his membership in the Red & White group. The town's other two Red & White grocers sold milk for eight cents a quart. When

Hendrik offered two quarts for fifteen cents, they protested to Lee & Cady. Hendrik explained that the North Side Grocery charged a nickel deposit on every bottle, while the other stores, selling Blanding's milk, charged no deposit. Besides, the milk they sold was pasteurized; Hendrik's was not. But Lee & Cady insisted that Hendrik not undercut his fellow Red & White grocers on such a significant item.

The wholesaler's representative delivered an ultimatum: "If you don't raise your price, we're going to take down your sign." The threat provided an early test of Hendrik's determination to be competitive. He would not raise his price. Instead, he went outside with a hammer and, with the salesman's help, took the sign down himself. Soon afterward, he began buying his groceries from a merchant-owned cooperative, the Grand Rapids Wholesale Grocery Company, and he called his store simply Meijer's Grocery. (To join Grand Rapids Wholesale, Hendrik bought stock for $250 from a grocer in nearby Clarksville. He borrowed $100 from a Greenville bank for the down payment, and the grocer agreed to take the balance in installment payments—often in groceries as well as in cash.)

Nor was milk the only item on which Hendrik had begun to establish a reputation for good prices. His margins were so low, he said later, that "we were called on the carpet for being unfair competition." It was the barbershop pricing battle all over again. "Nobody considered the customer," Hendrik noted, "but the customer found a reason to consider Meijer." Such aggressiveness began to pay off, but it was a struggle all the way.

"Henry had a hard time getting along for quite a while," recalled his friend George Smith. "One morning he stopped me and said, 'George, come on up to my office. I want to talk to you. . . . I've got to have some money. I wonder if you could let me have a couple hundred dollars on time . . . ? I've got some groceries coming in and I haven't got enough money to pay for them.' " He got his loan, but it was not the only time he needed one.

He bounced a check to DeFouw once when the young salesman was new to the territory and had never before had a check returned. "I had three choices," DeFouw reflected years later. "Put it through again and see if it cleared, get a new check, or get cash." The young man went to Greenville uncertain of which path to take. Hendrik watched him check through his products on the grocery shelves, then finally called him over.

"You don't look good today," he said. "Maybe I can help you."

"I've got a problem," DeFouw said. "Your check came back."

"That's no problem," Hendrik replied. "What are we going to do about it?" The salesman listed his three choices, and Hendrik asked him which one he preferred. DeFouw answered uncertainly, "I haven't got the check with me; how about the cash?"

"Come with me," Hendrik said, and they went into the back room, where Hendrik gave him the cash. Much to the young man's relief, this grocer did not react indignantly at what could have been an awkward moment. He told the author forty years later, "I never saw your granddad mad."

Even after two years, Hendrik was far from convinced that his destiny lay in the grocery business. He had started the store to save his building, and he brought to the venture no greater aspirations for the future. Pursuing every avenue the Depression permitted, he even applied for a state agricultural inspector's job. Johanna boarded with a professor from Greenville who had connections in state government. After she hinted discreetly that her father was interested in applying for an inspector's position, the professor said with a smile, "I told you your dad would end up being a politician." It was as though Hendrik never expected to do himself the things he sensed a smart grocer might be able to.

Although he was finally making a modest living from the store, he had not given up dreams of quicker riches. He leased out mineral rights on his farm north of Greenville and then waited anxiously as oil was discovered nearby. "We need a new car," he wrote to Johanna in Ann Arbor. "Maybe we'll strike oil, and then, look out." Later he added, "If they strike oil, Brother and I are going to follow the fleet and join the navy and see the world."

Hendrik, Zien, and Fred practically lived at the store. On a radio in the back room Hendrik listened to the funeral service for King George V of England and described it for Johanna: "I could hear the command of the officer of the guard and the silent movement of the throng of people—it sounded just like water splashing against the shore. . . . " At night he listened to Major Bowes or Father Coughlin or one of the classical music programs. He went to movies by himself or with Fred (Zien seldom cared to go) at Greenville's two theaters.

He loved the movies, and when he and Fred decided to go, as Zien wrote to Jo, "You could not hold them with a team of horses." (She might have said the same thing twenty years later, when "going to the stores" was as much a pastime as a livelihood, a team activity father and son both relished.) The store often stayed open beyond customary hours for farmers who stopped by on their way out of town. Late at night Hendrik would rest his head on a pillow on a table in the back room. Sometimes the radio played, and Zien would drape a coat over his shoulders when he fell asleep.

In high school Fred was shy and somewhat self-conscious, a little uncertain of himself in the world outside the store. To Jo, Hendrik related Fred's anxiety about learning to dance. "He takes after his ma, I presume," he wrote. "I know I used to shake them up once in a while." But in the store, where Fred fixed up a table in the back so that he could study between customers, it was a different story. Hendrik was happy to claim credit for his son's ability, noting in one letter, "Brother is counting money—a chip off the old block."

In 1936 Greenville experienced its harshest winter in twenty years, and the kitchen stove was the only reliable source of warmth in the farmhouse. "It is nearly 12 o'clock and we are all in the kitchen soaking in what little heat it radiates," Hendrik wrote to Johanna one night. "The wind blows outside; it is snowing; the pump is frozen; the sewer plugged. Isn't the suburban life wonderful? Our caveman ancestors did not have the modern conveniences to worry about, so why should we?" When the farm was snowed in and the car would not start, Hendrik and Fred hauled milk to the store on sleds. They shoveled snow off the roof of the drugstore next door to keep it from caving in.

Having joined the Grand Rapids Wholesale Grocery Company in the wake of the Red & White milk controversy, Hendrik applied for membership in the wholesaler's cooperative marketing group, the Associated Grocers—or AG Stores. Membership meant joint advertising again, and stores that reflected a consistent decor. Hendrik informed Johanna, "I have to start painting next week, ceiling and walls cream and green trimmings."

In Ann Arbor Johanna survived on a strict budget. Her parents sent a check whenever they could. When a tuition payment or medical bill was due, or Johanna needed a new dress, Zien reassured her. "Don't worry about the money," she wrote on one occasion, "Pa said it will be there if we have to rob a bank to do it."

Life was scarred by the Depression in a thousand small ways. Hendrik testified in the trial of a vagrant charged with stealing coal. "He came into the store and asked me if I could use some coal in exchange for groceries," he explained to Johanna. "I told him I could, so he says, 'I'll bring you some tonight yet.' He got some groceries and I did not get any coal. But we lived through it. He got about 75 cents in groceries, and the court paid me 85 cents. You know, it's hard to beat a Hollander."

He loved to play off the ethnic stereotype of the slow-witted Dutch miser. When he told Johanna about buying an adding machine, he said, "I think it is very essential for a couple of dumb Hollanders." By "a couple of dumb Hollanders" he meant Fred as well as himself, for although his son was still in high school, Hendrik was already treating him as a partner in the enterprise. Fred was his partner in other ventures as well. Hendrik had a fondness for horse trading, and he took Fred along when he made a deal. "Some Montana men shipped in some horses and we could not resist the temptation," he wrote to Johanna. "You know, the lure of the wild." Fred cast a less romantic eye on the bargains his father struck. When they bought two draft horses in the spring of 1936, he noted in his diary, "We have a good crippled team."

By 1936 the Model Dairy, operating only to supply milk to the store, had gone the way of the barbershop. Hendrik sold his cattle for considerably less than he had paid for them. Still, it was a necessary step. The store simply demanded everything he had, and he could buy all the milk he needed from one of his old competitors. The store was coming to dominate the family's life, as a typical entry in Fred's diary from August 1936 suggests: "Pa and I cleared the alley and hauled the rubbish to the dump with Einer's truck. We also cleaned the back room. Pa's painting the north wall of the store. I sent a check to GRWG Co. [Grand Rapids Wholesale Grocery Co.]. I tapped 2 vinegar barrels. Ma washed this afternoon. Sis had her name in front page of paper, about her renewed scholarship."

Once committed to selling groceries, Hendrik looked for ways to improve his thoroughly conventional little store. He flirted with buying a truck for delivering grocery orders and later considered a larger truck that would serve as a mobile store and would enable him to sell to farmers in rural Montcalm County. Even as he contemplated such innovations, however, the grocery business was changing in more fundamental ways. The Depression had brought new pressures to bear on the time-honored operation of the conventional food store, whether it was part of a chain or a struggling independent. In the case of a typical independent like Meijer's Grocery, the proprietor or his wife or son or daughter waited on customers behind a long counter, assembling orders—sometimes by phone—for people who were billed on a monthly basis, but did not always pay as regularly.

The typical customer—"Mrs. Smith," to quote one food chain executive—had to wait in line to be served.

> Each item was obtained by clerks from high shelving against the walls and a few promotional displays in the center of the store. Many items were in bulk and had to be weighed on an even-balance scale with its questionable accuracy. . . . When the order was completed, the prices were listed on a sheet of paper or on one of the bags in which the groceries were placed. If the clerk was adept at addition, Mrs. Smith had a reasonable chance of being charged the right amount [indeed, chain stores assured parents that they could send their children to a chain store and not be overcharged]. . . . So, loaded with her groceries, meats, fruits and vegetables, Mrs. Smith with some difficulty would push through the door and, in most cases, walk home. Stores were small and conveniently located for pedestrian travel.

But a Depression-driven determination to keep costs low, coupled with the mobility that came with owning an automobile, began to change the way people shopped. Old patterns of neighborhood shopping broke down. If a cash-only store could offer lower prices by eliminating credit sales and delivery service, shoppers had the means as well as the incentive to search it out.

Chain stores had pioneered the practice of selling for cash only a few years before. In 1936 Hendrik decided to follow suit. As Fred wrote in his diary in June 1936: "Pa and I went to Hastings and Battle Creek to look at some 'cash' stores. We were greatly encouraged by their effective and logical system of merchandising." Naturally, Hendrik worried about how his customers would respond to the change. Farmers had seen their crop values collapse, and many factory workers were still laid off. Howard Kipp, Hendrik's rival across the street, continued to sell on credit. But Hendrik was convinced that "cash-and-carry," as it was then known, was the way of the future—the only way ultimately to offer low prices without going out of business. "Art Johnson's grocery bill is $25 since last pay-day," he wrote to Johanna. "Do you blame us for going cash?" He knew instinctively the importance of meeting the low prices of the cash-and-carry stores operated by the big chains, and as he observed to Johanna, "On credit it can't be done."

On July 1, 1936, Meijer's Grocery stopped making deliveries and selling grocery orders on account. Most of Hendrik's customers accepted the tradeoff for lower prices and responded enthusiastically. (There were always exceptions. Ellis Ranney came into the store soon after the switch and dropped several receipts on the counter in front of Hendrik and Fred. "Why should I buy from you folks for cash when I can buy just as cheap from Svendsen and get it delivered?" he demanded. Fred separated Svendsen's receipts from theirs and compared the orders: the other grocer's prices averaged 15 percent higher. Ranney was impressed, even if the difference, in Depression dollars, was only seventy-five cents.) The price advantage proved highly persuasive. Sales rose, and suddenly a three-hundred-dollar day was not uncommon on Saturdays after payday at the refrigerator factories. "I hope you're still holding to the 'No Credit' slogan," Johanna wrote from Ann Arbor.

Indeed they were. Meijer's Grocery was undergoing a retail revolution in microcosm. A week after the switch to cash, Hendrik paid $26.50 for a neon sign that reflected the store's new competitive thrust—and gave it a name to go with its character: "Thrift Market." In July the store's first advertisement as the Thrift Market appeared in the *Buyers' Guide*. "It cost $6," Fred noted in his diary. "It sure looks good." Johanna came home for the summer and helped paint price signs for the shelves and mark prices on the goods for the next logical, although still more dramatic, innovation for a small-town grocery store—self-service.

Ellis Ranney, the industrialist who was otherwise so conservative, was now prodding Hendrik Meijer to convert his store to self-service, where customers were expected to help themselves to goods displayed within their reach. Hendrik quickly warmed to the idea. Nor was he the only one in the family primed for action when Ranney threw out an ingenious challenge. Ranney told Fred that if he set up a self-service system by a certain weekend that fall, he would take the boy along to Ann Arbor for a University of Michigan football game and a visit with Johanna. Fred accepted the challenge. He bought a dozen double-handled wicker baskets for a dime each,

SMASH!

GO PRICES

CORN FLAKES, Millers .... lge. pkg. 9½c
CORN FLAKES, Kelloggs .... lge. pkg. 11c
KELLOGG'S WHOLE WHEAT BISCUIT .... pkg. 11c
MOTHER'S OATS (with china) .... pkg. 22½c
POST'S 40% BRAN FLAKES .... pkg. 9½c
SHREDDED WHEAT .... lge. pkg. 11½c
WHEATIES .... pkg. 11½c
BIRD SEED, French's .... pkg. 11c
BIRD GRAVEL, French's .... pkg. 7c
CUTTLE BONE, French's .... pkg. 7½c
OATS, Quaker Rolled .... lge. pkg. 17½c
OATS, Quaker Quick .... lge. pkg. 17½c
PORK & BEANS, Van Camp's .... 31-oz. can 9½c
PORK & BEANS, Tall Boy .... 30-oz. can, 3 for 25c
GRAPEFRUIT, Mission .... No. 2 can 12½c
CATSUP, First Call .... full 14-oz. bottle 10c
SARDINES, Van Camp's, in tomato sauce .... can 8½c
SARDINES, Van Camp's, in mustard sauce .... can 8½c
LIBBY CORNED BEEF .... can 18c
CORN BEEF HASH, Broadcast brand ...... can 14½c
CHILI CON CARNE, College Inn brand ...... can 8½c
PEAS, Indiana brand .... No. 2 can 6c
SOAP, Yellow A-1 .... 6 bars for 17c
GREEN CUT BEANS, Stokley brand .... No. 2 can 8½c
KIDNEY BEANS, Stokley Dark Red .... No. 2 can 7½c
SUPER SUDS .... lge. pkg. 16½c
GOLD DUST .... lge. pkg. 15c
OXYDOL .... lge. pkg. 21c
OXYDOL .... small pkg. 8½c
RINSO .... lge. pkg. 20c
RINSO .... small pkg. 7½c
CRYSTAL SOAP CHIPS .... 5-lb. box 25c
GLOSS STARCH .... 3-lb. pkg. 17½c
CORN STARCH .... pkg. 6½c
COFFEE, Vacation Land brand .... lb. 15c
BREAD, Muller .... 2-lb. loaf now only 10c
BREAD, Muller .... 1-lb. loaf now only 6c
DOUGHNUTS .... Friday & Saturday, doz. 12c
DINNER ROLLS .... doz. 6c
KELLOGG'S BREAKFAST FOOD DEAL,
   42c value for only 31c

SAVE WITH CASH

THRIFT MARKET

H. MEIJER, Prop.
605 North Lafayette Street

OPEN SUNDAYS, EVENINGS AND HOLIDAYS

*"Save with Cash" was the slogan in this advertisement from October 1936.
The dramatic headline was a hint of things to come.*

and Hendrik helped him build a bin for the baskets at the front of the store. Above the bin, in time for the start of business that October Saturday, Fred lettered a sign that read, "Take a basket, help yourself."

Fred had met the challenge, and he rode to Ann Arbor in Ranney's Lincoln Zephyr. When he returned to Greenville that night, however, Hendrik showed him the empty basket bin. Self-service had caught on quickly with the Thrift Market's customers. They saw the sign and did indeed help themselves —to the wicker baskets; before the day was over, the entire supply had disappeared.

But people liked serving themselves. As Hendrik wrote to his daughter, "Frank Rasmussen was in again Saturday night and said, 'If you keep on you'll get so much business you won't know how to handle it.' " And Zien confirmed the efficiency of the new approach: "Those baskets sure are nice. I had a lady in with her husband and daughters. The order came to $4.80. I got the bacon and flour; the rest she got herself. In the meantime I waited on three, four customers; so you see it works pretty well."

The problem of keeping first wicker baskets, then drop-handled wire ones in stock persisted for another year, until the Thrift Market received its first baskets on wheels—shopping carts. As Zien observed, "Nearly everybody asks, 'How much are those baskets?' or wants to take one; they think we give them away." Even as the basket supply fluctuated, sales grew. "We had some mob Saturday," Hendrik wrote to Johanna in November 1936, "and as usual I was going around in a circle."

Because Hendrik endorsed Roosevelt's efforts to pry loose the grip of the Depression, the presidential election of 1936 posed an easy choice. "Roosevelt, born with a silver spoon in his mouth, can see both sides of the class struggle and is smart enough to combat the problem [the Depression] in a statesmanlike way," Hendrik observed to Johanna. Fred's diary, echoing his father's opinions, noted that support for Republican nominee Alf Landon came from men like William Randolph Hearst, J. P. Morgan, the Fords, and the Rocke-fellers. "If all those people support Landon," Fred wrote, "I think that's reason enough to support Roosevelt."

Hendrik sympathized with the Spanish Republicans in their civil war with Franco, who had the support of the con-servative church hierarchy. He contrasted their aspirations with the narrow-minded outlook of a local minister. "Brother [Fred] is just telling me about the armistice speech he heard yester-

H. MYERS

POCKET BILLIARDS   **BARBER SHOP**
CANDIES, CIGARS AND TOBACCOS

EX MILK MAN   GREENVILLE, MICH.   EX FARMER

NOW – GROCERY STORE   10-16-36
"THRIFT MARKET"

Dear Sister.

I was already to go bed, but changed mine mind I thought better write you a few lines This 10³⁰ and came just home all along. Pal met me and you know glad to see me. she Sundays stays home nice.

Sixteen-year-old Fred Meijer made these notations on his father's stationary.

day by the new Methodist preacher," he wrote to Johanna. "He said the foreigners causing unrest in this country should be deported on ships not seaworthy so they would sink in the middle of the ocean. What a fine exhibition of the Christian faith put in practice. When you hear such talk, you do not wonder at the bitter struggle in Spain against such bloodsucking parasites."

Friends sometimes had difficulty understanding the conviction with which Hendrik condemned the new German leader, Adolf Hitler. Was he not, some asked, just the man to rescue Germany from the hyperinflation and depression that sank the Weimar Republic? Hendrik knew better. A Dutch anarchist had been hanged for setting fire to the German Reichstag building—the incident Hitler used as a pretext to consolidate power. The victim's brother had visited Hendrik's in-laws, the Mantels, on his way home from the trial in Berlin. He had seen his accused brother, barely conscious from the effects of drugs and interrogation, break down on the witness stand and confess to a crime of which few believed him guilty.

Nor was Stalin exempt from Hendrik's criticism. Zien had held out idealistic hopes that the Soviet Union would live up to the promise of communism. But fascist or communist— Hendrik observed how easily the dictators changed their stripes. Look at Mussolini, he said. A socialist contemporary of Hendrik and Zien and once publisher of a popular progressive newspaper, Il Duce had started in politics as a spokesman for the left. When Mussolini's son wrote a book glorifying his experiences as a pilot in the Ethiopian campaign, Hendrik wrote Johanna cynically, "It was fun dropping bombs on the natives from low-flying planes." And this from "the son of the former editor of *The Advance*."

* * * * *

Hendrik's original "meat department" consisted of an eight-foot refrigerated case. Adding a butcher and service counter made the department more complete, but not significantly more profitable. Hendrik recognized his need for an experienced butcher to correct that department's deficiencies. Yet if the butcher performed poorly, the barber did not always recognize the fact. So Hendrik negotiated a lease arrangement whereby the butcher owned the department and paid 6 percent of meat sales to cover rent, grocery bags, and the use of the cash register at the front of the store. For better or worse (depending on the butcher's condition, for he drank too much), the meat department became a joint venture.

Hendrik's time was consumed by an endless succession of chores. Driving back from Grand Rapids one night with a side of beef in the backseat, he fell asleep at the wheel. "You know Sister, I nearly had a bad accident," he informed Johanna.

> I had to go to Grand Rapids after a [side of] beef at the packing house. Of course Ma says "come back quickly," so I wound up my dealing and started back. [While Hendrik was away buying or touring or meeting with the wholesaler, Zien often managed the store by herself.] Between GR and Rockford I got sleepy, or

rather, drunk with sleep. We had been up nearly every night
till 12 o'clock and I guess I could not take it any more. I thought
of driving onto the side of the road and snoozing awhile, but
I didn't, thinking of Mother being alone at the store. The traffic
was light, not a car in sight, and I must have passed out. The
first thing I knew the rail fences were flying in all directions. . . .

Hendrik escaped with a few bruises, but a running board and
fender were wrecked. In his diary Fred noted with relief, "It's
a good thing I didn't do that."

As Hendrik's explanation of his accident suggested, the
family worked interminable hours. But their effort seemed to
be paying off. Although Hendrik was still behind on even the
interest portion of his mortgage payments, the Thrift Market
was registering record sales. When Hendrik saw one of the
Kipp brothers tending the plot of grass between their store's
sidewalk and curb, he could not help but compare their tidy
exterior with the well-trodden path of broken concrete beyond
his entrance. As he boasted in an ad, "No grass grows in front
of the Thrift Market."

Hendrik relished a catchy headline, and the Thrift Market's
advertisements grew more and more aggressive. "We're going to put in *hot* specials every week now instead of everyday
prices," Fred wrote in his diary in 1936. Saturdays were the
busiest days, but Saturday's cash could not be deposited until
the following Monday. Without a safe in the store, Hendrik
brought the money home for the weekend. The heap of cur-
rency suggested at least a fleeting prosperity. "Ma's got $455.32
under her pillow and a shotgun next to her head," Fred wrote.
"The money makes such a big lump she really doesn't need
a pillow."

Even a pessimist had to admit that the store had come a
long way. In his capacity as bank director Ranney offered help
if Hendrik could not meet his interest payment. As Hendrik
wrote to Johanna, "You know, these gloomy guys don't always
mean bad; of course he knows we are trying to play ball."

Hendrik passed his fifty-third birthday without having
struck oil—indeed, without having paid all his bills—but the
little Thrift Market was poised for yet another change. Once
again, as when he emigrated, and later when he turned in
desperation to selling groceries, he was caught up in a current which proved irresistible. He was ready for the age of the
supermarket.

II

You know what papa always said, "What you really want to do, you can do."

—Gezina Meijer, quoting Hendrik
in a letter to Johanna, 1936

In Greenville, as elsewhere, the ingredients of change were already at hand. "Cash only," "self-service"—these innovations provided the foundation for a new way of selling groceries. The Depression had redoubled demand for a way to bring down grocery prices. Henry Ford's techniques of mass production had reduced the price of automobiles. Was there a correspondingly efficient means of merchandising that would reduce the family grocery bill?

The components of the modern supermarket first came together in 1930 in a vacant automobile garage (the Depression created those by the hundreds) on Long Island. There Michael Cullen, a former manager for the Kroger Company, proposed a large, no-frills store in a low-rent district outside New York City. His location kept his overhead low, and his strategy had a missionary ring to it: "I would lead the public out of the high-priced houses of bondage into the low prices of the promised land."

The stark setting of the old garage reflected the bargain prices found inside the "King Kullen" store. Cullen's idea was to sell a high volume of national-brand items at a very low mark-up—sometimes even at cost, with no margin of profit at all. His array of groceries, meat, produce, dairy products, and household items offered unprecedented variety. He had room for huge quantities—five times or more the space of a typical grocery store. Add enormous displays and the heavy advertising of rock bottom prices, and he was certain to draw a crowd—for which he provided free parking, because more and more Americans made their shopping trips by automobile.

King Kullen's first raucous ads identified the store as "the world's greatest price breaker." Cullen, in fact, was not above trading on the anti-chain rhetoric of the demagogues, for whom chain stores symbolized the subversion of small-town America by Eastern financiers. At the top of one ad was a warning directed to such competitors: "Chain stores, read these prices and weep. You Wall Street stores have been making millions from the public for years with your outrageous prices. Chain stores, drop your prices, give the poor buying public a chance.

I'm trying to prove to these Wall Street chain stores that the people . . . are sick and tired of paying any price you ask. Chain stores, play fair, lower your prices. You are a menace to the nation.''

In its first week of operation King Kullen rang up sales that neither a corner grocer nor a chain store executive could comprehend. No one even knew what to call this crudely fixtured behemoth and the horde of imitators it inspired until three years later, in 1933, when the president of the Kroger Company (who had spurned Cullen's proposal when the young man tried to interest his employers in the idea) left the chain to open just such a store himself in Cincinnati. He called it a "super market."

King Kullen and its offshoots acquired a reputation for cutting prices even below cost on a fast-moving product like coffee or oleomargarine just to attract a crowd that could then be exposed to the immense variety of the larger store. Picturesque names such as "Wild Tiger" and "Big Bear, World's Champion Price Fighter" emphasized the new stores' aggressively competitive posture. Traditional competitors were appalled. Some grocers declared that once the novelty wore off and prosperity returned, no one would drive twenty or thirty miles to fight the crowds at one of these cheap, self-service food barns.

Expansion of conventional chain stores had peaked in 1932, less from the advent of the Depression or anti-chain campaigns than from the changes wrought by Cullen's new concept. The Depression-bred need to conserve every penny made the supermarket's price advantage decisive. "This store will save every family from $2 to $5 on their groceries every week," Cullen promised. Week after week his price-oriented advertising spread a powerful message. One of his favorite slogans, emulated by others around the country, was compellingly simple: "Why Pay More?" Years later, Hendrik Meijer's company would adopt the phrase as its own.

The supermarket left traditional stores, independent or chain, far behind. As one pioneer operator defined it, "A Super Market was not a building merely in excess of a certain number of square feet; nor an operation that has a volume in excess of a certain number of dollars. I prefer to consider a Super Market as a new method of food merchandising, based on the theory of 'Pile it High and Sell it Cheap,' plus the elimination of service and introducing of self-service techniques." Pile it high, sell it cheap—and run ads featuring items sold below cost.

In Greenville, the Thrift Market's customers were hardly the carriage trade. As much as Americans anywhere, when the Depression struck they were forced to look for the lowest prices they could find. They were acutely receptive to appeals to their pocketbooks.

During the winter of 1937, auto workers in Flint made history when their strike shut down the General Motors Corporation. Always a student of current events, Hendrik Meijer reflected his interest in a Thrift Market advertisement in the *Greenville Daily News:* "Sitdown strikers will stand up for these prices." Prices—low prices—had been his obsession since he had come into the store on a full-time basis in 1935. He saw the future of his store tied to his ability to offer customers a bargain. After Fred put out the wicker baskets, Hendrik's ads began to encourage shoppers to "Serve yourself and Save." By 1937, however, it was increasingly apparent that "help yourself" baskets and clever advertising were not enough to keep the tiny Thrift Market competitive.

Although independent operators had been the first grocers to gamble on the supermarket idea, the chains were quick to exploit its potential. No longer could even A&P, with small stores on every Main Street east of the Mississippi—including two a block apart in Greenville for a time—be assured of success merely by undercutting the prices of other grocers in the neighborhood. In that respect, the supermarket was a product not only of the Depression but of the automobile. From 1920 to 1930 the number of licensed autos jumped from eight million to twenty-three million. Until the auto age, New Deal economist Adolph Berle noted, the same local merchants who had denounced chain store practices had sometimes enjoyed neighborhood monopolies. The car reduced the consumer's dependence on and loyalty to the neighborhood store, chain or independent. Shoppers were willing and able to seek out lower prices and greater variety. And the supermarket, with so much more space than a conventional grocery store, offered both.

A corner grocer's notion of aggressive retailing might have been to set out a bushel basket of turnips or potatoes with a good price on it. His one or two aisles were narrow and cramped to begin with, however, and ladies snagged their hose on the edge of the baskets. Indeed, the attitude of many traditional grocers toward their customers was, in the words of a salesman who called on Hendrik, "If they fell over it, it would sell better." The conventional grocer bought merchandise in small quantities, seldom marked prices on individual items, and lacked the space for variety or large displays.

In Ann Arbor, Johanna recorded her impression of one of Michigan's first supermarkets: "It is housed in a large garage comparable in shape and size to Tom Sharpe's [a garage in Greenville], if not a little larger," she wrote. "As you enter you take a basket and you come to the meat department. . . . Then they have long tables running the length of the store—I think seven, and each table is a sort of department, such as one for canned fruits, one for canned vegetables, and one for glass goods, etc. . . . Then as you exit you pass the fruit department. One thing I noticed was that the meat, fruit, and staples were separate sections. . . ." Southeastern Michigan proved a hotbed of supermarket activity. By 1936, as M. M. Zimmerman later observed, Detroit "had become quite a Super Market city," with eighty of the big stores operating there.

And by 1936, A&P, the biggest chain of all, had begun to stir like Gulliver on the beach of Lilliput, casting off its old stores to cash in on the new phenomenon. The company had pioneered high-volume retailing. Its founder's son, John Hartford, had once said, "We would rather sell 200 pounds of butter at a penny a pound profit than 100 pounds at two cents a pound profit." So, recognizing the magnetic appeal of the King Kullen idea, the A&P chain experimented with formulas that would satisfy the new criteria of low price and wide variety. A&P stores opened in old warehouses (Detroit was the site of the first such "warehouse store"), and the chain even tried selling groceries in dime stores. Stores of many sizes and designs were tested until A&P management hit on a format that set the standard for supermarkets for a decade to come: the 10,000-square foot store. The new format, first introduced in Ypsilanti, Michigan, and then in Detroit, was five times the size of the standard food market of the day. Hendrik Meijer's Thrift Market, by comparison, occupied little more than 1,400 square feet.

In the spring of 1937, A&P announced plans for nineteen big stores in western Michigan. In Grand Rapids they converted vacant buildings to supermarkets, and customers responded enthusiastically. Seldom did a competitor match the insurgent's prices. When A&P sold an item at a price lower than an independent retailer could buy it for wholesale, even Hendrik might drive to Grand Rapids and stock up on cans of fruit juice or vegetables, hoping he would not be recognized.

Indeed, Hendrik and Fred quickly became acquainted with the new A&Ps. Once they needed wallpaper cleaner, and A&P's price was lower than the Thrift Market's wholesale cost. They bought a dozen cans in Grand Rapids to take back to Greenville and sell themselves. The A&P cashier was surprised to see someone buying so odd an item in quantity. The white-haired customer, rather fastidiously dressed in a dark suit, had a hint of ministerial bearing about him, so the cashier ventured to inquire, "What are you going to do with all this, clean a church?" With a sly smile Hendrik replied, "In my father's house are many mansions."

After saturating larger cities with supermarkets, A&P fixed its gaze on small-town expansion. Shopkeepers trembled in Charlotte, Hastings, and Grand Haven; and Greenville was also on the list. Its two dozen small grocers, seemingly content to operate much as they always had, recoiled at the news.

In April 1937, Hendrik heard a speaker at a meeting of Grand Rapids Wholesale members predict that self-service, high-volume supermarkets like A&P would soon be the "only salvation" of other grocers. But the prices! A neighborhood merchant might go broke matching A&P's prices. Yet Hendrik saw no alternative, and that left him with no choice but to expand.

Admittedly, he had a few advantages when he decided to double the size of the Thrift Market by removing the wall that separated it from the cafe next door. Although his mortgage payment was sometimes late, he owned both the storefronts. The man who ran the cafe agreed to move into the basement and operate a tavern called the Rathskeller.

Though the Thrift Market still struggled from payday to payday, Hendrik's low prices had built a steady trade. And competitors were beginning to feel the effects of his growing volume. As a clerk for one nearby food store recalled, "The concept of self-serve which [Hendrik] instituted . . . shook the surrounding community grocers. Basically they said, 'At those prices he won't last long.' " Across the street Kipp pressured a local wholesaler to freeze the Thrift Market out of certain brand name products Kipp bought. Later on, however, the wholesaler wanted to distribute Cream White shortening, a brand Hendrik bought directly from the producer in Tennessee. Hendrik bought so much of it for his one store that before the producer would sell to the wholesaler, he asked Hendrik if that would jeopardize the company's lucrative relationship with the Thrift Market. Although Hendrik was tempted to say yes, he resisted. He told the shortening company it could sell the wholesaler all the shortening he needed.

Hendrik liked to stack up big displays of coffee or Crisco just as the supermarkets did: an old snapshot shows the front window of his store nearly filled with bags of coffee. And self-service and the elimination of credit were cornerstones of his success. But only by enlarging the store could he achieve the sales volume that would enable him to keep his prices low enough to do what seemed only natural—challenge the A&P.

He felt he had to act quickly too, before the new A&P reached Greenville; otherwise, he would be just another small grocer with somewhat lower-than-average prices. In May he informed Grand Rapids Wholesale of his expansion plans and how he would lay out the store. One of its executives listened carefully and said, "You remind me of a dumb fox." A&P was much too large to take notice of a single small-town competitor. Had they taken notice, however, the chain might have been flattered, for Hendrik's strategy took flattery's sincerest form— imitation.

When he set out to remodel the store, he still owed the lumber company across the street several hundred dollars from earlier projects. Its manager, openly skeptical of Hendrik's latest scheme, asked how the remodeling work would be financed. "I told him as far as I knew now I could do it myself," Hendrik wrote to Johanna, "and I believe we can. We keep the wholesalers paid up. In fact, we only owe them $1.25, and that's not due till Saturday." But he had to pay cash for his lumber and paint, "Hoover stuff," as he called it—pay as you go.

Hendrik and Fred did much of the expansion carpentry themselves, but they turned to part-time helpers—"Henry's henchmen," as his barbershop apprentice once described them—for additional manpower. "Rudy Schwartz is building the stairway [to the new cafe downstairs]," Hendrik wrote to Johanna. "Herman Kunz does the plumbing and Wash Nielsen the cleaning up. I run around in a circle as usual." Johanna would soon be home for the summer, and as Hendrik informed her, "There will be plenty of work for you also, so roll up your sleeves."

He had trouble finding someone to put an opening through the basement wall for the steps leading downstairs from the street to where the tavern would be. So he offered ten dollars to one man, then another, and each took his turn with a sledge hammer before giving up. Then Schwartz took up the offer. He neglected to mention, however, that he planned to create the doorway with dynamite—a small, well-placed charge. The family was working in the store upstairs when they heard a muffled thumping sound, a rattle, and another thump; the floor trembled and the front windows shook. Then Rudy Schwartz trudged up the stairs and said, "Well, Henry, you owe me ten dollars. The hole is in the wall." After checking out a customer, Hendrik stuck his head downstairs to investigate. Schwartz had blown a hole in the concrete—blown it directly below the checkout counter, Fred remembered, "right while we were doing business upstairs!"

In late July 1937 they tore out the wall between the old store and the space where the cafe had been. Hendrik had a clear idea of his strategy for arranging the store; what remained were the specifics. He and Fred drove to Grand Rapids and Big Rapids, Muskegon and Charlotte, to see what A&P was doing. Fred had never been inside an A&P store before his father went into the grocery business. Now father and son both became students of the huge chain's success. Everywhere they went they carried a tape measure. In Grand Rapids they studied the aisles at the A&P on Grandville Avenue and measured the shelves in the store on Stocking Street. One fact stood out: A&P was using the same general layout everywhere.

Sometimes they conducted their research clandestinely; on other occasions they had the blessing of the A&P manager, who amused himself by divulging his chain's techniques to a small-town merchant with a heavy Dutch accent. Either way, Hendrik saw exactly how he might set up a supermarket: where the meat and produce went, what aisle was best for bread or cereal, where the cookie counter belonged, and so forth.

The new A&P stores went first class. The store planned for Lafayette Street in Greenville (the town's smaller, older A&Ps would be closed) would be located in a new building. And the chain's acquisition of new equipment meant bargains for buyers of the old. Hendrik bought five used A&P meat cases. They were not as shiny and modern as the newer models, but they cost only twenty-five dollars each, and they enabled Hendrik to boast that the expanded Thrift Market would have the biggest meat department in Montcalm County.

By the end of July 1937, the soon-to-be-doubled store was taking shape. In his diary Fred wrote, "We've got Edna K.

sacking and Pa and I are fixing the counters into place while Ma, Sis and Dorothy S. sweep and wait on trade.'' Three weeks before the enlarged store was scheduled to open, Grand Rapids Wholesale shipped the largest order the Thrift Market had ever placed. Fred answered the back door when the truck arrived, read the invoice, and ran to show his father. To their horror, they discovered that they had exceeded the credit limit of $300. The order had been sent COD—and the bill was nearly $600. They had nowhere near that kind of money in the cash register, or in the checking account.

"Get it unloaded,'' Hendrik told his son. ''We'll argue about it afterwards.''

The driver was at the end of his route. When all the cases were off, he discovered to his irritation that the order was a case or two short. So upset was he at the foul-up that he jumped into the cab cursing the invoice and drove off. When he returned to Grand Rapids without a check, the credit manager called Greenville. ''The driver left before we could pay him,'' Hendrik explained. Then he crossed his fingers and hoped for a busy weekend. The following Monday, Hendrik and Fred drove to Grand Rapids with a check. There still was not enough money in the bank to cover it, but the check had to make a four-day circuit from Grand Rapids to Chicago and back before clearing the bank in Greenville—time enough to sell more groceries and run to the bank with a new deposit.

On August 2, Hendrik erected a massive sign with ''Thrift Market'' painted in bright yellow letters on a red background. The sign was forty feet long and spanned what had been two storefronts. ''There were four of us with a rope from the roof and four men shoved up from the bottom,'' Fred wrote. ''It sure is a beautiful sign.''

Shortly before the expanded store's grand opening, Hendrik explained his operating philosophy to a reporter from the *Greenville Daily News.* ''No delivery service, no telephone business and everything strictly cash is the basis of my business,'' he said. ''For these reasons we are able to offer extremely low prices. . . . '' Self-service, the reporter added, meant that ''customers who wish to do so may take a large basket and choose their supplies as they wish.'' Improvements as a result of the remodeling included ''a new rack of the large wooden type . . . installed at the rear of the store for fresh vegetables.''

ANNOUNCING THE

GRAND OPENING
OF A NEW FOOD CENTER
- SATURDAY, AUGUST 21 -

SHOP AT YOUR LEISURE OR SERVE YOURSELF INSTANTLY

605 NORTH LAFAYETTE
2 BLOCKS NORTH OF THE BRIDGE

THRIFT MARKET

NO WAITING SERVE SELF AND SAVE

LOADS OF BARGAINS

The Answer To Your Food Problem Is Right Here!

Greenville's Newest Comple Food Market

PLENTY OF PARKING SPACE

WATCH THE DAILY NEWS FOR VALUES EACH WEEK

CATSUP 14 oz. bottle "Alice" 9

Corn Flakes "Kellogg's" **2** lge. boxes **19c**

BLISS COFFEE lb. tin **21½c**

Wheaties Breakfast Cereal box **10c**

DEL MONTE COFFEE Pound Tin 25c

MILK Swift's tall can **4** cans **25c**

FIG BARS 2 lbs. 19c

CAR LOT PRICES!

Salmon Tall Can **21c** Libby's Fancy Red

GRAPEFRU

JUICE Very Finest Premier No. 2 size can **9**

Uxydol or Chipso	large box	19c
JELLO ALL FLAVORS	pkg.	5c
Heinz Soups MOST VARIETIES	2 cans	23c
VINEGAR Pure Cider gallon		**15c**
Sunbrite Cleanser	box	4½c
Balloon Soap Flakes	5-lb. box	35c
Baking Soda ARM & HAMMER	box	6½c
Tomato Juice LIBBY'S	50-oz. giant size	21c
SUGAR Pure Cane	10 lb.	**49c**

QUALITY MEATS at SELF SERVE PRICE and YOU GET THE 'COUNTER SERVIC

FREE! FREE! FREE!
ONE RING OF BOLOGNA WITH EVERY 50c PURCHASE OR OV

Sirloin, Round Steak lb **22**

BEEF ROAST	lb. 16c	BEEF RIBS	lb 12½c
FRESH GROUND BEEF 2 lbs.	29c	PURE PORK SAUSAGE lb	18
PORK CHOPS	lb. 28c	PORK LOIN ROAST lb 28	

LARD Pure Kettle Rendered With Meat Order **2** lb. **29**

BACON SQUARES lb 19c		BACON, sugar cured, lb 25	
BACON, 1½-lb. cello wrapped pkg.	16c	MINCED HAM, sliced lb	15
PICNIC HAMS Sugar Cured	Small Skinless		Large
19c	WEINERS 20c lb.	FRANKFUI 15c lb	

Pineapple "Del Monte" Crushed No. 2 Size Can **15½c**	Loganberries "Del Monte" No. 2 Size can **23½c**

BANANAS 3 lbs. 14c

Carnation Milk Tall Can **7c**

Gold Medal Flour 24½-lb. Sack **99c**

Reflecting supermarket-style aspirations, this ad for the expanded Thrift Market's grand opening featured "car lot prices." (Greenville Daily News)

Two days before the opening, the Thrift Market ran its first full-page ad—a big step toward the sort of powerful advertising that characterized supermarkets (and which became a Meijer trademark). That same afternoon, however, one of the bargain-priced, ammonia-cooled meat cases—an A&P relic—sprang a leak. The store Hendrik would soon be promoting as "Greenville's newest complete food market" had to be evacuated.

Two days later the meat case was still out of action, but the fumes were gone and everything else was ready. Fred used a wax pencil to make signs for the new display counters. On the two doors opening onto the sidewalk hung hand-lettered signs for *in* and *out*. Hendrik hired extra help, and on August 21, 1937, grand opening day, the Thrift Market rang up its best day ever.

Eleven days later, on September 1, A&P opened the doors of its gleaming new "Master Market" a few blocks down Lafayette Street. "Big news for the people of Greenville and vicinity," its ad proclaimed. "Today America's specialists in food economy open the greatest market ever seen in this part of the country. . . ." And the newspaper reported an innovation everyone had to see: "Very convenient rolling carriages, equipped with two wire market baskets, are available to each customer upon entering the store." Thus did the shopping cart make its debut in Greenville.

The Thrift Market's customers were not immune to the lure of the new A&P. Crowds streamed downtown to explore this enormous store that promised hot prices and "rolling carriages" and was even larger than Hendrik Meijer's establishment. Even Fred admitted in his diary, "It sure looks nice."

It was not long, however, before Hendrik counterattacked with a newspaper ad that summed up his response to the Master Market: "We don't meet competition, we make it." As Maurie DeFouw recalled, "Whatever A&P sold it for, that's what he sold it for. It didn't make any difference what it cost him." Sometimes he was a bit reckless. Michigan's fair trade law required merchants to sell certain brand-name products at or above a minimum price. Among these was Miracle Whip salad dressing, which was many a grocer's staple. Its fair trade price was 35 cents, but competitors caught Hendrik selling it for 33 cents. "That was a mistake," he explained later. But mistake or not, it typified his style.

"He was the best customer I had," said DeFouw. "If we had a special [promotion on a certain item] coming up, I asked him how many he wanted. He was able to sell, and sell at a [low] price." His biggest question always was, " 'What's A&P going to sell it for?' " DeFouw added. "A&P *was* the grocery business. Whatever A&P was doing, that's what he would do. He couldn't have had a better pattern."

Along the way Hendrik learned some things about buying. He did not hesitate to drive to Bay City for a deal on peanut butter or to a little mill near Lansing for cheaper flour. And as the price war raged, the Thrift Market's customers came back. On one occasion a man brought in a ten-cent box of cereal—A&P's private brand. The man's wife had intended to get another brand, and now he wanted a refund from the Thrift Market. At the cash register Fred started to explain that the cereal could not have come from their store, but Hendrik stopped him. As Fred recalled, "He took me to one side and told me: 'We can eat it ourselves; don't send him back to A&P for a dime.' "

If North Greenville residents were a little surprised when they found out that the new A&P could not improve on Thrift Market prices, they were still more surprised that the giant national chain had patterned the aisle and shelf arrangement of its Greenville store on the very layout Hendrik used. More than one regular customer, upon reaching the cash register at the Thrift Market, called to its ebullient proprietor, "Hey, Henry, looks like A&P copied you." Hendrik Meijer would affect a thoughtful pause before replying, "Why yes, isn't that something?"

6

First Link
in a Chain

*Some people could not see a changing world if they were dropped off
on Mars.*

—Hendrik Meijer, 1937

The Depression introduced grocers to a new medium of
exchange: welfare orders issued by the government. When
relief payments were inaugurated, many merchants regarded
them with suspicion and disdain; and many newly impover-
ished Americans shied away from government "handouts."
Especially in small towns, public assistance was a last resort.
But as the ranks of the unemployed increased, proud men and
women were forced to turn to the government. Their
neighbors, including their shopkeepers, did not always understand their dilemma. "Every possible stigma was attached to
aid," wrote William Manchester in *The Glory and the Dream.*
One community tried to bar welfare recipients from voting.
Elsewhere, groups objected to the admission of children from
welfare families to their public schools; families were even
discouraged from attending some churches.

In the grocery stores, public assistance could mean public
disgrace. A customer stepping up to the cash register to pay
for groceries with a government welfare order self-consciously
anticipated the merchant's raised eyebrow or the sidelong
glance of a neighbor. "Where's the welfare register?" a cashier
might call out to the clerk or the owner, and the customer
would cringe as everyone within earshot turned to see who
was "on the dole."

The thought of that cruel ritual made Hendrik Meijer
wince. Although Ranney warned him not to accept government relief orders because "welfare" was a Roosevelt scheme
that would bankrupt the country and shortchange its merchants, Hendrik encouraged welfare customers from the start.

Indeed, he posted a sign in the window of the Thrift Market that read, "Welfare orders welcome." He told his cashiers never to refer to welfare orders by name. At the Thrift Market such transactions were recorded as "due bills." (Ironically, the poorest customers were not the only ones presenting due bills at the checkout. When Ranney advanced Hendrik cash for mortgage payments, he was paid off with groceries, and he also used a "due bill" to make a purchase. And Hendrik employed due bills when he bartered groceries for equipment or repairs.) Thus the Thrift Market appealed not only to the pocketbooks of the unemployed, but to their self-respect as well.

Hendrik could not have predicted that his instinctive response to the needs of customers on relief would also prove to be good business. By the late 1930s, however, the Thrift Market was accepting nearly 60 percent of all the relief orders in Montcalm County—a staggering percentage for a single store in a county with thirty grocers. "In those days I heard grocers say they didn't want any welfare business," Hendrik said later, "but welfare families were welcome at my store." A later newspaper account added: "As the word got around, welfare families—four families to a car—drove to Greenville from miles around to buy from Meijer." And Hendrik recalled, "I could understand their problem because I was just as hard up as any of them, being in debt and on the verge of losing everything."

Late in 1937 he wrote Johanna: "I got bawled out for putting too much bread on one [relief] order. You know, the poor do not need too much bread. W. Lincoln [a Greenville farmer] is mad that the government's buying too many apples to give to the needy. I told him every apple bought by the government would go to people having no buying power and would help his market because it would take care of the surplus, but he saw red and he is too good a Christian to be mistaken. You know, religion and Republicanism give that self-satisfying, never-to-be-wrong feeling."

The following year, Johanna wrote from Ann Arbor, "Every time I get a letter it says mama's doing welfare orders." Welfare trade was significant because in Montcalm County, as elsewhere, unemployment continued at record levels. For a few months in 1936 the Depression went into remission, but in 1937 the dark days returned. On October 19, Fred wrote, "The stock market took a fall today; it looks like we're in for another depression." Union organizing efforts brought auto plants to a standstill in Flint and led to bloody confrontations in Detroit. In Greenville, the refrigerator factories became targets of union activity. At a local plow works, two men agitating for a union were laid off when health examinations revealed spots on their lungs. "Maybe that's a good way to get rid of the CIO members," Hendrik wrote cynically. "The dieticians know how to be diplomatic."

*　　*　　*　　*　　*

With the Thrift Market battling for business, Hendrik was always on the lookout for a deal. He paid sixty-four dollars for the inventory of a grocer who had gone bankrupt, advertised "hot" prices every week, and even raffled off a bicycle. He watched what A&P did and tried not to let a low price go unanswered. In one competitive skirmish, he determined not to let A&P undersell him on vinegar. He learned of a producer near Grand Rapids named Van Maldegan, who was too small to supply A&P, but who had built up a surplus. Hendrik and Fred drove down to see him.

"'I hear you've got a lot of vinegar," Hendrik said as they came in the office door.

"Yep."

So Hendrik asked, "Would you sell me some for nine cents a gallon?"

Van Maldegan, suddenly turning red, looked up at him. The wholesale price was a dime or more, and even A&P was getting seventeen cents a gallon retail.

"That's what's wrong with you goddamn grocers," Van Maldegan sneered. "Then you want to sell it for a quarter; you don't care whether we're losing money; you don't care about us at all. . . ." On he went in a withering tirade against greedy merchants who did not care about their suppliers.

Hendrik listened for a moment, then turned abruptly and walked out of the office, slamming the door behind him and abandoning Fred to the irate vinegar man. Hendrik could not go far; Fred had the keys to the truck. A long moment later he reappeared in the doorway. In a calm voice he said, "Mr. Van Maldegan, may I start over again?"

The vinegar man drew a deep breath and nodded.

"I know when you say grocers get a quarter for a gallon of vinegar, that's true," Hendrik began. "I also know that A&P sells vinegar for seventeen cents a gallon. I'd like to buy a truckload [ten fifty-gallon barrels] from you. I'd like to take that vinegar to Greenville and sell it for ten cents a gallon. That'll really stir up the market, please the farmers, and bring in business. Will you help me?"

The vinegar man's expression softened.

"You'd be willing to haul it to Greenville, unload it yourself, and pump it—all for a five-dollar profit?"

Hendrik nodded.

"Then I'd be glad to sell you my vinegar at nine cents a gallon."

Van Maldegan unloaded his surplus. He was willing to work with the struggling Greenville grocer who was ready to take on A&P even if he lost money on the deal. The vinegar man never would have cooperated if he thought the merchant was trying to take advantage of his surplus to make a killing. But Hendrik had enlisted the seller on the side of the buyer. Later students of business might call the technique "buying by objective."

Hendrik dealt with potentially disastrous customer problems in a similarly engaging way that even complemented his discerning eye for shoplifters. Once when he noticed a man with a can tucked under his mackinaw waiting in line at the checkout, he squeezed by him and patted his chest. "Say," he told the would-be shoplifter casually, "you've put on some weight."

As the lowest-priced stores in town, the Thrift Market and the A&P vied for the business of farmers who bought groceries on their Saturday trips to town. Much as Hendrik tried, however, there were times when he failed to please some of those customers. In the late 1930s both the Thrift Market and the A&P were licensed to sell oleomargarine, the cheap and still somewhat controversial alternative to creamery butter. Oleo appealed to the Thrift Market's welfare customers and others forced to stretch their dollars, but it was anathema to many farmers, some of whom had dairy herds themselves.

When a farmers' union decided to boycott stores that sold oleo, the Thrift Market became a target. A&P was too big to be intimidated by a local boycott, but an independent grocer was vulnerable. The president of the local union had a farm near Hendrik's north of Greenville. Although he had been a steady Thrift Market customer, he refused to shop any longer at a store that exercised its license to sell oleo. He traded instead with a small grocer at a crossroads north of Greenville. The rural grocer dared not register with the state to sell oleo, even though some of his customers might prefer the cheaper spread. Rather than take out a license, he supplied oleo to those customers by buying it out of the dairy case at the Thrift Market—and signing his receipt as a wholesale purchase so he would not have to pay sales tax.

Hendrik grew indignant when the boycott persisted and more farmers began to trade with the other grocer. He offered to show the other grocer's receipts for oleo purchases to the officers of the farm union: the grocer they were patronizing was indeed selling oleomargarine—he was just bootlegging it into his store. But the farmers remained adamant; they refused to look at the sales slips. Hendrik too was adamant; he continued to sell oleo. Finally, after several weeks, the farmers abandoned the boycott when their failure to win the sympathy of other Greenville consumers became apparent.

Whether the battle was fought over vinegar or butter or corn flakes, the outcome of the grocery store war as Hendrik perceived it turned foremost on low prices. He needed the lowest wholesale costs he could find. With a Swedish immigrant supplier he argued over the price of a load of oleo. When they failed to reach agreement, he unloaded the product from his car and drove off in a huff to buy from another wholesaler. As he explained in a letter to Johanna, "You know, I hate to have a Swede fool a Hollander." Salesmen often warned him that he was cutting his margins too thin. He received their advice skeptically, however, because his low prices irritated, even infuriated, his competitors, and they frequently complained to salesmen who also called on the Thrift Market.

Hendrik's determination to meet the competition of the A&P store was paying off. His sales volume grew. "We are gradually getting out of the red," he wrote to Johanna late in 1937. "That is, we figure we are between $10,000 and $11,000 better off than we were when Brother, ma, you and I started in here." All in all, that was not bad news only three years after their desperate debut in the grocery business. Across the country consumers were responding enthusiastically to supermarkets committed to low prices. The number of such establishments more than doubled in 1937, growing from 1,200 to 3,066 stores nationwide.

It was not always easy to appreciate the promise of the big picture, however. When the butcher was drinking again, Hendrik heard a rumor that the *manager* of the Thrift Market was "reported to be hitting the bottle heavy." He assumed that he was the target of malicious gossip. His first reaction, he told Johanna, was "Too bad they can't leave me alone." When the rumor persisted, however, he "woke up to the fact that [the butcher] passes himself off for the Thrift Market manager, and no wonder people get confused [mistaking the butcher for the grocer], but what of it?"

Hendrik also tried to rid himself of one of the butcher's men, another heavy drinker. "I fired him Thursday for being drunk," Hendrik wrote, "but [the butcher] needed a man, and he is back." After the butcher himself disappeared on a bender, Hendrik fired him. But the man started sobbing and Hendrik took him back. That scene was played out more than once, for Hendrik, like many entrepreneurs whose businesses were built on their own enterprise and intuition, was uncomfortable with the management role that sometimes called for a painful termination. As soon as Fred became old enough, such matters fell to him.

The butcher also operated a meat market in Ionia, and he tried to persuade Hendrik to join him in a combination meat and grocery store there similar to the Thrift Market. Although Hendrik turned down that offer, he was not averse to the idea of a second store. In 1937 Fred graduated from high school and joined his parents in the store on a full-time basis. The Depression showed signs of easing, and with Fred to help run things, a second Thrift Market no longer seemed like such a remote ambition.

By the Meijers' standards, sales had begun to boom, topping $400 on busy Saturdays. Hendrik was encouraged. "I'll be glad that someday we'll be able to lift the mortgage and show the bank that we don't have to kiss their feet," he wrote to Johanna. Despite the progress, however, the bank turned down his request for a hundred-dollar loan and refused to finance the purchase of a used truck because his mortgage payments were still overdue.

To save money, Hendrik, Zien, and Fred moved into the apartment over the drugstore in January 1938. At least they would not be snowed in there. Hendrik nearly sold the farm north of Greenville—until a nearby farmer struck oil, reviving the grocer's dreams of a gusher of his own. Sometimes at night in the apartment he played clarinet duets with Fred. As Zien noted on one occasion, "Good thing the drugstore is closed, otherwise they would drive him out."

In June 1938, Hendrik appeared before the Greenville City Council to support the widening of Lafayette Street north of the Flat River bridge. The improvement would encourage development of the north side, and make the Thrift Market accessible to more Greenville residents. As Hendrik related it to Johanna, a doctor who endorsed the road work "made a speech about growing North Greenville that made them all take off their hats, and you take out the Thrift Market and what have you got left?"

For several months, after adding a "wet rack" with a hose for fresh fruits and vegetables, the Thrift Market relied on a peddler from Ionia for produce. One week the man quoted Hendrik a good price on fifty bushels of peaches. The Thrift Market ran a big ad in that Friday's *Daily News* advertising peaches for fifty cents a bushel. The peddler had promised delivery before the ad was scheduled to appear. But Friday night came, and there was no sign of the peaches; and as customers began responding to the ad, Hendrik could not track down the peddler. By midnight they still had no peaches, so at dawn Hendrik and Fred drove their new truck to the farmers market in Grand Rapids and brought back fifty bushels. They arrived in Greenville before the store opened—and just before the peddler arrived with his order. The price was hot enough, and the store busy enough on that Saturday, that by noon all one hundred bushels were gone. But they drew a lesson from that scare. From then on, Hendrik bought his produce "on the market." He and Fred rose almost every day at 4:30 a.m. and managed to be back in Greenville with their load by noon.

On one trip from Grand Rapids with a trunk full of flour, Hendrik and Fred had almost reached Greenville when they had a flat tire. In order to jack up the rear end of the car, they had to unload the flour and stack the twenty-five-pound bags in the ditch. They finished reloading moments before a cloud-burst. Had the job taken any longer, the flour would have been lost.

On their innumerable trips to Grand Rapids, Hendrik seldom drove, preferring to ride with Fred. In fact, there was not a single aspect of the business in which he did not involve his son—from foisting off the firing of a clerk to scouting out real estate. Buying was an important part of their shared experience. One day a salesman came in as Hendrik was writing a letter to Johanna. He "pushed him onto" Fred, who was just a year out of high school, he explained to his daughter, because "I'm supposed to have an appointment with you." It may in part have been self-consciousness about his accent, one friend said later, that prompted Hendrik to encourage a partner's—and a spokesman's—role for Fred even at an early age.

Hendrik had once expected to teach Fred how to cut hair, thinking his son might use the skill to finance his education. But that option was long forgotten as Fred wrestled with his plans for the future. On the one hand, he was curious about college and felt as though he should follow Johanna to the university; on the other, there was no shortage of challenge for him in the store. Casting a shadow over any decision was the growing threat of war in Europe: by late 1938 hostilities appeared imminent. War joined politics and religion as a common topic of conversation with the salesmen who came to Hendrik with a deal on soap or news of a price change at A&P. Typical was this entry in Fred's diary after one such visit: "We talked to the Seminole man about business and socialism."

Two of Hendrik's favorite newspaper columnists, O. O. McIntyre and Arthur Brisbane, died in the late 1930s. Of McIntyre Hendrik wrote, "He knew the turmoil; he knew life." Brisbane was his favorite for political commentary. After Mussolini's invasion of Ethiopia, he observed, "I would like to hear what [Brisbane] would say about the Anglo-Italian mix-up."

In November 1938 the Thrift Market acquired its first shopping carts, thus catching up with A&P's innovation of the year before. And business continued to grow. It was big news for the family when Fred made a $1,100 bank deposit ("the most we've ever banked at one time," Hendrik noted) following a weekend's rousing sales in the wake of payday at the Gibson Refrigerator Company, which had supplanted Ranney as Greenville's largest employer. Added Hendrik, "We paid the interest in full at the bank and [I] told Mr. Miller [the banker] he should congratulate me on this event—so unusual, you know." Although the factories were not yet back to full shifts, paydays were becoming more regular for more people, and merchants felt the upswing. The Thrift Market had become so cramped that Hendrik rented a small building up the street for additional storage.

For Hendrik the store had begun to offer unanticipated promise. It had become something of an adventure. One Saturday, in one of his boldest promotional gambits yet, he gave away a pound of coffee to each customer. The response, he informed Johanna, was overwhelming. "They are coming from far and near," he wrote gaily, "some with crutches and some in wheelchairs. You give something away and they come for it. We have a nice ad in [the newspaper] this week, and the cash register plays a tune all the time."

With more space and shopping carts and big promotions, the store was taking on a new image. And Hendrik changed its name—or amended it—to reflect what was going on inside. He called it the Thrift Self-Service Super Market.

The economy was picking up—albeit in the shadow of a second world war—and black smoke poured from the stacks at the refrigerator plants. Hendrik was gambling and winning, and his own circumstances were converging with a national current of recovery and expansion. Fred was assuming greater responsibilities—in fact, was fully capable of running the store, though he was not yet twenty years old. The lessons Hendrik had learned about buying and merchandising, combined with his ambitions and those of his son, suggested that by 1940 thoughts even of a second store need not be idle speculation.

Hendrik anticipated the turbulence of changing times in the "weekly messages" that headlined his advertisements in the *Daily News*. The message was sometimes melodramatic, sometimes whimsical. One week in the winter of 1940, for example, a tie-in with Hollywood caught his fancy. "Gone with the Wind" were the pennies of shoppers who failed to trade at the Thrift Super Market. A few weeks later, under the heading "Modern Times," Hendrik observed, "Like the auto replaced Old Dobbin, so has modern merchandising changed. We buy and sell the modern way and share the savings with you."

When Fred decided to stay with the store, Hendrik made him a partner in legal terms as well as in spirit. During the winter of 1940 they began a second major addition to the store, taking over the third of the three storefronts Hendrik owned on North Lafayette Street—the corner building with the drugstore on the ground floor and the Meijers' apartment upstairs. "Today is the first Saturday we've had since the whole store opened up (120 feet long)," Fred noted in his diary of March 16, 1940. "Last Saturday we had the whole meat department in the front yet. We moved it back last Monday morning. . . . This week we started moving the shelf stock into the new part. We're probably going to move the checking counters Monday, and then we will have three checklanes."

Three days later Fred drew a diagram to accompany his diary entry, noting, "We moved the soap bin from the back to the middle of the store and the feed to the back. It was a big job, but I think a great improvement. . . . We started placing the salad dressing, etc., and the baby foods tonight. Pa painted all evening on the new bread rack." The chronicle of renovation continued the next day—when they moved the pickle and olive table—and entered its final stages after Hendrik took along a carpenter to study the fixtures at an A&P store in Grand Rapids. The carpenter disappeared when Hendrik hailed the store manager to ask if they might measure the dimensions of his cookie table. The manager nodded his approval just as the carpenter crawled out from under the table with a tape measure in his hand. That same day the Thrift Super Market took delivery of a dozen new shopping carts.

Workdays were long. After closing, Fred would put together their advertisement for the *Daily News*, with Hendrik often contributing the headline. On March 27, Fred wrote, "We put an ad in the *Buyer's Guide* as well as the *Daily News* this week." They were spending more to promote the store, and sales grew proportionately. As Fred added, "We got a check today from the welfare for $715.19 [as reimbursement for relief orders sold by the Thrift Market]; we sure can use it." Although 1940 proved to be Michigan's most prosperous year since 1929, "the welfare" remained a significant source of trade. The Thrift Market gave prominent space to announcements stating, "We do not charge for cashing PWA checks, unemployment checks, old age pension checks, dairy or cream checks."

In late March, Fred wrote, "The carpenter built in the toilet tissue bins for the north wall today and is lowering the shelves. Pa and Wallen [the carpenter] are still working—it is now 15 minutes to 12 midnight. . . ." And the next day Fred added, "Pa worked until 2 a.m. getting the north wall shelf done and painted. We packed breakfast foods on it this morning."

*   *   *   *   *

In the spring of 1940, Germany added Denmark and Norway to its occupied territories. America's role in the European war remained uncertain, although Roosevelt had initiated efforts to aid Great Britain. FDR asked Congress for authority to sell munitions to friendly powers on a basis Americans understood from shopping for groceries: "cash and carry."

In Greenville, Hendrik's newspaper advertising reflected popular awareness of the widening conflict. "Aeroplane Quality! Submarine Prices!" a Thrift Market headline boomed. In his diary Fred added, "Today's headlines are that Germany is marching her troops toward the Netherlands. Britain admitted today that Germany's air force overwhelmed her sea power and that her battleships are now no match for Germany's airplanes."

Business demanded that Hendrik and Fred spend an increasing share of their time in Grand Rapids. As the Thrift

Market grew, its owners' errands multiplied. An entry in Fred's diary in the spring of 1940 recorded a trip to the city that began at dawn and ended late at night—after seventeen stops. Father and son visited two A&P stores, stopped twice at the produce wholesaler, and made the rounds of the Grand Rapids Wholesale Grocery Company, a rubber stamp company (for price markers), the welfare office, the bakery that sold them bread, a wrecking yard where they found building materials at bargain prices, a glass company, a music store, the farmers market (where they sold twenty-five cases of eggs received as barter from Greenville farmers), the Salvation Army, a store where they bought sign fabric, and a doctor's office, where Fred received shots for a hernia he had suffered while doing exercises taught him by the man who installed the Thrift Market's refrigeration system.

When Johanna visited friends in Chicago in July, she received a letter from her father. "Well, we are at the store again," he wrote. "Brother is talking over the phone about a flour deal. Before I forget, we took inventory. We took it at shelf price and it figured up to $13,700, so that is not bad taking into consideration the start we had. That leaves it about $12,000 wholesale, not including fixtures." He added that he "had to go uptown to the school playgrounds. We are going to have a bunch of boys do some advertising for us tomorrow— house-to-house canvassing."

At one point two western Michigan grocers were caught underpaying their taxes. "You know [a grocer in a nearby town] paid a $1,000 fine for sales tax and what Raymond from Luther paid we don't know," Hendrik wrote to Johanna. "I just can't see why those guys can't play it straight. The accountant complimented us on our books and the way we take care of this end of it." Yet "that end of it" cried out for Johanna's help when she visited Greenville. Attention to detail has always been a characteristic of successful retailing, but the bookkeeping part was a detail Hendrik attended to as little as possible.

His enthusiasm was reserved for what was happening in the store or what his next ad would say. The Thrift Market had been Greenville's dominant grocery advertiser since its first expansion to a "super market" in 1937. Not even A&P ran ads as large on a weekly basis. In August 1940, a nearly full-page Thrift Market ad broadcast "Carloads of Bargains! . . . Take your pick from the largest retail grocery stock in the county." There lay the excitement for Hendrik: in the merchandising.

As it expanded into the former drugstore building in 1940, the Thrift Market could call itself a supermarket without being accused of wishful thinking. As a friend wrote of Hendrik's achievement, "He has competed with and beaten the chain stores and inspired the more progressive independent grocers."

As the store grew, so did Hendrik's campaign to match the prices of the ubiquitous A&P. His advertising preached the low-price gospel: "The average family spends more dollars of their paycheck at a grocery store than at any other single store," one ad observed. "Three times a day most of us eat. That means, three times a day you can either save or waste money. Did it ever occur to you what a saving like that means over the period of a year? Figure it out! Let's say you only save ten cents a meal, three times a day, 1,095 times a year. That saving alone would mean over $100.00 a year. If you think $100.00 or more extra each year might be useful, then the Thrift Market is your complete answer."

In September 1940, Hendrik and Fred attended their first meeting of the three-year-old Super Market Institute. The pioneers of this new species of food retailing were gathering in Kansas City to compare notes on what they were convinced was the store of the future. Hendrik made the trip at the suggestion of a supermarket operator in Detroit. His first response was that he could not afford to be away from the store so long. Then fly, the other grocer advised, because the meeting would be too valuable to miss. Hendrik did not admit his more basic concern—whether he had the money to make the trip at all. The other grocer prevailed, however, and Hendrik and Fred took the train to Kansas City.

The morning after they arrived, Hendrik rose early, as was his habit, noting in a letter to Zien that "you are missing a lot by lying in bed. It is 5 a.m. here, 6 your time. Fred is still in bed, and I woke up maybe because at this time on Monday we are on the market. Maybe I slept all I needed to. . . . We had plate lunch at the hotel and it was a fine affair. . . . After that we had speeches and entertainment; three girls, one with accordion, one violin and one bass. . . . But today the big day starts. We've already met the Lurie Brothers of Detroit and the gentleman from Green Bay. . . . You can buy a big glass of orange juice for five cents and do we like it. . . ."

A Grand Rapids grocer, L. V. Eberhard, had accompanied the two Meijers from Grand Rapids through Chicago to Kansas City. "Mr. Eberhard took us to see some of the most beautiful window displays I've ever seen," Fred wrote. "The windows were about ten feet high by eight feet wide and just filled with head lettuce, grapes, oranges, pears, peaches . . . everything in the fruit line. Then we walked to Walgreen's largest and most beautiful drug store. . . . Mr. Eberhard said 'come on' and we all rode up and down the automatic stairway."

In meetings with the other grocers, Hendrik said little. He preferred to talk privately with Fred, then encourage his son to ask questions. Although he could be something of a raconteur in one-on-one situations, he grew reticent in larger groups. This approach allowed Fred to play a larger part than he might have otherwise. Thus, when they began to acquire real estate, Hendrik would coach Fred on how to deal with the seller, then let him close the deal. But he seemed never to have tried to mold Fred in his own image—in itself a triumph over a strong father's ego. If the son's role as partner pushed him through adolescence too quickly, it also bestowed on him a sense of worth and purpose.

In a pause between sessions in Kansas City, father and son fell into conversation in the hotel lobby with a supermarket operator from Pennsylvania named Sigfried Weis.

"How many stores do you have?" Hendrik asked the other man.

"Forty," Weis replied. And how many did Hendrik have? "One."

The people with ten stores dreamed of twenty, and those with forty aspired to sixty. As Fred said later, "We came back with the bug to put in another store."

In the two men's absence the Thrift Self-Service Supermarket was managed by Zien and Johanna. "We had all kinds of excitement in the store yesterday, but I enjoyed it," Johanna wrote the Sunday after they left.

> We weren't very busy until about seven o'clock and then we hopped to it. Mother gave Hank [a clerk] his letter [of termination] last night. [Hank] didn't say much but Roy [another clerk] came back and said he and Hank decided to stick together and so he thought he would quit too. I didn't quite know what mother would say but she said that was just fine. "He knew what was best." Then she walked away. . . . When we came back to the office, Roy was still there and asked mother if she wanted to see him.
>
> Mother said, "No, you have made up your mind and that's all there is to it."

Hank fully expected her to ask them both back, because he waited for Roy. Then, when we were just about to leave, Hank and Roy came back for their social security cards. Hank was real snotty. Mother said they would have to come back and get them from you.

Saturday was always the busiest day, starting early and ending late. "When we got home," Johanna continued,

we talked over the day's work. A whole pile of prune juice was spilled and cases of Spry toppled on some cases of mustard.

This morning [Sunday] we got up and at 10 o'clock we were in the store. We asked Whitey [another clerk] to come because Mother wanted to check the prune juice that fell. . . . While Mother took care of the money, Whitey and I carried cases of stuff to the floor for the girls to fill shelves in the morning. Then we checked the prune juice. There wasn't a bottle broken. Nothing was damaged at all. Then we proceeded to straighten the back room for the order you said might come. We worked until 1 o'clock. . . . Dick Baird is coming to work after school [on Monday] and Betty is coming mornings so everything is jake. . . .

"Sister" closed with a postscript: "Learn everything you can."

Hendrik and Fred followed her advice. Wide-eyed and not a little awed by the scale on which some of the other grocers were operating, they were attentive students in Kansas City. It was not so much a matter of absorbing instruction as of becoming infected by a spirit. Those operators of big new supermarkets seemed to have a tiger by the tail.

Father and son flew home in a DC-3 that encountered turbulence over Chicago. Fred found it exciting, but Hendrik's white knuckles grasped the armrests tenaciously. When Fred laughed, his father, flying for the first time, said curtly, "It's not funny."

*　　*　　*　　*　　*

Operating a high-volume independent supermarket made Hendrik something of a public figure in Greenville. Late in January 1941, he spoke on behalf of his adopted hometown at a "Greenville Night" promotion broadcast over a Grand Rapids radio station. He described the evening in a letter to Johanna, who had graduated from the University of Michigan and was teaching school in Mount Pleasant. "It was at the Keith Theater before a show full of people," he began. "I told them about the 196 lakes in Montcalm County and Baldwin

[Lake] within the city limits, about potato growing, and I gave away two sacks of potatoes [from] the Thrift Market.

"I also told them we had 2,000 people employed in the various factories and there was no house to be had. . . . In the summer we see cars from nearly every state in the union." He took questions from the audience and was asked if business was good at the Thrift Market. As he wrote to Johanna, "I told them it could not be better." Radio listeners included merchants in Grand Rapids and Thrift Market customers in Greenville. Those who tuned in late wondered if the voice with the accent belonged to Hendrik. Said he, "I told them if they wanted my autograph, all they had to do was just ask me."

In late May, Hendrik, Zien, and Fred—with Fred driving—took a Sunday drive through neighboring towns—Sparta, Coopersville, Ravenna, Cedar Springs. They wanted to see what other grocers were doing, but they also wanted to see, in the wake of their experience in Kansas City, whether one of these communities might be a suitable place for their second store.

Meanwhile, Hendrik's weekly messages in the *Daily News* fought for attention with the ominous news from Europe. Juxtaposed against urgent controversies over Roosevelt's Lend-Lease program and aid for beleagured Great Britain was the reassuring humdrum of small-town Midwestern life, where a Thrift Market customer received thirty agate marbles free with the purchase of a jumbo bag of Lily White flour. Against the backdrop of imminent war, the Thrift Market barraged shoppers with happier news.

"We are first again," a banner headline proclaimed in an advertisement introducing vitamin-enriched bread. If that news was not particularly compelling, it could be made more so by appealing to the patriotism of consumers: "Our United States government has asked all bakeries to 'vitamin enrich' their products for the general welfare and good health of its citizens. In England and Germany the governments just passed a law. In our democratic USA the government has only asked the bakeries to do this. Therefore in full cooperation, our Muller Grocers Baking Company is the first in this area, to our knowledge, to comply. All our bread products are now vitamin-enriched." For a nation often undernourished during the depths of the Depression, the news was not unwelcome.

As one halting step after another drew the United States closer to war, many Americans wondered about the guile of a president who had pledged to keep his country out of conflict. "The people are called upon to arouse for war, when only last October they were assured again and again in the plainest words, that we should be kept out of war," the *Daily News* editorialized in late May 1941. "When the country was dismayed by its lack of preparation to defend its own borders it was told that its future duty was to carry the Four Freedoms into every part of the world! The attitude of the public should not be interpreted as dumbness when probably it is only numbness caused by contradiction, vacillation and confusion."

Confusion showed itself in Fred's dilemma. He was twenty-one years old—old enough, as Hendrik's partner, to assume more challenges than their single store in Greenville offered. He was also a prime candidate for military service if the United States entered the war. In order to open a second store, Hendrik would rely heavily on Fred. But if war broke out, Fred would presumably be gone. To settle the question, Fred tried to enlist; father and son reasoned that if he went in right away, he might do his duty and be back in Greenville a year later. Therefore, in the early summer of 1941 he tried to enlist, consecutively, in the army, the navy, and the army air corps. In each office, when the recruiters learned of the hernia for which he was still taking shots and wearing a belt, the answer was the same: they would not take him. Hendrik accompanied Fred on visits to doctors in Grand Rapids and reported one physician's conclusion to Johanna: "He told us that the army was very particular about such things, as the last war taught them that it was a bill of expense after the boys got out, so that's that."

*   *   *   *   *

The day Hendrik wrote that letter, L. V. Eberhard, the grocer from Grand Rapids, walked into the store with one of his managers. Eberhard belonged to the same wholesale cooperative that supplied the Thrift Market, and he had come to survey the recent changes in the store. "He spoke very highly of our venture," Hendrik wrote to Johanna, "and he is not the man who believes in patting someone on the back. He also asked us if we would attend the Super Market Institute convention in Philadelphia and fly—he got a kick out of my behavior on the last and only ride."

In Thrift Market ads for the early fall of 1941, Hendrik acknowledged the growing prospect of war. "For Your Defense" was the headline on September 4: "The nation of which we are a part is working day and night for our defense. . . . Our everyday low prices are the best home defense for your food budget." Advertisements urged consumers to join the "V" crusade: " 'V' is for vitamins—and victory too—victory over malnutrition, the 'fifth columnist' in health."

The best response to a climate of anxiety seemed to be a redoubling of normal activity—just doing something. Prices were rising, some products were growing scarce, but Hendrik found satisfaction in pressing ahead. "We are putting an inch of insulation board on the ceiling in the warehouse and soon start on the big produce cooler which is urgently needed," he wrote to Johanna. "You can get along without these things, but doing it right is something else. Everything calls for streamlining and smooth operation, and we must have it, and when you say must, that is what it means."

Streamlining became a byword of the early supermarket movement, and ceaseless innovation was the key to a grocer's capacity to expand and multiply his markets. Soon Hendrik was remodeling the Thrift Market again; eventually it was to undergo nine major alterations. One grocer who came up from Grand Rapids to see what was going on "was very much in love with our layout—in fact, he did not expect to find things as they were," Hendrik wrote. He delighted in the praise: "We call that our reward for the effort." His enthusiasm was confirmed by his counterparts at the supermarket convention in Philadelphia. "The whole feeling," Fred recalled, "was to expand."

Saturday sales at the Thrift Market now regularly exceeded $1,000. Merchants in the neighboring town of Belding complained of intense competition from out of town. "Their loudest cry," a friend told Hendrik, "was over the Thrift Super Market in Greenville."

In late September Harold Albaugh, a real estate developer from Grand Rapids, took Hendrik, Zien, and Fred for a drive. "He gave us a ride this week showing us some of his latest creations," Hendrik informed Johanna. "As we talked, he asked me if at any time we had thought about putting in another store. We told him we had no idea at present." Indeed, they had no idea of *where* to put another store, but since that first convention in Kansas City, since they had remodeled the Thrift Market and seen its volume grow, and especially since the meetings in Philadelphia, their urge to expand was becoming irresistible. Albaugh owned a building—a soon-to-be vacant garage—in Cedar Springs, a village twenty miles north of Grand Rapids and fifteen miles west of Greenville. The man's offer, Hendrik reported, was that "we could buy it for $3,000, almost nothing down. It is now occupied by the Chevrolet dealer—who bought the building now used by the Ford dealer."

Hendrik was clearly interested. He registered the Thrift Market name in Kent County, and he described the property to Johanna: "The building is 60 by 90 feet and we have to make some changes and buy a house in back of it for $1,200 and that solves the parking problem. . . . We looked it over again yesterday and it does not look bad. . . . Should you come home a week from tomorrow, we shall show you what it is all about . . . providing we go through with it."

And indeed they did go through with it. Within a week, they had agreed to buy the building. Barely had they begun to plan the new store, however, when a rival grocer opened "Nielsen's Thrift Market" across the street. Hendrik had registered the "Thrift Market" name, but the other grocer had used the term "thrift" in some of his advertising. Nielsen offered to take down his "Thrift Market" sign—for one hundred dollars. Hendrik turned him down. Registering the name "Thrift Market" had not precluded someone else's use of it when it was preceded by a proper name. So as plans went ahead for the Cedar Springs store, Hendrik added "Meijer" to the name of his store in Greenville: the name became "Meijer's Thrift Super Market" ("Self-Service" was no longer necessary, because customers took that for granted in any store that called itself a supermarket).

But the name was not the only stumbling block to a successful store in Cedar Springs. When the Kroger Company announced that it would replace its small conventional store there with a supermarket, Hendrik's anxiety intensified. A wrong move might jeopardize all that he had built up in Greenville. When those second thoughts set in, he asked a lawyer if he could withdraw from the deal. He offered to forfeit the down payment and give back the building. The land contract was binding, the lawyer declared, but then he added, "Now there's always something wrong with every title, and we can say he doesn't have a clear title. You can almost always find defects" (this before he had seen the title document). "I'm not going to do that," Hendrik told him. "If I bought it, I bought it." Fred said later, "If we'd had an easy way out, we'd never have built the Cedar Springs store. Yet if we hadn't, would we ever have built the third store, or the ones that would follow that?"

Once committed to the building, Hendrik brought carpenter Dennis Guernsey over from Greenville to help with the renovation. Guernsey tore out interior walls and set to work removing a chimney. But that proved to be a challenge: the chimney's topmost section of brick was supported beneath the roof by two boards that were bisected by a third. Hendrik and another workman cleared away debris at the base of the chimney, while Guernsey and the other workman's son hammered away on another project at the rear of the building. The chimney protruded only a foot or two above the roof and had long ago fallen into disuse. Most of the mortar was gone, and the bricks merely rested on one another.

Hendrik was never one to pass up a quick solution. He proposed simply knocking out the supporting planks and letting the chimney fall straight down. "No," Guernsey said adamantly, "it can't be done. You can't knock both of the planks out at the same time. It'll tip over and go right through the roof." Hendrik was disappointed with the answer. He merely nodded, and Guernsey and the boy returned to work at the rear of the building. Minutes later they heard a rumble, and the building shook; they were afraid for a moment that the roof might cave in on top of them. "We ran to the front of the store to see what happened," Guernsey recalled. "And this boy says to his dad, 'You damn fool, didn't you know any better than that?' " The chimney was a pile of rubble. Dust was still rising from the floor, drifting through a gaping hole in the roof. The other workman looked at his son and then at Guernsey and said, "Well, Henry made me do it." Hendrik had already turned and walked away. The others heard a car door slam and the sound of an engine as he drove off.

It took three days to patch the roof; they could have taken the chimney apart brick by brick in two hours. Despite such setbacks, Guernsey observed, there was always one thing about Hendrik: "If he told somebody to do something and they did it the way he said and it was wrong, he never said a word about it."

In early October, as German troops advanced to the outskirts of Moscow, and A&P completed a remodeling of its store in downtown Greenville, an item in the *Daily News* noted:

Hendrik Meijer, whose Thrift Market in Greenville has had an almost phenomenal growth, plans to open a new supermarket in Cedar Springs. Associated with Mr. Meijer in the business is his son, Fred. The Cedar Springs Thrift Supermarket will occupy the building now known as Denton's Garage, which Mr. Meijer and his son purchased from Harold Albaugh of Grand Rapids. The building has a frontage of more than 60 feet and is considered an ideal location for a store of the Thrift Supermarket type. A home near the store was also purchased by the Meijers for use in any future expansion needs.

Under the subhead "Example of Independent Merchandising," the story continued: "Possession of the Cedar Springs building will be taken on November 1, although it will be a month or so later before the store can be opened to the public. Extensive alterations are planned, including an all new storefront, ceiling, skylights and fluorescent lighting equipment. The Cedar Springs market will be operated on the same plan as that in Greenville with everyday low prices."

As Hendrik's renovation proceeded, the economic climate improved in direct proportion to the threat of war. Gibson Refrigerator received its first defense contract, a $589,000 munitions order, and Secretary of State Cordell Hull issued an ultimatum to the Japanese. Hendrik headlined a two-page ad in the *Daily News*, "We serve the alert."

On the first Saturday in December, the *Daily News* reported optimistically, "Crisis Eases, Japs See Peace." And that was not the only good news. For Greenville, the Depression was virtually over. The newspaper announced that the rising value of real estate had made possible the termination of bank receiverships that had existed since the bank holiday of 1933. The next day, Sunday, December 7, 1941, dawned clear and cold in Greenville. It was Fred's twenty-second birthday. By the end of the day, however, neither economic prosperity nor a young man's birthday celebration was much on anyone's mind.

The Japanese attack on Pearl Harbor gave the military second thoughts about how selective it could afford to be. It also created a climate in which such deep-seated feelings as the pacifist inclinations of Zien and Hendrik—and their antipathy to military service—were subordinated to an abhorrence of the Axis powers. For Fred there was the added pressure of watching friends and classmates go off to war. Again and again he expected to be drafted. Four times he rode the bus to Detroit, where Michigan inductees received their physical examinations. He became almost a regular on the run, and was assigned by one driver the thankless task of supervising the rowdy contingent that drank and sang its way across the state in what was usually their last outing as civilians.

Finally, Fred cleared what he thought was the last hurdle to service: the army now seemed inclined to repair hernias and would allow him to enlist despite his condition. Only the swearing-in ceremony remained when he was spotted in the line by an officer, a salt salesman in civilian life who had called on the Thrift Market and knew of Fred's medical problem. "Come with me, you've got to see another doctor," the man said. The other doctor looked at Fred's case history and never even bothered to examine him. He just said, "Throw him out." Moments earlier, Fred had called Hendrik to say he was about to be sworn in; now he had to call back, tell his family, "I'm out again," and stand to one side as the other inductees raised their right hands. It was as close as he came to going to war. The next day he was back in Greenville, and soon in Cedar Springs, where the work went ahead slowly.

The year ended with a nation at war and a sudden surge of prosperity. A scarcity of goods replaced a scarcity of dollars. The cash drawers at the Thrift Market seldom overflowed, but then, neither did the nail on the back room wall where new invoices were impaled. Hendrik wrote to his daughter nine days before Christmas: "Brother is having a good laugh. The Grand Rapids Wholesale office just called and said we had them all paid up, and we still have a $7.00 check in the mail on top of that, so they owe us this time. He laughs and says it can't be true."

After Pearl Harbor came more confusion, as the fever and excitement of war filled the air. The newly organized Greenville Defense Council offered a page of advice in the *Daily News* headlined, "What to do in an air raid." To skeptics who ignored the alarmist talk, an advertisement for war bonds answered a decisive yes to the question, "Can the Japs bomb Michigan?" A map showed that, via Alaska, the Straits of Mackinac were little farther from Tokyo than the Golden Gate Bridge was. Although change was difficult to detect from day to day, the world would never be the same again. What Hendrik observed of the world at war applied to his grocery business as well: "I look for some change after the smoke clears away."

"War's effect on the super market" was the theme of the Super Market Institute convention of 1942 in St. Louis. Shortly before the grocers convened, the government's Office of Price

Administration (OPA) unveiled its food rationing plans. Americans were queuing up at their nearest elementary schools to register for coupons entitling each person to half a pound of sugar per week. Food store customers needed help sorting out ration points and planning meals that kept them within their ration limits. So bewildering was the array of rationing plans, allocations, price controls, and paperwork that operating a grocery store became a diplomatic chore.

An official of the OPA assured the grocers in St. Louis that his staff did not want to put them out of business. Indeed, when retail food prices were frozen, the new price structure worked to the advantage of the lower-priced supermarkets because they were given the lowest ceiling on what they could charge. Stores that had charged more before Pearl Harbor had higher ceilings, and they could charge more after prices were frozen. The lower price ceiling posted in supermarkets only enhanced their reputation for saving customers money.

But with war came shortages—sometimes real, sometimes imaginary. "In the first few days of the war," wrote William Manchester, "grocers were selling sugar in hundred-pound sacks, canned goods by the case, flour in fifty-pound bags." And a good cut of meat was a prized commodity. One customer, a Methodist preacher, recalled the day he waited in line at Hendrik's meat counter. Anxious female customers jostled for position, pushing ahead of him in the line, until the butcher, Leonard Kurtz, spotted the minister and called out his turn. In St. Louis the nation's grocers fretted over the availability of staple items. Hendrik wrote Zien that "the coffee, tea and cocoa situation will become slightly better instead of worse. But in canned goods and salmon there will be a definite shortage."

Yet shortages in basic commodities sometimes played into the hands of more creative and aggressive merchants—who in the retail food business usually operated supermarkets. With prices frozen within a narrow range, competition shifted from price to product. Before the war, one grocer's selection of canned goods or crackers may have differed little from another's; but now the variety of groceries the shopper found on the shelves could no longer be taken for granted. A grocer might measure his success or failure by how much of his inventory he kept in stock. Hendrik foraged for deals and experimented with all sorts of substitutions. If a popular product like grape jam was temporarily unavailable, the smart grocer ran a special on guava jelly.

Government calls for conservation and thrift also sometimes worked to the benefit of a low-priced store, particularly
one called the Thrift Super Market. One of Hendrik's advertisements asked customers to return used bags; and along with
other grocers, he seldom missed an opportunity to identify the
interests of the store with the goals of the nation. "Resolve
to be Thrifty," said one ad. "It's both patriotic and wise."
When price ceilings took effect in May 1942, he announced:
"We pledge our support to any steps the government finds
necessary to win this war." Another ad reminded customers
that although there were price controls, there was "no ceiling
on savings." When Singapore and the Philippines fell to the
Japanese in the late winter and spring of 1942, Hendrik advised
Daily News readers that "lost ground can always be regained,
but lost dollars . . . never."

Although war left the completion of the Cedar Springs
store in limbo, Hendrik and Fred remained eager to expand.
Their counterparts in St. Louis confirmed their ambitions.
"One speaker talked on exactly what we are planning to do,"
Hendrik wrote to Zien. And a tour of stores included a very
impressive, "very large one away from the congested area and
entirely depending on auto shopping. We were told [it] had
to do $60,000 a week to pay expenses. And believe it or not,
the checkers tell us they register $2,000 on one register on
Saturday. So mother, don't blow up, but see if you can do a
little more next Saturday. . . ."

Material and manpower shortages bedeviled their expansion plans, but by the fall of 1942, after a year's delay, the Cedar
Springs store was finally ready for business. The manager of
the newly opened Kroger supermarket bluntly declared that
the town wasn't big enough for Kroger *and* Meijer to survive—
and Kroger was not going to be the one to leave.

Hendrik was not without his doubts, either, but he had
a sense of what people wanted from a grocery store. After planning his opening week advertising, he paid a visit to the *Cedar
Springs Clipper* and spoke with the editor, Nina Babcock. Hendrik was almost sixty then, and his hair was white; but he had
the vitality and bearing of a much younger man. Forty years
later, Nina Babcock recalled her first impression of the tall
Hollander as vividly as if it were yesterday. He was the kind
of person, she thought to herself, who "must lie awake at night
thinking of things." And she was right. This was only his second store; it was possible to dream that there might be more.

7

The
Golden Age

*If you are a customer of one of the Meijer food stores you will from
time to time see a tall, gray-haired man with twinkling eyes and a
kindly manner wandering among the stalls of the store you patronize.*

—Grand Rapids Herald, 1954

T he new Meijer's Thrift Super Market in Cedar Springs was
just the sort of supermarket one expected to find in a small
town in the 1940s. The entrance opened on the sidewalk of
the town's main street, and the parking lot remained unpaved.
Across the street stood the Cedar Cafe; a Standard Oil filling
station occupied the nearest corner, and behind it Hendrik had
had an old house torn down to provide more parking.

The opening of a new supermarket—even one located in
an old garage—was a major event in the life of a small town.
As is common even today, suppliers and salesmen were on
hand to provide free samples and the attendant hoopla. But
the sounds of the store were different then: there was no inter-
com or electronic whir of the cash register, no melodic blur
of Muzak. Register keys tapped irregular rhythms. Customers
placed the produce and meat and canned goods from their
"rolling carriages" onto the wooden checkstand, and cashiers
shoved the items behind them down the "lane" to a "packer"
or "bagger"—usually a young man in a white apron—who
placed the order in boxes or bags and carried it out to the
customer's car. Inside, the store was bright with the harsh
white light of fluorescent tubes. The atmosphere was sufficiently festive, and the prices so special, that customers seldom
complained if the line at the checkouts snaked back into the
grocery aisles.

Amid the hubbub, the Pillsbury salesman promoting a new
pancake mix played "The Wabash Cannonball" on his squeaky

portable phonograph. He dropped the needle onto that plat-
ter again and again, until one of the cashiers, twenty-three-
year-old Lena Rader, asked in exasperation, "Can't you play
anything else?"

Only one strategy came naturally to a store called Meijer's
Thrift Super Market: offer the hottest prices in town. For
example, grapes had been an important item in the first few
weeks after opening. The new Kroger store was selling two
pounds for 19 cents; Fred wrote an ad featuring two pounds
for 17 cents, and Kroger retaliated by dropping its price to 15
cents. Meijer dropped to meet that, and down they went until
Kroger was selling its grapes for five cents a pound. Later,
when the Kroger manager paid Hendrik a visit in the easy way
competitors once did (today they would be suspected of price-
fixing) to propose an agreement on shorter store hours, Hendrik would have none of it. "You know how you cooperated
on the grapes?" he asked. "Well, we're going to cooperate the
same way on store hours."

Soon after the store opened, Hendrik fired its original
manager—the company's first outside manager. In his place
came Johanna, then in her mid-twenties, who left behind her
teaching career in Mount Pleasant. At a time when war had
created a shortage of able-bodied workers, particularly men,
Johanna took over a store that would flourish in defiance of
the Kroger manager's prediction.

*   *   *   *   *

When the war ended in 1945, fruits and vegetables quickly
came off the rationing list. But price controls remained in effect
until the OPA felt that the danger of postwar inflation had
passed. Nonetheless, when the OPA finally removed controls,
food prices rose more than 30 percent in a single year. By mid-
July 1946, wholesale food prices hit their highest point in
twenty-six years. Controls were soon reimposed—as they
would be periodically until 1948. Building materials were no
longer diverted for defense needs, however, and wartime
impediments to expansion began to disappear as soldiers
returned home eager to resume civilian careers.

In the summer of 1945, Hendrik bought a parcel of land
in Ionia, the small city south of Greenville where he had once
installed Holland Furnaces, and the family was soon deep into
planning its third store. In Cedar Springs, Hendrik had
remodeled an existing building. The Ionia store, by contrast,
he started from scratch. And he undertook its construction with

enthusiasm, as he always did with projects that appealed at once to brawn and ingenuity. He hired neither architect nor engineer, preferring to contract out the project himself. He decided to tile over a creek that ran across the future parking lot and to fill in the gully around it. After acquiring surplus wheelbarrows from the Works Projects Administration, he discovered that the job required heavier equipment. But then a bulldozer he rented nearly sank in the soft clay, and he had to bring in a crane to lift it from the mire.

A few weeks later, Fred was working in Greenville when his father called. A truck and trailer delivering twenty tons of cement had just arrived at the site—with no one but Hendrik to meet it. The driver informed the grocer that his contract said nothing about unloading cement. Although Fred drove down from Greenville as quickly as he could, by the time he reached Ionia, his sixty-two-year-old father, stripped to the waist in the hot sun, had already unloaded two-thirds of the sixty-pound bags.

The building in Ionia was nearly completed when, on the evening of May 21, 1946, Hendrik caught the last showing of *Tomorrow Is Forever* at the Silver Theater in Greenville. (According to a newspaper report, the movie was "the vibrant, pulsing story of a woman escaping her past." Claudette Colbert was the woman, starring with Orson Welles and George Brent.) At home after the show, he felt as if he had just fallen asleep when the whistle sounded from the roof of the fire barn behind city hall. Across town, one of his friends heard the whistle and had a premonition. "I woke right up out of a hard sleep and heard the truck going up Lafayette Street and I said, 'Oh, I bet Henry Meijer's store is on fire,' " George Smith recalled thirty years later. Smith threw on a shirt and trousers. Out on Lafayette Street half the town was streaming north, following the sirens toward the plume of smoke that rose high in the unnaturally bright night sky.

Awakened by a policeman, Hendrik hurried to join the growing crowd of onlookers. It was the wrong time—as if there is ever a right time—for a fire. The back room, which doubled as a warehouse, was piled high with merchandise, including cases that had already been delivered for the new store in Ionia. Fred and a co-worker broke through a brick wall at the rear of the building to rescue ledgers and account books.

"Hundreds of persons were attracted to the scene as flames swept through the store, sending smoke spirals hundreds of feet into the air," the *Daily News* reported. "All was destroyed by fire which gutted the interior and left scattered piles of what was a few hours earlier precious supplies of foods."

From the street Hendrik watched the flames jump behind the front windows. Then the big plates of glass popped out in a series of explosions. When the fire reached the cereal aisle, it flamed up like a torch and tore through the ceiling to the roof. The crowd gasped. Spectators remarked on how the cereal had literally exploded, while the toilet paper and tissue a couple of aisles away, too densely packaged for the fire to ignite them, could be found the next day floating in a lake of water from the fire hoses.

Hank Doornbos, a salesman for the Hekman Biscuit Company, stood at Hendrik's side as the fire raged. He was expressing his sympathy when Hendrik pointed toward a smoldering corner of the building. "Look, Hank," he said, "those Hekman saltines you sold us won't even burn." Said Doornbos later, "Regardless of how bad things would look, he always had a sense of humor and was planning for the future."

The structure was a total loss—the original little grocery store, the corner building Hendrik built in 1923 for his barber shop, and the half dozen additions that made it the largest supermarket in the county. As the *Daily News* reported, "A few boxes of crackers and canned goods stood grotesquely in the north corner of the front part of the store, pointing to the spot where firemen stopped the blaze's advance." So quickly did the fire spread that one volunteer fireman said flames that had been confined to the middle of the store when he started attaching a hose to a hydrant had enveloped the building by the time he finished the connection.

The store's white-haired proprietor did not know how to react at first. "Stunned by the fire when called by firemen," the *Daily News* reporter wrote, "Mr. Meijer was unable to report any definite plans on rebuilding his store or for providing a temporary store." He was only beginning to sift through his possibilities. At least no one was hurt; the tenants in the two apartments upstairs had escaped without injury. "It could have been worse," Hendrik observed—just a little too casually for a few townspeople, who did not understand that it was not in his character to be troubled by circumstances beyond his control.

Damage was estimated at $125,000. Two hundred cases of beer were destroyed, as well as 5,000 pounds of beef and pork—a newsworthy loss because meat was still scarce so soon after the end of rationing. Although the merchandise, valued at $40,000, was fully insured, the building itself had appreciated far beyond its insured value of $5,000. The loss was nearly as great as the total net worth of the fledgling chain. Suddenly, weeks away from the day the company was to become a three-store chain, it was reduced to a single store. The only cash flowing in came from sales at the Cedar Springs store. Hendrik had to borrow money from both Greenville banks to complete the Ionia store and reopen in Greenville at the same time.

The Meijer's Thrift Super Market had been Montcalm County's busiest store as well as its largest; so there was never any question that Hendrik would rebuild. Years earlier, when the store was already cramped, Hendrik had bought property across the street. The week of the fire, he took a grocer from Grand Rapids through the rubble of the old store and then across the street to the new property. The ruins were still smoldering as he described in glowing terms his plans for a new supermarket. As they stood on the curb and Hendrik waxed enthusiastic, the other grocer interrupted him. "Henry, don't smile so much," he said. "People will think you burned it down."

Hendrik understood well enough the extent of the loss and the lean days he faced trying to compensate for it. But he told his friend, "I'm not going to go around crying just to prove I didn't burn it down." Nor was his optimism unfounded. The fire had ravaged his store early in the predawn hours; later that morning came word of a prefabricated Quonset building that was disassembled and loaded on a flatbed trailer up in Newaygo. Hendrik immediately arranged to have it hauled to the new site across from the burned-out store on Lafayette Street.

The Quonset building was a steel, arched-roof structure of the sort that had been mass produced during the war for use as anything from a barracks to an aircraft hangar. The first load of beams and supports was delivered at four p.m. on that Wednesday—less than twelve hours after the fire had been reported. The next day the *Daily News* reported, "Hendrik Meijer, whose Thrift Market was destroyed early Wednesday in a $125,000 fire, would run a close race with Army and Navy reconstruction battalions famed for their genius at rebuilding bombed out bridges and command posts."

That same day Hendrik opened "Meijer's Produce Market" in a makeshift wooden structure on the new site. Not much more than a screened-in shed, it sold produce and a few dry groceries, with baskets of fruit and vegetables set out on the sidewalk in the fashion of an outdoor market.

And fourteen weeks after the original supermarket was destroyed, a new one was in operation. As always seemed to be the case, this store had its jerrybuilt aspects. The new checkout counters were not counters at all but tracks of steel rollers down which canned goods and packages rolled in big wooden trays from cashier to bagger. On a busy day the rollers set up a continuous clatter, adding to the din of the cash registers themselves, with their clackety keys and cash-drawer bells.

The city permitted Hendrik to widen Lafayette Street in front of the site to improve traffic flow to the new store. A row of stately maples had to be sacrificed to provide an extra lane of traffic. Hendrik instructed the road crew to remove the trees very early one morning, before anyone saw what was happening. The day they came down, a customer stood outside the store with the old grocer and lamented, "What a shame they had to take down all those trees." Hendrik's response was a blend of feigned innocence and sincere regret as he said with feeling, "Yes, isn't that a shame."

In January 1946, after a courtship that took place under the watchful and sometimes amused eyes of their co-workers, Fred married Lena Rader, a shy brunette cashier from a German Lutheran farming community near Lakeview, Michigan. Six months later Johanna moved back from Cedar Springs and married a scholarly former business instructor she had met at the University of Michigan. Her husband, Don Magoon, had just returned from occupied Japan on terminal leave as an army captain. He joined the budding chain on an equal footing with Hendrik and Fred—at least that was the intent of all parties.

The Ionia store opened in August 1946, one week before the huge Ionia Free Fair. A grand opening circular advertised steaks at fifty-five cents a pound, hamburger at thirty-three cents, and bread at eleven cents a loaf. The parking lot was unpaved, and Don Magoon spent much of that steamy summer day pushing out cars that had become mired in the soft earth.

In Ionia, as in Greenville and Cedar Springs, the company built its reputation first and foremost on low prices. The family was learning the lessons of high-volume retailing: if an item did not sell, they marked it down quickly. The same discipline of taking painful mark-downs that was critically important later when Meijer sold general merchandise also served a supermarket operator well. As Fred wrote from a grocers' convention in Florida, "Our cost-cutting policy on certain poor or high-priced items is correct. . . . I'm glad we started it when we did."

Not long after the fire, a vacant potato storage building north of the Greenville store became the company's new warehouse and general office. For family and employees, conditions were somewhat primitive and hours were long. Lena and Fred visited stores on their honeymoon and laid out ads on their dining room table; Johanna and Don spent an anniversary taking inventory. In the anteroom outside Don's cramped office—he was grocery buyer as well as corporate treasurer and manager of the office—salesmen waited their turns on worn wooden folding chairs from a shoe store whose seats read "Blue Goose Shoes."

Sunday June 20 - 1948

Greenville Store

Dad- Lena wanted the front all red + you weren't here to defend your yellow, so it's all red now. It looks good too, Lena says so.

Fred

On a snapshot of the Greenville supermarket sent to Hendrik in Europe, Fred described the informal way a decision was reached when the store was painted in 1948.

The Mantel family had come through the Nazi occupation of the Netherlands unharmed—although Wilhelm and Ferdinand had been on the list of suspicious persons rounded up by the Germans because of their socialist-anarchist activities, and both spent several weeks in a prison camp.

In 1947 Zien's oldest brother, Wilhelm, became the first of the Mantels to visit America since Zien's arrival in 1912. Hendrik and Fred gave him a tour through their three stores. Sitting in Hendrik's Buick outside the new Ionia building, they told Wilhelm about all that had happened since the war—the debts and the fire and their ambitions for the future. Wilhelm, like Hendrik, was in his sixties; he had been a tailor all his life. He listened to Hendrik and Fred's exuberant account. Their sales had nearly doubled—to $1.8 million—in a single year. It was heady stuff, but they were skating over thin ice, going deeper into debt, gambling the company at every step. Wilhelm interrupted with a note of alarm: "But you could go broke!"

Hendrik paused and turned to look at his brother-in-law. "Yes," he said deliberately, "we could." Of course they could; but the idea hardly struck terror in his heart. If he had worried about such things as a young man, he might never have come to America. Without risk, there was no adventure. The Mantels had taken fewer risks: they had stayed in the Old Country, and they had waited too long, despite Hendrik's encouragement, to expand their tailor shop to include ready-to-wear clothes. Meanwhile, Hendrik was pioneering his Greenville supermarket. Like many successful merchants, he had no great fear of starting over. He had done so more than once already.

*　　*　　*　　*　　*

In 1948 Hendrik celebrated his sixty-fifth birthday. Fred and Don were taking on greater responsibilities. Fred, at twenty-nine, was general manager and supervised the operation of the three stores. Don, then thirty-eight, was grocery buyer and supervised the office and financial areas. He introduced payroll checks and business machines to a bookkeeping system that had once relied on invoices piled in bushel baskets. Finance had never been one of Hendrik's strengths: the only cash register he ever learned how to run was the one he used in the first store in 1934. He cared not at all for numbers, although he grudgingly recognized the necessity of adequate bookkeeping if the company was to grow; and he was not content to stand still.

Beginning in 1948, winter meant a drive to Florida for the older Meijers. With Hendrik behind the wheel of the Buick, Zien kept hour-by-hour notes on a tiny pad. She was a selfless diarist who recorded Hendrik's every observation of scenery or livestock. When he found a cabin for the night or stopped for coffee, Zien quoted him. "Henry is singing 'Ring Around the Roses,' " she would write, as they rolled south. It was an extraordinarily intimate relationship, and their personalities were complementary. Zien was amused and charmed by her husband's good-humored energy and ambition; he drew strength from her discipline and fortitude.

But Hendrik never considered retirement; at the office he preferred instead to look ahead. Accompanied by Fred and Don, he scouted sites for future stores. The company had been successful thus far with a strategy, as much instinctive as consciously reasoned, of expanding from Greenville to neighboring towns. A number of prospective markets in small towns in central Michigan presented themselves—St. John's, Big Rapids, Owosso—but they were not the only alternatives.

Vivid in Fred's mind was the day he flew from Grand Rapids to Chicago with fellow grocer L. V. Eberhard. As they took off, banking low over new subdivisions on the south side of Grand Rapids, Eberhard swept his arm toward the view from the window. "Look at all those houses," he said. Look at all those potential customers, he might have added. The impression was not lost on Fred, and when he got back from Chicago he shared it with Hendrik and Don. Like other cities, Grand Rapids was enjoying the prosperity of the postwar boom. Sprawling suburban neighborhoods beckoned retailers. If Hendrik and his family really wanted to build the kind of supermarkets they kept hearing about at the conventions—and generate the sales volume to support those stores—Grand Rapids, where in 1948 a young lawyer named Gerald Ford was running for Congress, seemed the most logical target.

Their search became serious shortly before Hendrik and Zien left Greenville for a trip to Europe. "As to buying in GR," Hendrik wrote his son and son-in-law from the Netherlands, "I wish you would wait until I get there."

*   *   *   *   *

Hendrik and Zien returned to Europe in 1948 for the first time since 1920. Once again, as he had been for *Recht door Zee* as a young immigrant, Hendrik became a correspondent. He carried a letter of introduction from Michigan Governor Kim

Sigler stating his plans to write "a series of letters for the *Greenville Daily News*, one of this state's leading small town daily newspapers." On board their Holland-America Line ship, passengers were forbidden to speak German, so deep did the scars of war remain. The crossing was rough, and Zien and Hendrik were both seasick—Hendrik five times, Zien noted in her diary.

Hendrik brought his new Buick along with him to the Netherlands. He derived no end of satisfaction from driving the big American automobile, in all its chrome-trimmed, white-sidewalled splendor, through the narrow streets of his childhood. He would draw the car to a stop alongside a ragpicker or streetsweeper, share a brief conversation in the old Hengelo dialect, and relish the thought that he was defying the rigid divisions of social class he had known as a young man.

In Hengelo's bustling marketplace he observed the universal way in which people responded to the right merchandise offered at a good price and felt his faith in the future of the high-variety, self-service supermarket confirmed. "We are on the right track as long as our prices are right," he wrote.

Although they spent most of their time with Zien's family, Hendrik was also curious about his relatives. All of his immediate family had emigrated, but there were aunts and cousins and old friends with whom he had lost touch. Walking in the woods one day, he encountered a man in wooden shoes who was carrying a hoe. The man looked dimly familiar, and indeed Hendrik discovered they had served in the same infantry battalion; he had been a boilermaker and remembered Hendrik's father from the Stork factory. He directed the American grocer to a farm where the house had been destroyed during the war. The old woman there turned out to be his father's half-brother's wife—Hendrik's aunt. "We had a long talk," Hendrik wrote. "She lived in a large chicken coop" with a daughter and eight grandchildren; they had been farmers and were struggling to rebuild. Hendrik returned the next day with some clothes for the family. "They were nice people . . . ," he wrote. "They did not cry on my shoulder."

The devastation of World War II was still much in evidence. In 1940, German bombing had rendered familiar Hengelo neighborhoods unrecognizable. One day Hendrik went for a walk and lost his way. And yet, for all the destruction, some things still sparked memories of forty years before. A funeral procession passed with the men wearing traditional stovepipe hats. "Strange how certain customs change so slowly," he observed. The new American tycoon with the expensive suit and big Buick was escorted through the de Monchy textile mill by the proprietor himself, a member of the family whose earlier generations were regarded in Hendrik's boyhood as exploiters of the working class. The irony of the situation did not escape the visitor. The owner introduced him to the older men in the plant, some of whom, now close to retirement, had been Hendrik's contemporaries. De Monchy, like Hendrik, was a Rotarian, and he took the grocer to a meeting of the club that was, in Hendrik's words, "very exclusive here."

Now that he enjoyed a measure of affluence, Hendrik began to indulge a passion for collecting paintings. Dutch landscapes were among his favorites. As he and Zien prepared to return home, he wrote ahead to Fred, who was to meet their ship in New York, asking him to bring along a small trailer. Hendrik was bringing back five paintings, along with two trunks and five suitcases. "I'm afraid the car cannot hold it all," he wrote. "Bring no suitcases of your own if you can do without."

When Hendrik returned, the family tried to put a supermarket in one of Grand Rapids' first shopping centers. But the developer had already committed the site to another grocer. Looking elsewhere, they found property on South Division Avenue, a main artery through the city's southern suburbs.

As they completed negotiations for the site on South Division, the developer of the shopping center called. His deal with the other grocer had fallen through, and he offered to lease Meijer the unfinished building. Hendrik had already borrowed $25,000 to buy the first site, but the second was equally tempting. He discovered, however, that to open not one but two stores in the big city required more money than skeptical Greenville bankers were willing to lend. Yet Hendrik, Fred, and Don seemed to have few doubts that the risk was worth it. For the first and last time, they agreed to a mortgage on their merchandise—along with fixtures and other equity—to finance the second Grand Rapids store. That arrangement gave the bank a lien on everything they owned. If the company's suppliers were to try to recover their merchandise because Meijer could not pay for it, they would discover that the bank had a prior claim to the goods.

The company hoped to keep the arrangement confidential, but word leaked out to suppliers. With uneasy creditors and insistent bankers, neither Hendrik nor Fred forgot the words of the Greenville bank president who concluded, after reviewing their financial statements, "You're OK, if nothing stops the train." With that warning in the backs of their minds, they plunged ahead with the two projects. As a salesman observed, "They saw a market and they jumped into it."

Hendrik lectured on his European travels to service and social clubs in the towns where he did business. He told Rotarians in Greenville some of the stories he had heard about Nazi atrocities in the Netherlands—mass executions, starvation tactics, deportation and execution of Dutch Jews (among them the elderly doctor who had performed Zien's surgery in 1911). "When they do things like that," Hendrik concluded, "human beings are not human beings any more." Seeing the devastation in the Netherlands and Germany, from the rubble in Hengelo's market square to the ruins that surrounded Cologne's magnificent cathedral, again wakened his pacifist impulses.

When a retired general addressed the Greenville Rotary Club on the need for universal military training for young men, Hendrik's passions were roused. He wanted to make sure an opposing voice was heard. Immediately after the general's speech, he approached a fellow Rotarian, Greenville's Methodist minister. "Do you know anyone who could give the other side of this issue?" he asked. "Get someone here; I don't care how much it costs."

This Methodist preacher, Hendrik's sparring partner in theological discussions, later organized a fund-raising drive to rebuild his church after a fire. As a local businessman whose customers included many Methodists, Hendrik contributed to the church's rebuilding fund—but, in the eyes of the clergyman, only a paltry sum for one of the town's leading merchants. The minister, Verner Kilgren, paid Hendrik a visit and related to him a parable, intimating that Hendrik had neglected to share the fruits of his success. Hendrik grew livid at the implication. Here was another side of the man about whom some employees and salesmen have told the author, "I never saw your granddad mad." Kilgren provoked from Hendrik a tirade on the sins and hypocrisy of the church; he, in turn, responded with hints of a boycott. Hendrik ordered the preacher off his property. Soon afterward, Kilgren wrote him a letter: "I am very sorry that I have offended you. I did not mean to wish misfortune upon you by citing the parable of the farmer who built greater barns, not at all. Only to cite that as you prosper and grow don't forget to share with the Lord and His work as you reap the benefits of your labors coupled with his blessing. . . ."

But Hendrik and the minister remained friends. Kilgren, a progressive clergyman in a conservative town, observed later that "the average businessman tends to be conservative. With Hendrik I could have a free, unhampered conversation."

In an address to Greenville Rotarians—after another trip back to the Old Country—Hendrik reported that Europeans could not understand Americans who supported the red-baiting tactics of Senator Joe McCarthy. Hendrik looked at his audience and said, "I understand there are people in this room who have supported him financially—shame on you." Said Kilgren of the Rotarians' reaction, "They had to respect him even though they didn't agree with him, but later some of them really chewed him out."

If the word "thrift" was no longer the Meijer stores' middle name, the idea of thrift remained at the heart of Hendrik Meijer's approach to retailing—and was symbolized in the cartoon figure of "Thrifty," a little Dutch boy. This character, whose name was suggested by a customer in a Meijer contest, became a fixture of the company's advertising in 1949 with the opening of the store on South Division Avenue.

At the turn of the century, the great department stores had vied with one another to unveil the latest technological advance or modern gimmick. They exposed many Americans to their first elevator or escalator or lighted sign. At mid-century, supermarkets had become the most conspicuous innovators in retailing. As a writer for *Collier's* observed in 1951, "All over the U.S., supermarkets—the prodigious issue of a marriage between brilliant showmanship and the world's most modern distribution techniques—are springing up almost faster than they can be counted. Last year [1950] they opened at the rate of better than three a day."

Each store boasted that it was more luxurious, more sophisticated, and of course lower priced than its competitors. The Meijer store on Division Avenue was the first in the chain with electric-eye doors that swung open automatically when a customer approached. Advertisements also boasted of radiant heat: "More healthful and comfortable for our customers and employees." In addition, there was a "special produce preparation room" and "21 feet of latest type frozen food cases." For the grand opening of the second store—every opening, of course, was "grand"—Meijer exhorted shoppers to "come out and see Western Michigan's most gigantic food shopping center," adding that "naturally, every fixture and piece of equipment in this huge market is the last word in modern design and efficiency and, when you enter its 'Magic Eye' door, you will cross a new frontier in food shopping ease and economy. . . . Truly this mammoth market gives the people of Grand Rapids 'some place to go and something new to see.' " An ice machine produced a ton of crushed ice daily for use in the produce department. The checkouts featured "highly accurate" new cash registers. All around the store were signs and banners stressing the Meijer philosophy of "thrift, courtesy, cleanliness."

In a survey of Hendrik's stores, *Self-Service Grocer* magazine observed:

> The new Eastern Avenue outlet [the second Grand Rapids store] is perhaps the most impressive. The exterior is enhanced by a redwood tower in natural finish. In keeping with his Dutch background, Mr. Meijer has placed a small flower garden at the entrance to the store and the approaching shopper is at once impressed with the neatness of the place. . . . Across the front of the market are six check-out counters. The ceiling is of tile and the upper walls are decorated with interesting murals depicting Cape Cod scenes. These will be changed from time to time to fit the seasons.

Beyond the physical changes, the operation remained distinctly a family enterprise. "The whole family has always pitched in and pulled together in running the business," the *Self-Service Grocer* reported. "Today, besides Mr. Hendrik Meijer, founder of the business, there is his wife, Gezina, who has charge of real estate; his son Fred, who is general manager; Fred's wife, Lena, who is responsible for pricing and advertising; Donald Magoon, his son-in-law who is buyer, and his wife, Johanna, who is in charge of personnel." The reporter exaggerated, but Hendrik always did encourage the inclusion of the others in publicity about the company. As Fred put it, "Our motto is share and share alike, and we believe this is responsible for most of our achievements." Added the reporter: "The six members of the family all work together and put back into the business their earnings. Thus it is truly a cooperative family enterprise."

In a letter to her parents when they went back to the Netherlands again in 1950, Johanna's summary of her activities suggests just how closely the lives of the family were interwoven with the business. Even after her son was born, she was helping supervise the stores: "Monday I went to Cedar [Springs], Tuesday I made the Grand Rapids rounds . . . and Thursday, with Elbert [her three-year-old son] in the back seat, I made the complete swing around."

The supermarket had become a force in food retailing during the desperately cost-conscious days of the Depression; during the bouyant economy of the 1950s it emerged as a characteristically American institution. Expanding beyond the bounds of the early A&Ps, stores like the 15,000-square-foot Meijer's on Eastern Avenue rapidly became the standard. Remodeled garages yielded to expensive new suburban markets.

Between 1946 and 1958 the number of supermarkets in the United States quadrupled. The baby boom meant more mouths to feed, and the burgeoning postwar economy gave lower- and middle-income Americans more money to spend than ever before. These factors combined to produce a climate ripe for supermarkets. Meijer's growth, one consultant observed, reflected a "trend to bigger and bigger stores that has continued to sweep through the nation since 1946 [the year Hendrik opened his 12,000-square-foot Ionia store, which one industry pioneer warned him was too big]. Even the single unit tends to become bigger and the multiple-store chains find a success formula and expand on it with seemingly no end."

To finance the headlong expansion, many chains made public offerings of their stock. Although sharing fully in the impulse to expand, Hendrik and his family preferred the control and flexibility of a privately held company. Given that preference, Hendrik could undertake new projects such as the first two Grand Rapids stores only if he was not reluctant to go into debt. And that was one thing he had never been timid about.

Hendrik was abroad when Fred completed negotiations for the purchase of a third Grand Rapids site—at the intersection of Michigan Street and Fuller Avenue on the city's northeast side. The father had willingly transferred authority to the next generation—although his children were always more comfortable when he participated in their decisions. As Johanna wrote while he was in Europe, "They'll be glad when you get home to share the responsibility."

Work on the third Grand Rapids store began in 1951. This project included a second story at the rear of the store for the chain's offices. With half their stores and over half their sales soon to be concentrated in that city, the family decided its offices should be there too. And from their desks upstairs, Hendrik, Fred, and Don could survey the aisles of the supermarket below.

The outbreak of the Korean War and its accompanying shortages confirmed the wisdom of moving the company offices to Grand Rapids. As head buyer, Don worried about being isolated in Greenville while salesmen based in Grand Rapids exhausted their allocations of scarce products locally. And as Harvey Lemmen, the young office manager who joined the company in 1949, later observed, "It was obvious that Grand Rapids was going to be the biggest area for us. It was the center of the grocery business in western Michigan. And people who were most convenient to it got the best deals."

Hendrik's children and their families moved to Grand Rapids before he and Zien did. He tried at first to commute from Greenville, where he had lived for nearly forty years. His friends were there, and he was deeply involved in fund-raising for a new Greenville hospital. He turned sixty-seven in 1951; with Fred and Don on the job, he hardly had to make the trip every day if he chose not to. And he was also mildly reluctant to relocate to a city with neighborhoods where working in the yard on Sunday was anathema. But his resolve did not last. He wanted to be close to his family and close to the office. In 1952, he and Zien moved to Grand Rapids.

Expansion had exposed the company's modest financial underpinnings. A grocer could survive for a long time on his cash flow, but the Meijer company was woefully undercapitalized to be building more stores. As a consultant noted in the mid-fifties, "In a sense they are always working on the capital of others and their cash position is always close to a negative quantity."

As expenses mounted after the Fuller Avenue opening in 1952, Hendrik and Fred found their bankers reluctant to provide further financing. Their accountant suggested they meet with another client of his, Frank McKay, a notorious political operative, former state treasurer, and kingmaker in Michigan Republican politics. McKay, he said, could arrange a loan through another bank. Hendrik and Fred were leery of favors, though: "We'd want to pay him," Fred told the accountant. "Don't worry," was the accountant's reply.

First time Albert Einstein has made the page. He is Meijer's favorite public personage.

International Political Football Game

Watching this game is his favorite sport.

Once served in the Netherlands Army Infantry.

We Have With Us Today

HENDRIK MEIJER, President, Meijer's Super Markets.

Boyhood ambition was to travel and see the world.

Reading is a hobby with Hendrik, and he likes to eat spareribs & sauer kraut.

Lives in Greenville where he is active on Hospital Board & School Planning Commission. A member of Greenville Rotary & Saladin Temple Shrine.

Born in Hengels Overysel, Netherlands.

Attended grade & factory schools in the Netherlands.

Interested in music, plays accordion, clarinet & ocarina.

Or did in his younger days.

Earned his first dollar working in a cotton mill.

10 hours a day for 10 days to earn one dollar.

Never get rich this way

Director of Produce Dept. G.R. Wholesale Grocery Co.

A Grand Rapids Press cartoonist sketched this profile of Hendrik in 1950.

At their first meeting, Hendrik and Fred told McKay they needed $175,000 to cover costs on the new store. "I'll get you $200,000," McKay told them. He offered to arrange $200,000 in mortgage financing through the Michigan National Bank—for a fee of $5,000. (Michigan National was unaware that a fee had been charged in the arrangement of its loan.) Hendrik and Fred wanted the money, but they felt that they could not afford the fee—until McKay agreed to take out his commission in groceries. The wily old politician relished his status as the only customer who could walk into a Meijer store and tell the cashier to charge his order. When rumors of his privilege spread, he told Hendrik and Fred, "I don't know why people think I have an interest in your company."

McKay's efforts relieved the short-term problem, but when Hendrik and Zien were back in Hengelo again in the summer of 1953, Fred wrote, "We still spend money faster than we make it, so if you find a rich uncle with a million dollars send him along with his check book."

Although their profits had fallen below the $88,000 they had earned in 1950, the opening of the third Grand Rapids store helped double Meijer's share of the city's retail food sales—from 10 to 20 percent—in the next four years. With growth came a need for greater sophistication. At the age of sixty-nine, Hendrik joined other Meijer managers in a training seminar offered by Michigan State College. In 1954 he marked his twentieth anniversary in the grocery business. The little chain had changed considerably, but more in size than in character. The anniversary advertisement included a portrait of Hendrik and Zien and a bilingual Dutch-English headline that echoed an earlier age: "Hours, days, months or years . . . fly by like a shadow." Hendrik had employed the expression once before—when he was begging Zien for patience while she waited for his proposal of marriage more than forty years earlier.

The fourth Grand Rapids Meijer supermarket opened on the southwest side in 1953, followed in 1954 by a much smaller store in the basement of a women's clothing store in downtown Grand Rapids. The company pinned its hopes for the downtown location on traffic from nearby offices and shops; but sales never materialized. The store lacked two essential ingredients of a modern supermarket: abundant variety and convenient parking. In addition, consumers preferred to shop near their homes, not their jobs. The Meijers closed the downtown store four years later.

In its place came larger, more conventional supermarkets. Two stores opened on the west side of Grand Rapids in 1955, bringing the chain's total to ten and spreading Meijer supermarkets throughout Grand Rapids and its suburbs, before expansion was stalled by Meijer's chronic undercapitalization. In 1954 the consultant had said, "Thus far, every store has succeeded." That would not always be the case. Not only did the downtown store fail, but in Standale, on the western edge of the city, McKay had sold Hendrik and Fred property in an area where he had envisioned a large-scale residential development. Only 50 houses were built, instead of the 500 promised, however, and the store there would lose money for most of the next three decades, before being closed in 1984.

In addition, other members of the Grand Rapids Wholesale Grocery Company, many of whom were Meijer competitors, were upset by the company's refusal to buy more wholesaler-label products. In a fit of pique, the wholesale group gave Meijer sixty days to leave—an impossibly short time in which to establish a new distribution system. But the company proceeded to call the wholesalers' bluff. Thirty days later, under Harvey Lemmen's supervision, Meijer was operating its own 70,000-square-foot warehouse in a vacant foundry. Asked by a food broker if it was true that his company had decided to quit the wholesale group, Hendrik replied in the accent that became particularly pronounced when he was upset, "Don't you beleef it. Vee vas kicked out."

For three years—the longest interval since they had opened the third store in Ionia—the company added no new stores. Hendrik grew frustrated as his competitors, Eberhard and Kroger among them, beat Meijer to good locations. "Goddammit, Fred," he growled once as they drove past a competitor's new supermarket, "if I'd been this conservative I'd never have opened the first store." Hendrik was impetuous at times, and decisive to a fault. He was never content to stay where he was.

Finally, in 1958 the company opened a store in a dramatic arched-roof building at 28th Street and Kalamazoo Avenue. The following year the chain grew to a dozen stores with the addition of a supermarket next to a Miracle Mart discount house in a renovated factory on Plainfield Avenue. Ten years after entering the market, Meijer supermarkets saturated Grand Rapids.

In the basement of the Michigan and Fuller store, Don Magoon researched the value of devoting more space to non-food items. By expanding the selection of health and beauty aids and kitchen items in its "home centers," the company created what was, in effect, a variety store or small department store annex that enabled the supermarket upstairs to take advantage of the typically higher markup on nonfood merchandise.

Meijer employees established the Consolidated Independent Union, Local 951, in 1951, but the company was continually subjected to organizing attempts by the national Retail Clerks Union. In an era when the Teamsters influenced the local retail clerks, a friend told Hendrik not to worry should an organizing raid succeed, because Jimmy Hoffa would cooperate, and he was said to be a man who kept his word. But the Teamsters who met with Hendrik and Fred in a Grand Rapids coffee shop spoke with contempt of the employees they hoped to bargain for. Given to dark suits and black Buicks, they solicited the company's help in organizing in exchange for a promise of cooperation. "You're in the union business and we're in the grocery business," Hendrik replied. "If you think you can organize, then go ahead. I'm not going to help organize them for you."

Although he identified with the historic role of unions, experience and his perspective as employer led him to question the benefit of union membership. "I had a thought," he told Fred in a letter from Europe. "Maybe you could have a vote. Have question boxes in the store, give each employee a slip that you can recognize that they could put in the box to tell whether they could do away with the whole thing [the union—still independent at that stage]. They would save $5 per month [in dues]. . . . See how many really would like to keep the union—if for no other reason than to find out where they stand. At least the union may sit up and do some thinking."

Such a vote was never taken. Nor did repeated raids persuade employees to abandon their independent union. In 1976, however, the Retail Clerks—now the United Food and Commercial Workers Union—finally achieved their objective when independent union members were persuaded to affiliate with the national union.

*   *   *   *   *

In 1954, Hendrik, then seventy years old and somewhat overweight, had suffered a heart attack. He had been warned of his coronary condition months before: his doctor ordered him home to rest, but he would do so only under pressure from Fred, and he insisted all the while that he had more stores to visit. After the attack he made a rapid recovery, although not without changing some of his habits. On his doctor's advice, he began to take a sip of wine with his dinner and to watch his diet more closely. Among the wellwishers during his convalescence was Frank McKay, who wrote a rambling get-well letter: "To have steadily and surely gained and kept the devotion, respect and loyalty of your family, friends and competitors bespeaks the goodness of a heart that became overtaxed. . . ."

He suffered a second, milder attack in 1961. This time, however, an artery was blocked in one leg, and a doctor broached the possibility of amputation. In his heavy accent he told a friend, "They want to take the leg off; I'm not going to let them." Nor did he. To recover, he walked and walked, not just in the stores, but through the neighborhoods on the northeast side of Grand Rapids. At Butterworth Hospital he had been a favorite of the hospital staff. As he was fond of musing, "I fell asleep to 'Perry Mason' and woke up to 'The Nurses.' "

Hendrik hired his grandsons to paint the long white fence surrounding his yard; but he still mowed his own lawn and, even in his seventies, drove to the office nearly every day. He sat in on meetings and looked for ways to challenge complacency. Believing, as Montaigne wrote, that "there is no conversation more boring than the one where everybody agrees," he liked to shake people up a little. As the organization grew, Hendrik was sometimes ill at ease with the extended lines of authority and communication. He could be "uncomfortable articulating problems," according to Earl Holton, later president of Meijer, who was a young store manager in the 1950s. But if a weekly sales meeting grew dull, he tried to provoke one of the managers with a leading question or sarcastic remark. When he succeeded, he winked at colleagues as if to say, "Here we go again."

He worked all his life yet would never have considered himself a "workaholic." When Holton was suffering from an ulcer, Hendrik talked to him about the importance of striking a balance between job and family. A manager was expected *not* to sacrifice his home life for his career. "If you're going to be late," Hendrik reminded his managers, "you owe your wife a call."

Soon after Holton became manager of the Michigan and Fuller store, managers of two competing supermarkets were indicted for short-weighting customers in their meat departments. The day after the story appeared in the newspapers, the phone line from the general office upstairs rang in Holton's cubbyhole near the checkouts. Holton picked up the receiver and answered, "Kent County prosecutor." The phone was silent. Moments later, Hendrik came clambering down the stairs and marched over to Holton's office with a gloomy expression on his face. Holton braced himself for a scolding, but Hendrik brightened suddenly, smiled, and said, "Did I ever tell you about my practical jokes? Some of them work, and some of them don't."

Hendrik's penchant for dressing well was recognized in 1956 when a national tailoring organization named him to its best-dressed list. Although he delighted in finding bargains, his tastes sometimes clashed with Zien's more frugal style. When he bought an expensive suit he might store it at Fred's house until the right time came to bring it home. (Grand Rapids Press)

In 1955, Meijer purchased commercial time on a children's television program called "Romper Room." The local station assigned a young salesman to help the chain's buyers obtain cooperative advertising money from suppliers. "My first encounter with Hendrik Meijer was early one morning," recalled the advertising man, Charlie Johnson. "I was on my way to the cafeteria for a cup of coffee. All of a sudden, a hand reaches out and claps me on the back. And there's Hendrik Meijer, admonishing me for walking stooped over. He said, 'There can't be any problem so bad that you don't stand straight and tall.' "

Television advertising might also require adjustments. On one occasion, Hendrik relayed to Johnson a complaint from Zien about a cartoon on the "Romper Room" program. She was upset over an animated shooting incident. "Well, it was a *cartoon*," Johnson said later, "one of those silly little cartoons, where I guess one of the characters was shooting a cannon. But from then on I screened all the cartoons coming in, to make sure that there was no shooting or violence." The teachings of Domela Nieuwenhuis had not been forgotten.

Hendrik had made his radio debut as a spokesman for Greenville in 1941. His television debut came when he was seventy-one, and he wore an incongruous little beanie on "Romper Room." The hostess, Miss Jean, conferred on him the title of "Best Do-Bee of all."

Television was only one means by which supermarkets generated promotional excitement. Grocers were the most extravagant merchandisers of the era, and they left no gimmick untried. One California operator promoted a wedding that drew 10,000 guests. Another advertised that the customer with a lucky ticket would win a "white baby." Civic groups rose up in indignation over the announcement, but on the day of the drawing the baby was revealed to be a squealing white suckling pig. When the Meijer store at Michigan and Fuller was remodeled, Hendrik and Fred drove three-wheeled Isettas, Italian compact cars, down the aisles to demonstrate how much room customers had to maneuver their shopping carts.

A store opening was a twentieth-century circus-in-the-suburbs, replete with beauty queens, television celebrities, and giveaways. At the opening of one of the early Grand Rapids supermarkets, Meijer gave away 2,000 orchids, 1,000 dolls, and 15,000 balloons. High school bands offered performances featuring "comely drum majorettes with twirling batons," and Buck Barry, the cowboy host of a local children's television show, rode through the parking lot on his palomino, Thunder. Later Hendrik's grandson, Elbert Magoon, dressed up in a "Thrifty" Dutch boy costume to pass out candy to younger customers.

But the most enduring promotion of all was the trading stamp. Few of the aggressive chains of the 1950s were without stamps. Meijer bucked the trend at first. "We turned down the S&H Green Stamp plan more than two years ago," an advertising circular explained in 1954. "We have turned down over a dozen similar stamp plans in the past year." Hendrik regarded stamps as a sort of medicine show: they were messy for the stores to handle and provided the customer with no real savings. "Savings on stamps are not savings on food," one of his ads declared. A checklist "notarized by an accredited 'notary public' " compared Meijer's prices with those of stores that offered stamps and showed that in many cases customers saved 10 percent or more at Meijer.

When partisans of trading stamps argued compellingly that collecting the stamps was a powerful incentive to customer loyalty, Hendrik was still not convinced. But neither did he have the day-to-day responsibility to make that decision. Although it was not always easy for him to adjust to the growing company's managerial hierarchy, half the secret in delegating authority lay in allowing other people to make mistakes. In 1956, against his better judgment, the company initiated its own stamp program, called "Goodwill." Suddenly, and perhaps somewhat uncomfortably for Hendrik, the thrust of Meijer advertising changed. "Goodwill stamps cost you nothing," Meijer ads insisted. The basement of the Michigan and Fuller store became a stamp redemption center where customers could select their premium toaster or blanket or bicycle.

In all the promotional hoopla, however, Hendrik never forgot the circumstances of his entry into the grocery business. One day a young woman stopped him as he walked through one of the Grand Rapids stores. She shook his hand and said, "I used to live in Greenville. I attended the same classes as your son, Fred, did. Now I live in Grand Rapids and I have four little girls. My husband is a truck driver. I have traded at your store ever since you opened here, and I want you to know that the considerate manner in which you handled our relief orders when my father was out of work in Greenville is still very much appreciated."

As newspaper ads were being laid out, Hendrik was known to walk over to the layout table and ask, "Have we got any beans for the poor people?" It was not a calculated question. It reflected one of his sources of satisfaction as a grocer. By allowing for the widest possible distribution of the widest variety of goods, supermarkets were, in their way, wonderfully democratic institutions. Gimmicks were fine, but Hendrik's supermarkets were also in the business of providing life's necessities. The Kent County Welfare Board selected Meijer to distribute surplus food to the needy. And Meijer advertising continuously emphasized basic virtues like courtesy. "More friends meet at Meijer's than at any other supermarket in Western Michigan," one ad declared. Next to a photo of a handshake was the copy: "Friends gather at Meijer's for good reasons . . . because they are treated as friends, fairly and squarely." From those efforts, not from gimmicks, came loyal customers. As Hendrik said in one ad, "It is our aim always to bring you more of the best for less. We perform no sleight-of-hand acts . . . pull no rabbits from hats."

That attitude carried over into the sale of merchandise other than food. Sections like Meijer's home centers, featuring non-food items from kitchen utensils to sewing notions and sneakers, became increasingly important to the supermarkets of the 1950s. Don Magoon toured stores around the country and reported back to Hendrik and Fred on the sales potential of these nonfood sections. In that way, he helped pave the way for the company's later expansion, because, as an employee newsletter explained in 1961 (in a tone of inevitability hardly supported by fact), a discount store was "a natural outgrowth" of the home center.

The buyer for Meijer's home centers was a Hollander named Al Meijer (no relation to Hendrik), who had started with the company as an immigrant window washer. "I sincerely believe that profit was not the first thing Mr. Meijer was thinking of," he recalled. "It was secondary. Customer service and competitiveness were given priority—so much so sometimes that profits were knowingly and seriously affected. Mr. Meijer believed that an item should be in stock at all times, even when we were selling it at a loss. . . . Sometimes we would restock an item within hours but pay a premium by buying from a local wholesaler."

One facet of customer service was honest advertising—not just technically truthful, but plausible, credible advertising. "Statements had to be true," Al noted, "but more than that, they had to be believable. I remember I had a men's tie sale with a sign stating, 'Sale price fifty cents, regular price $1.99.' Mr. Meijer questioned the truth of the $1.99 regular price. I tried to explain that these ties did indeed sell for $1.99, but were bought at a very special close-out price." Hendrik was not satisfied with that explanation. "The customer doesn't believe that," he told Al. So the "regular price" designation was removed. Hendrik also disliked hyperbole in advertising. Words like "unbelievable," "tremendous," or "fabulous" he rarely tolerated—and they remain suspect today.

If customers deserved respect, so did salesmen. A textile manufacturer called at the Meijer offices one sweltering summer day in the late 1950s. As a result of his encounter with Hendrik—insignificant in itself, one of thousands of impressions that go into forming any company's history—he wrote the old man a letter. "It was after five o'clock on a very hot afternoon . . . ," he began.

> One of my salesmen and I were "sweating it out" in your outer office—waiting to see your Mr. L. A. Hansen. It was my first trip to see you people, and we had been discussing your portrait on the wall, so I recognized you when you came through, apparently on the way to the comforts of home, and, no doubt, hot and tired. (Incidentally, I liked your informal attire—coatless and open collar.)
>
> As you started down the stairs, you glanced our way, hesitated a second, and came back and asked if there was anything you could do for us. We told you we were waiting for Mr. Hansen, and, inasmuch as your switchboard operator was off duty, you volunteered to go and tell Mr. Hansen that we were waiting. . . . Your concern for two total strangers was very refreshing.
>
> I was sorry immediately after you left that I had not dared introduce myself to you, and tell you how much we appreciated this generous gesture. Those things simply do not happen too often with top-flight executives. The least I can do now, having failed to do so at the time, is to tell you that two then hot and tired "peddlers" will always remember you and think kindly of you.

In their daily routine, Hendrik and Fred were nearly inseparable. "You never saw one without the other," a friend observed. When Hendrik insisted on making decisions by consensus, however, arguments sometimes arose. Once, when Fred and Don Magoon disagreed about buying a site for a store in Battle Creek—Fred wanting to buy it and Hendrik wanting to make sure Don agreed—they drove for an hour in frosty silence.

Although Hendrik occasionally had trouble solving problems through appropriate levels of management, he cherished the freedom to set his own schedule around the office and in the stores. Morning coffee was a ritual for him, and a way of keeping up with industry gossip. He chatted with salesmen, customers, employees—anyone who frequented the cafeteria at the Michigan and Fuller store. When he and Fred visited stores, they often parted company as soon as they entered. Fred tended to operations, while Hendrik might wander into the back room to see the butcher or strike up a conversation with a customer at the front of the store.

It was Fred's role to check in with the manager and supervise the store, but Hendrik remained a stickler for detail. Nothing seemed to escape him. Was the back room neat? Was someone pilfering from the receiving dock? "It behooves you to check now and then," he wrote. "I believe in control and more control."

As the organization grew, of course, less and less of the control was his. He was president, but only Fred reported to him directly. And there were times when he became almost paranoid about the intentions of people in the organization who no longer looked to him as their supervisor. Of one manager he wrote to Fred, "If he thinks he's got you in the bag and to hell with the old man, then I better stay home. I can get along good with people as a rule, but he gets in my hair, and I am telling you he is not the man you think."

Hendrik's head was sometimes turned when one of the Dutch immigrants—perhaps one he had sponsored—had a complaint. He got angry about petty things; yet when one of his stores burned down, he just said calmly, "We can build another."

II

Meijer's is not a one-man show. The family worked hard as an unselfish team. We know that in harmony there is strength.

—Hendrik Meijer, 1953

Sam Dicks, the same consultant who had found the company's cash flow chronically deficient, had nothing but praise for its management team. In 1956 he wrote: "We find it an interesting admixture of venture and success. The founder of the organization is in his early seventies and is tapering off in his controls. His son and son-in-law make an aggressive, hard-hitting and well balanced pair of executives.'' It was true that Hendrik was ''tapering off''; but the impression of the ''balance'' that existed between his son and son-in-law proved to be more illusory. In the summer of 1960, Hendrik's vaunted family harmony was shattered—and that was not even the first surprise of the decade.

In 1959 the company had opened its first supermarket in Muskegon. The year before, a Muskegon-based chain, Plumb's Ranch Markets, had opened a store in Grand Rapids. Plumb and Meijer both belonged to the Topco cooperative buying group, which sold grocery products under the Food Club label. Their expansion plans were on a collision course, and the two chains, both family-owned, harbored ambitions of building stores throughout western Michigan. As the owners discussed their plans, there seemed to be no reason not to consider a merger: together they could form the dominant chain in the region. Negotiations took months, but Fred and Don were enthusiastic.

On May 31, 1960, the two companies issued a press release announcing their tentative merger agreement. Hendrik and Zien had already set sail for Europe to attend a supermarket conference in Berlin. Hendrik remained as skeptical of this new commitment as he had been of trading stamps. Once again, however, he acquiesced to the impulses of the younger generation. It was not in his nature to be the conservative adviser, putting the brakes on the plans of younger men. He was usually the one willing to rush in, and he looked to others to temper his enthusiasm. But he was never entirely comfortable with the idea of a merger.

Meijer was the larger company: it had thirteen stores to Plumb's ten, and annual sales of more than $15 million to Plumb's $9 million. Although the Meijer bloc dominated the stock, a new organizational structure was designed to blend the two management groups: Hendrik would be chairman of the board for a term of five years; the founder of Plumb, already retired, would be vice-chairman, his son president, and Fred executive vice-president and general manager. After five years, the chairman and vice-chairman were to step down, with the younger Plumb becoming chairman and Fred taking over as president. Don Magoon was to be second vice-president in charge of finance, planning, and research; he was also designated corporate secretary. And as the press release emphasized, "No major changes are contemplated in the operation of the present Meijer and Plumb supermarkets."

Offices were to be consolidated at the Meijer office behind the Michigan and Fuller store, where workmen had begun installing ceiling tiles in a portion of the grocery back room that was available for office expansion. The press release noted: "By eliminating duplication and combining the office, buying and warehousing facilities, the two firms expect to achieve substantial economies which should result in improved services and lower costs to Western Michigan consumers."

The principals—except Hendrik, who was abroad—gathered in a lawyer's office to sign a forty-six page agreement. All they lacked was a final consensus on real estate values. Hendrik arrived in Rotterdam under the assumption that he was soon to be chairman of the board of the merged chain. Back in Grand Rapids, however, the merger was coming undone.

Plumb insisted on a higher value for his real estate than the Meijer people had anticipated. But if the merger was a sound idea in the first place, Fred argued, the adjustment Plumb demanded was no reason to scrap the deal. They were only $250,000 apart on a multimillion-dollar package. The family needed a consensus on a decision of such magnitude, however; and when Don vetoed a compromise on the real estate values, Plumb rejected the merger altogether.

Hendrik was almost relieved at the turn of events. And the family quickly would be grateful that the company's independence had been preserved. For Don Magoon, however, the merger issue was a watershed of another sort. His belated opposition revealed a long-standing and more deep-seated anxiety about his role in the company. Within a few weeks of joining the company—upon his marriage to Johanna in 1946— he had talked about leaving. At that time, Hendrik had persuaded him not to; he wanted his family in the company. He sensed great opportunities, and he assumed that the rewards inherent in a good job with a good salary in a business he enjoyed would be satisfying to others as well. But he misunderstood Don's position, and that lack of understanding was the most serious miscalculation of his life.

In the mid-1950s, Don confided his unhappiness to the company's attorney, Arthur Snell. "Don let his hair down" at that session, Snell recalled. "He didn't want to spend his life working in the retail business. . . . He was trying to do his best for the company. There didn't seem to be any real animosity." From an academic career before the war, he had been thrust into the midst of this vigorous small-town enterprise, hell-bent on expansion and defined by the dynamic personalities—Johanna's among them—of an ambitious, close-knit family. Forced or invited, depending on one's perspective, to find his niche in the management of the small chain, Don was never entirely comfortable.

Fred was unduly sensitive about not having gone to college. He regarded Don's learning almost with awe, and took it for granted that his brother-in-law belonged in the council of family decision making. "Fred did more to try to involve Don than anybody I ever saw," Harvey Lemmen noted years later. "Don was not the type to walk in. Fred had to pull him into things." However, Hendrik's admiration for Don was never so unalloyed. Said Lemmen, "They were oil and water."

In a setting calling for skills that came more instinctively to Fred than to himself, Don felt that he was never fully appreciated. Although his salary had been equal to Fred's in the past, the merger would have upset that balance. And Johanna and Don were both afraid that Plumb might dominate Fred—to the detriment, if he chose, of their interests.

Hendrik was abroad when Don's frustrations found vent in conversations with other employees. In his absence, Fred felt compelled to confront his brother-in-law with remarks he had received from people in the stores. Both men wept, so fraught with emotion was their encounter. Fred's tentative broaching of the subject, then Don's apologies and explanations for his comments, seemed to clear the air. And later, when Don complained bitterly of his situation in a letter to his in-laws in the Netherlands, Hendrik was quick to downplay the seriousness of the rift. He told Zien he would get both sides of the story when they returned home. Zien suspected, more accurately, that the problem was bigger than they knew.

To the extent that the situation was a result of the merger talks—at that time still continuing, to Hendrik's knowledge—he cautioned Fred, "Do not go overboard for Norrie [Plumb]. . . . Johanna and Don both seem to think he needed us badly." If Fred thought he had reached an understanding with Don, however, he was mistaken. Johanna was furious with him when she learned of their confrontation. What right did her little brother have to reprimand her husband—particularly in the absence of her father, who would have been expected to mediate any dispute? Johanna flew to New York to meet her parents at the boat. On the flight home, she loosed a floodgate of emotion. With Hendrik and Zien in the seat behind her, she described a situation she considered intolerable. Years of stifled bitterness were apparent in her frustration and indignation. Later, father and daughter would feud, but it was Fred's behavior that upset Johanna initially.

Hendrik hardly knew how to react. He tried to calm her down. The situation could not be as bleak as she imagined it, he argued; he had to get back to Grand Rapids to hear both sides of the story. Ironically, while Fred, physically and in other ways, may have resembled his mother more than his father, Johanna drew somewhat more on Hendrik's characteristics. That the relationship between father and daughter had been a close, affectionate one is apparent from the years of correspondence between them. Indeed, Hendrik wrote more letters to Johanna than Zien did. But father and daughter were both strong-willed, gregarious people—simply dominating personalities.

Although making certain judgments is terribly difficult, it seems in retrospect that Hendrik, the puritanical parent, had always been rather strict with his daughter and elder child. Fred had stayed behind in Greenville to work in the store while his sister was away in college or teaching, and inevitably shared more of his father's experiences. More by default than design, then, he received more attention from Hendrik than Johanna did. Hendrik and Zien may have been freethinkers, but they expected their daughter, so bright and able, to fit into a traditional female role though she was capable of so many other things. And Hendrik expected his son-in-law to be happy with a life that was an extension of his, when Don's ambitions lay in vastly different worlds. It was Johanna, finally, who delivered Don's resignation—in effect a joint resignation from a situation too intensely emotional for any other resolution. After that, Don embarked on consulting projects abroad. He and Johanna later moved to Ypsilanti, Michigan, where he became a professor of business on the faculty of Eastern Michigan University. Johanna, who raised three children, became active in social causes—from civil rights to arms control—that reflected the progressive values of the Mantels.

At the time of the family crisis, Hendrik owned about 20 percent of the stock in Meijer, and his two children with their spouses held 40 percent each. When Don and Johanna decided to sell their holdings, the burden fell on Fred to buy their shares if the company was to remain private. Hendrik was seventy-six years old and in no position to increase his estate. But he was upset with the commitment Fred made in agreeing to pay Don and Johanna nearly as much as the book value of the entire company—when the Magoon share was still a minority interest. It was an obligation that would hang over the son long after his father was gone. "That's too much money," Hendrik warned Fred.

But Fred insisted: "I want to do it."

Snapped Hendrik, "You're crazy. You'll be working for him [Don] all your life. The company just isn't worth that much money."

The episode was traumatic for the company as well. It was, as Lemmen noted, "a big wrenching." As employees pondered the effect of a split in the ranks of ownership, a friend warned Hendrik, "Don't die before this problem is solved." Although the emotional scars did not heal in Hendrik's lifetime, the corporate wound did. Hendrik and Fred came to be grateful that Don's misgivings had torpedoed the merger talks with Plumb. Plumb could have—and admitted later that he would have—exercised his veto over the dramatic changes that were on the horizon. In a similar, if far more agonizing way, Don's departure may have been something of a catharsis for the company. From his direction too had come a not unwarranted skepticism about the gamble father and son were contemplating.

* * * * *

Three years after they adopted trading stamps, Fred came to share Hendrik's distaste for the promotion. Stamps were a gimmick that did not belong at Meijer. Raising prices to support the cost of the program ran counter to Hendrik's every thought and impulse. He was convinced that his company was better off competing as it had since the days of the first store—by offering low prices. In 1960, Fred and his associates concluded, with Hendrik's enthusiastic assent, that stamps had to go. Meijer stores closed for a day while clerks marked down prices. When the stores reopened, it was as though the company had been born again. In an undercurrent of change invisible to customers, but increasingly clear to those directly involved, the company had put behind it the flirtation with merger and the schism in the family. Now the company had cast aside the most widespread promotional gimmick of the day. Meijer advertising "exposed" the fuss and expense of trading stamps: when the program was dropped, big newspaper ads announced that "all day Monday some 300 Meijer employees were busy reducing hundreds of prices to the new level made possible by the elimination of trading stamps!''

The new slogan in Meijer ads was, ''You take your savings home in cash.'' And cash, as the ads noted dryly, was ''redeemable anywhere.'' In a sort of confession, the ads went on to tell customers: ''When Meijer issued trading stamps, we paid approximately $10,000 per week for these stamps. This $10,000 had to be added to your food costs. As is necessary in most stamp plans, about half of this amount was spent for overhead, NOT PREMIUMS! Meijer has reduced prices to save you this entire $10,000 in CASH each week.'' This cash ''discount,'' to use an increasingly fashionable word, was an approach to merchandising that Hendrik cherished. Needless to say, it had the potential of much wider application.

In the last six months of 1960 the company had been racked by change. The merger plans had fallen through, ownership was consolidated (although plans for the buy-out of the Magoon stock were not completed until 1963), and low prices triumphed over stamps.

In the midst of this turmoil, new stores opened in Battle Creek, Grand Haven, and—in a kind of prodigal's return that Hendrik savored—in Holland, Michigan. That store, like the others, was closed on Sundays. That was the only way a merchant did business in De Kolonie, even in the 1960s. (Over the years, however, with Meijer often leading the way, that would change.) For the grand opening, Hendrik invited family and friends, including the survivors among his crew at the Holland Furnace Company, to the store for a reunion. His two living sisters, Anna and Griet, were there with their families. The ribbon-cutting took place on a bright spring morning, and Hendrik was a dapper, gregarious host. He welcomed John Huizinga, who had traveled to Yakima with him in 1911, as well as other men who had remained all their lives within blocks of the house where Hendrik had first made his home in the New World. Sitting on lawn chairs outside the entrance as customers streamed by, they reminisced over coffee and doughnuts.

Even as Meijer was opening more supermarkets, however, a hybrid form of retail merchandising was evolving that would cause the biggest stir in the American marketplace since the supermarket pioneers had introduced their concepts thirty years before. There were clues that Hendrik, now in his late seventies, was thoroughly receptive to the changes that were coming. One day a few years earlier, for example, he had been raking leaves when he picked up a scrap of paper that had blown onto the lawn from across the street. It was a receipt for a shipment of watches from a New York jewelry wholesaler. Hendrik tucked the paper in his pocket and later gave it to Fred. ''Keep this,'' he said. ''Maybe someday we'll be in the watch business.''

8

The World and
Twenty-Eighth Street

They were thinking men, who had an insight into the requirements of the time—what was ripe for development.

—*Hegel*

The final act of Hendrik Meijer's business life—and the innovation that became his legacy—was the marriage of a supermarket and a discount house in a single store. In the spring of 1961, Hendrik and Fred attended a convention in New York for operators of discount department stores. These maverick ''mass merchants'' were applying supermarket concepts of self-service and high volume to items other than food. Their low-priced assault on traditional department stores offered prospects of growth tantalizingly reminiscent of the supermarket explosion of the 1930s.

Hendrik and Fred returned from the meetings fired up with all the enthusiasm of their pioneering days in the self-service grocery business. Discount houses were springing up everywhere, and people loved the bargains. ''It looked like a regular gold rush,'' Fred recalled. ''We got the fever.''

In October of that year they announced plans for the addition of a discount department store next to their arched-roof supermarket Number Eleven at 28th Street and Kalamazoo Avenue in Grand Rapids. Here they plotted the company's debut in the brave new world of discounting, transforming themselves from grocers to mass merchants in a ''fever'' that nearly broke them.

Perhaps there was a kernel of truth in their employee publication's claim that ''this move is a natural outgrowth of our present Home Center Departments, in which we have been selling children's wear and household items for the past eight years.'' But almost nowhere was an example to be found of a supermarket operator making the successful transition to selling nonfood merchandise. Hendrik had been unsuccessful selling paint at the Ionia store, and paint was a straightforward merchandising proposition compared to fashion apparel or toys.

Perhaps, as the company publication observed, ''the public's overwhelming acceptance of our no-stamp, low-overhead style of merchandising'' made the new venture possible: ''You might say that our first step was to become a discount house for groceries.'' Until Meijer entered the discount department store field, however, no one in Grand Rapids would have thought to buy lettuce and lingerie in the same store. The challenge of this new institution was to break down traditional barriers between selling groceries and selling clothes or hardware. Indeed, Meijer planned to offer such a variety of items in so much space (more than two acres) that they called the store simply Thrifty Acres. After describing all the fashion and hardgoods departments envisioned for the expanded building, the company's employee publication *Cracker Barrel* concluded, ''Look out Downtown, Meijer has everything.''

Until the 1950s there had been no store for selling nonfood merchandise comparable to a supermarket. A shopper for slacks or a lawnmower had three choices: the traditional department store—often located downtown, without convenient parking; the smaller specialty store; or a catalog. Discounting changed all that. The movement's most prominent pioneers started stores in vacant factories and mills in New England. (Atlantic Mills was the name of one early chain in the region that became known as ''the cradle of discounting.'') These merchants dispensed with such niceties as service and decor; they were promotion-minded cousins of the old department-store bargain basements, with plain pipe racks for garments and rickety wooden display tables. They priced their inventory below the ''suggested retail price'' that traditional stores used to obtain higher markups. Like the supermarkets, discount houses compensated for narrower profit margins with higher sales volume.

Like the early supermarkets, the first discount houses were spartan, unprepossessing establishments. At first, wrote Godfrey M. Lebhar in *Chain Stores in America*, ''their sole appeal was offering standard products at less than standard prices.''

Only because complacent conventional merchants had stayed so long with "standard" or "fair trade" prices—usually those set by the manufacturer—did discounters have a reason to exist. "Ironically enough," Lebhar continued, the "Fair Trade laws, which [traditional department stores had] relied upon to make such [discount] merchandising impossible, had just the opposite effect. For wherever Fair Trade prices prevailed, the discounters had a ready-made, authentic yardstick by which to demonstrate to the consumer how much lower their prices were" on items identical to those in the department stores.

With prices that ranged from 15 to 25 percent below conventional retail, the word "discount" began to take on significance. Major manufacturers whose goods were being discounted, including General Electric, Westinghouse, and Sunbeam, spent millions of dollars seeking injunctions and trying other legal maneuvers to maintain their right to enforce Fair Trade pricing.

Meanwhile, conventional retailers sneered at the discount houses. "Do you know what discounting is?" asked one New York department store executive. "It's nothing more than selling inferior merchandise on Sundays." Others condemned discounting as everything from "a malignant cancer" to "an unsound method of distribution." But the armies of the status quo were fighting a losing battle: by 1962 the Fair Trade law had been so successfully challenged that it had become unenforceable in half the country—including Michigan. "As it was," Lebhar concluded, "Fair Trade had remained in force long enough not only to give discounting its original impetus but to enable it to pick up considerable momentum."

This momentum brought a westward expansion of the discount idea. Chains such as Arlan's and Miracle Mart opened outlets in Grand Rapids. Every aspect of their approach was geared to selling goods cheap—and, frequently, to selling cheap goods. Some discount houses were shoddy operations, and others were guilty by association. At some stores, items were never in stock when a customer wanted them; at others, self-service meant no service at all. Yet shoppers liked the low prices, and the early discounters proved that by eliminating frills they could produce substantial savings.

Hendrik was in his seventies then, but he was also the man who had saved the watch receipt that floated into his yard. He was one of the grocers who had pioneered low-margin retailing. And the lessons of Zola's story of Au Bon Marché had not been lost on him. The great department stores owed their original success to wide variety and low prices; they made shopping efficient and exciting. Discount stores could apply the same formulas. Add to these impressions Meijer's tentative success in its own home centers, and Hendrik and Fred reached the same conclusion: the discount house was here to stay.

Nor were they alone. In Detroit, the S. S. Kresge five-and-dime chain altered its course decisively by introducing K-Marts, the first of which would open—as the first Thrifty Acres would—in the spring of 1962. Kresge's dime-store rival, F. W. Woolworth, announced plans to build a Woolco store in Columbus, Ohio. On Fifth Avenue that same year came the first E. J. Korvette store; in tiny Bentonville, Arkansas, Sam Walton opened the first Wal-Mart; and in France, a company called Carrefour introduced Europe's first great discount store.

With the entry into discounting of major retailers came wider public acceptance. The Woolworth annual report of 1961 observed a "consumer willingness to dispense with certain services in exchange for cash savings and the comforts of shopping for all manner of goods under a single roof, with self-selection and checkout counters."

En route to Europe in 1959, Hendrik and Zien had met a group of German exporters who sold to the new discount houses. These men reported on the potential in discounting, and Hendrik was impressed with what they had to say. "Maybe someday we can buy goods directly from an outfit like this," he wrote to Fred—over a year before they had committed themselves to the Thrifty Acres idea. "You almost have to get into the discount business; food may eventually be secondary, the way it looks to me."

Hendrik and Fred worried, moreover, that if discount chains located their stores next to supermarkets, the combination would be formidable competition for conventional, free-standing supermarkets like theirs. Worse yet, a discount house might subsidize a supermarket of its own just to lure shoppers into the discount house with low food prices. In either case, they reasoned, their supermarkets stood to suffer.

On Grand Rapids' northeast side, a Meijer supermarket shared a building with a Miracle Mart discount department store. Originally, the landlord had offered to lease the entire building to Meijer—if the local chain was prepared to open a discount house of its own. Fred and Hendrik tried unsuccessfully to get a downtown clothing store to join in the experiment, but when the clothing store declined, father and son were unwilling to commit to all that floor space themselves.

Next to the Meijer supermarket on 28th Street the company owned several acres of land. Hendrik and Fred had planned to develop a strip of stores there, but negotiations fell through with a local drugstore, the most important of the small center's prospective tenants. At the same time, an opportunity arose from an unexpected direction. A Grand Rapids realtor, Ben Muller, had placed an advertisement in the *Wall Street Journal* for the sale of a Plumb supermarket building in Grand Rapids. He was seeking a sale-leaseback arrangement, and he received several inquiries. He sold the property soon afterward, but a Swiss investment group, having failed to acquire the Plumb building, expressed interest in similar investments and invited Muller to find a deal for them. He in turn approached Fred and Hendrik about selling their 28th Street supermarket to the Swiss group, then leasing it back. Later Muller would say of his contact with Hendrik and Fred, "I happened to hit them at a time when they needed money."

The Meijers were enthusiastic at first: the company always seemed to need money, and the last couple of years had produced flat earnings. By the time they had second thoughts, Muller had already arranged for one of the Swiss bankers to visit Grand Rapids to discuss the prosposal. The more they thought about the offer, however, the more Hendrik and Fred hesitated to sell the store. Father and son were conveniently absent from the office the day Muller and the Swiss investment banker came to call. "I remember tracking them down," Muller said later. "They were literally hiding from me. It was, to say the least, embarrassing." Told that the grocers might be found at their store on Plainfield Avenue, Muller and his visitor "went over there and caught them behind the pickles."

To encourage Hendrik and Fred to reconsider the Swiss proposal, Muller offered to help them attract a discount store to the vacant site next to their supermarket. Then the Swiss concern would buy the whole complex. Not only would Hendrik and Fred get their money out of the property the drugstore had rejected, they would build more traffic for their supermarket with a discounter located next door. When they approved of Muller's offer, he undertook the search for a discount house for the 28th Street site.

"I vividly remember one particularly irritating conversation I had with Miracle Mart in New York," Muller recalled. He had suggested that the discounters locate next to a Meijer store, as they had on the northeast side of Grand Rapids. But this time Meijer was initiating the project, and the response

Muller got was, "We're Miracle Mart; we're big. Who the heck is Meijer?"

There were, in fact, no discounters beating down the doors to put a store next to the supermarket. Yet the money for such a venture was available: the Swiss were interested. (Over the years rumors concerning the company's financial backing have suggested sources ranging from Republican boss Frank McKay to Queen Juliana of the Netherlands.) Hendrik and Fred did not lack confidence in their retailing acumen. And they had seen what Miracle Mart had done on the other side of town and were less than impressed. Discounting was a gamble; general merchandise retailing posed pitfalls unknown to grocers. But there were problems inherent in anything new. Solving them required judgment and work, not a special genius. Besides, it was inconceivable to them that they could not run a better store than Miracle Mart.

The Swiss went along with the project—although their representative told Ben Muller, "Meijer doesn't warrant that kind of investment," based on the company's balance sheet. Still, the European was convinced "by some sixth sense," Muller recalled, that these grocers would be winners. "If their credit wasn't all that great," the realtor added, "they were great operators." Indeed, Hendrik and Fred had painted a rosy picture for themselves. But their confidence derived in part from their naiveté. "Many discounters had a lot of experience and were doing well," Fred noted. "We thought, 'Hey, this is great'—except we knew nothing about it."

"The fever," as Fred described the impulse to open discount stores, was easy to contract. Many discounters did not even operate most of the departments in their stores. The discounter often became a glorified landlord who leased each department to a separate retailer who had experience in that specialty. That merchant in turn, like an independent shopkeeper, hired his own employees, ordered his own merchandise, and established his own prices, paying a percentage of his sales to the discounter. Starting this way required relatively little capital—the inventory belonged to the individual tenants—and a grocer who went into discounting did not have to become an expert overnight in sporting goods or shoes or plumbing supplies.

Hendrik and Fred hired a consultant, Tom Reges, to study the Grand Rapids market and advise them on the wisdom of joining the discount "gold rush." Reges was skeptical: "If Meijer is to go into the discount business, it would endanger their supermarket business,'' he wrote. A big problem was cash flow: in a supermarket, inventory turned over quickly; not so with general merchandise. Only if the grocers leased out virtually all the nonfood departments could they avoid the danger of a cash drain so severe that it might break the company. The lure of discounting had touched off a stampede among eager merchants. If the market became saturated, Reges warned, smaller chains might be squeezed out. Meijer was small *and* lacked experience; and finally, neither S.S. Kresge nor the other retail giants who were opening the new breed of discount stores were going the final step of combining food and general merchandise under one roof.

By late summer of 1961, however, their planning had passed the point of no return—or so Fred thought. ''We decided to go,'' he said later, ''but we were still looking for reassurance. We were pretty far along when I asked my dad one last time, 'Do you think we should do it?' '' There followed a long pause. They were sitting in Fred's car—they had just come from a tour of the stores—outside the office on Michigan Street. Fred looked across the seat at Hendrik, and the old man said no.

''I was really surprised,'' Fred recalled. ''I asked, 'Why would you say no?' . . . I knew he was in favor of it. And he said, 'Because I'm too old to see it through. . . . If we go broke in this deal, I don't want you to tell yourself, ''I did it because my dad wanted it.'' ' '' Then Fred, who was forty-one years old, asked Hendrik, ''Well, what would you do if you were my age?'' To that the old man answered decisively, ''I'd jump in with both feet.'' That was all Fred needed to hear. And Hendrik, who was nearly seventy-eight, jumped in with both feet too. ''He was impetuous in a way,'' said a friend. ''He wasn't afraid.''

In the fall of 1961, bulldozers moved onto the 28th Street site. To their 20,000-square-foot supermarket with the arched roof, Fred and Hendrik committed to an addition of 80,000 square feet. Still something of a mystery—to themselves as well as to employees and customers—was the manner in which they proposed to stock a 100,000-square-foot expanse of space. ''The store was actually under construction,'' Fred recalled, ''and we still hadn't made up our minds how it should be laid out.''

They studied other discounters and discerned three alternatives for selling food and general merchandise under one roof. One option was to put a partition between the supermarket and the discount house and use two separate rows of cash registers. That approach appealed to grocers concerned about the typically higher wage rates commanded by food store cashiers, and it eliminated the potential housekeeping problem of laying a sweater on a checkout counter that was wet from a head of lettuce or a carton of ice cream. A second solution was to put a concourse down the middle of the building with checklanes on one side for food and on the other side for nonfoods, thus achieving the same physical separation of merchandising categories. A third approach was to install a single long row of checkouts with all the departments grouped behind it. That way had its operational complications. Would customers feel comfortable buying a blouse or fruit along with their motor oil? Could cashiers cope with the volume of grocery traffic combined with the awkwardness of checking out garden supplies or a bicycle?

These were all questions that awaited answers, but the convenience of a single row of checkouts—"one-stop shopping" would soon be the favored phrase—was unrivaled. Regardless of the variety of goods purchased, customers could pay for everything in a single transaction. Of all the stores Hendrik and Fred investigated, only one, in Middletown, New York, had taken the single-checkout approach. They liked what they saw, and that format became the core of the Thrifty Acres idea.

Hendrik described the new facility as a "super general store." He regarded it as the inevitable convergence of the supermarket approach to food retailing introduced in the 1930s and the century-old idea of the general store, where a customer could find virtually everything he or she needed. "It is a logical combining of the self-service principle and an all-inclusive department store," he said at the time. "The obvious advantages are less overhead and a subsequently lower price structure."

Before the 28th Street store was even laid out, however, the stakes were raised still higher. The Meijers had long planned a third supermarket for Muskegon, and when the developer there wanted to put a discount house next door, Hendrik and Fred said they would take that on too. After all, if most of the nonfood departments were leased out, adding another store was hardly an overwhelming proposition. Then, when the same situation presented itself next to their store in Holland, Hendrik and Fred agreed to locate a third discount house there. No one told them that they had bitten off more than they could chew. "I can remember the amazement of the supermarket employees at the time," recalled Meat Director

Darrell Steinke. No one could comprehend what the company was going to do with all the extra space. The three new stores, all scheduled to open within a five-month stretch in the summer and fall of 1962, would have more square feet of building, more brick and mortar and retail space, than all the rest of the chain combined.

As construction progressed on 28th Street, the company built in some insurance that hinted at the riskiness of the venture: an extra-thick, five-inch concrete floor that would make the cavernous addition suitable for an auto showroom or a warehouse if the new store failed. Inside the shell of the vast building, confusion prevailed: a snow fence separated the area under construction from the existing supermarket, which continued to operate even as its cases and shelves were being rearranged. Customers peered into the dark reaches of the newly enclosed space and followed signs to relocated grocery aisles. The company printed fliers with a map and a "certificate of membership" in the "Thrifty Acres Sidewalk Superintendents Club" that offered customers "free guide service if lost in this jungle and an unlimited opportunity to meet otherwise well-informed folks who are just as confused as you are as to where to find anything."

The big store *was* a novelty, and the town was beginning to talk. A *Grand Rapids Press* photo showed a contractor riding a bicycle through the open expanse of store clutching a blueprint to the handlebars. Meijer, "a pioneer in the development of self-service supermarkets," the newspaper reported, had announced "the first of 'several' self-service department stores in Central and Western Michigan."

If there was curiosity and confusion on the surface, behind the scenes there was chaos. Outside managers had been hired to supervise the new general merchandise departments, which appeared distressingly disorganized as opening day approached. "What they didn't know," said a friend of Hendrik and Fred, "they weren't afraid to hire someone who did know." The New England discount store manager brought in to oversee the nonfood operations was unaccustomed to the informality of the "food men." This was a small-town company by his standards. He was accustomed to being addressed as "mister," but at Meijer, people called each other by their first names. (The only exception was Hendrik himself, who was always referred to, through no insistence of his own but simply because of his age and demeanor, as "Mr. Meijer.")

Visiting the store one day, Hendrik and Fred were disturbed to find Earl Holton, the young district manager responsible for the supermarket, sitting in the back room placidly sipping a cup of coffee. Much of the store was a mess, yet he was acting as if everything were under control. "My supermarket's all set," Holton explained, "but when I stick my head on the other side of the snow fence they tell me, 'Mind your own business, food man.' " Meijer people were beginning to sense difficulty in reconciling their way of doing business—the aggressive and efficient way of the supermarket, always so concerned with "streamlining"—with the habits of discount merchandisers.

Wariness prevailed on both sides of the fence. Early discounters, somewhat like early supermarket operators, were regarded in some quarters as pariahs of retailing. To traditional department store and speciality store merchants, the discounters, with their pipe racks and warehouse locations and their self-service tables heaped with cheap goods, were schlock artists. Such was the reputation of the early discount house that *discount* was itself a dirty word. "In the first place," Fred said, "the term itself is becoming less realistic all the time. When fair trade [laws] held sway, a written-in lower price on a manufacturer's price tag meant something. The customer could see the difference. But this never did hold true on soft goods [wearing apparel and domestics], and now manufacturers are abandoning the old price tag anyway." Yet they knew they had to provide customers with discount-style value, whatever they chose to call it. Fred described the store to a *Modern Retailer* reporter as a "self-service department store," and the distinction he drew between "department store" and "discount house" went "deeper than just labels," the reporter noted, "reflecting a basic attitude of Meijer management."

Although the appeal of the store was tied to bargains, its spirit was not supposed to be cheap. Other discounters had come to town with standards that did not always conform to the particular impulses of western Michigan's shoppers. Hendrik and Fred understood the need, to them not at all contradictory, of a combination of low-priced merchandise—for the Hollanders who comprise the area's dominant ethnic group are a notably frugal people—*and* a clean, attractive store. "It was a stigma to trade in a discount house," Ben Muller recalled. "But I don't remember ever having a stigma about shopping at a Thrifty." (Others would disagree. The author's wife remembers her seventh-grade teacher expressing surprise and distaste at the idea that anyone "would buy *milk* in a discount store that sold *clothes*.")

According to *Modern Retailer*, the company's reputation in the grocery business would help overcome shoppers' doubts about discount stores: "Checks of customer attitudes toward discount operations around the country have often uncovered views of 'poor quality,'. . . so the Meijer name was seen as important in its contribution to the wanted quality image."

At least that was the response Hendrik and Fred and their associates hoped for when the store opened on June 5, 1962. Although there was a splash of advertising, the company dispensed with the customary ribbon-cutting and beauty queens when the doors swung open well before the scheduled hour of 9:30 a.m. Banners across the front of the store proclaimed Thrifty Acres as "the only discount department store with the 'hometown' touch!" The store boasted an unheard-of eighteen checkout lanes, stretching the length of what had been the original supermarket. For children there were nine one-cent pony rides.

Grand opening excitement subsided quickly, however. Although many people came to see the new store, sales were disappointing. "It wasn't a howling success from the day it opened," recalled Art Snell, the company's attorney. The magical touch that Hendrik and Fred had seemed to bring to the grocery business was not magic at all when applied to general merchandise. The organization's skills were not automatically transferable. Instead, father and son staked their reputation and their fortunes on an institution they could not control at the crucial level of customer contact—where success or failure would be determined.

With a different operator in control of each department, the company was helpless to correct deficiencies in stocking, service, or even cleanliness. And equally important, Hendrik and Fred were determined to have low prices; but the outsiders who ran the infants' or paint departments thought more about their own bottom line. Their only concern was to make their own departments profitable. In pricing, as in service and quality, there was no consistency. One lessee even employed a bait-and-switch come-on in his advertising. To get him out quickly, Hendrik told a salesman one day over coffee, "I wrote the biggest check of my life." The operator of the paint department was forced out after his manager was abusive to a customer who returned a can of paint.

Father and son soon came to a disturbing, if inevitable, conclusion: the lessees who operated most of the departments would have to go; indeed, in some cases they would have to go even before the Holland and Muskegon Thrifty Acres stores were to open three or four months later. Some of the apparel department operators saw the writing on the wall and balked at expanding to the new locations.

As Meijer started taking over the leased departments, the complexion of the adventure changed. Where would the money come from to buy out the leased-department inventories and order new goods? Reges had been right. Just as early supermarkets had taken over meat and produce departments that had originally operated as leased concessions, Meijer now was faced with the necessity—it was a necessity, a *requirement* of Thrifty Acres' ultimate success—of operating its own shoe and menswear and sporting goods departments. "Don't hesitate to tackle the new departments," Hendrik advised Fred. And what if selling shoes and menswear and sporting goods remained a mystery? The grocers would have to learn by doing. "Just give the customers the kind of merchandise, services and prices you would like if you were the customer," Hendrik wrote in the *Cracker Barrel*.

Although Hendrik had little trepidation about buying out his original leased department—his first butcher—back in Greenville in 1935, now the stakes were far greater. The company taxed its resources nearly to the breaking point buying merchandise in categories its buyers knew little or nothing about. And they started with fashions, the trickiest of all, on a scale larger than they had any business contemplating. "The leased departments were making the money," Ben Muller recalled. "I had an inward feeling that bringing in outside people with plenty of expertise wasn't right. What impressed me was the speed with which they converted from the leased departments to their own."

Suddenly a man like Al Meijer was given the job of buying goods for apparel departments the company took over. The closest he had ever been to Seventh Avenue was ordering neckties or T-shirts from a local jobber for the supermarket home centers. In the late summer of 1962 he went to New York with instructions to obtain a $300,000 inventory for the ladies' departments of the three new stores. "Fred just told me to go to New York and buy," Al said later. "Realizing we didn't have time to prepare for such a trip, and without a New York buying office, and on top of that lacking fashion-buying experience, all I could say was, 'Fred, I don't want to lose my job.' His answer was, 'You won't,' and I went to New York.'' To Al fell the task of explaining to wholesalers, manufacturers, and credit managers just what a Thrifty Acres store was. No, it was not exactly a discount house. Or maybe it was a discount house. And it sold *food* with the dresses?

Nor did it help that Thrifty Acres had been set up as a separate corporation. (At first the name Meijer did not appear on signs or advertising.) ''By the end of the week we ran into a real problem,'' Al continued. ''The manufacturers refused to sell to us because we didn't have a credit rating. 'Thrifty Acres' was unknown in the market. I called Fred and he gave me the okay to place orders for 'Meijer' [as in supermarkets] instead of Thrifty Acres.'' But even that did not carry much weight with New York credit offices—especially after September 1962, when the company's best supermarket, at Michigan and Fuller, was gutted by a fire started by a burglar's welding torch. (That store was another under Holton's supervision. When Hendrik arrived to survey the damage, he tried to calm the young supervisor down. ''Right now,'' he said, ''there's nothing you can do. If you can't change things, don't butt your head up against a brick wall.'')

In New York, wholesalers wondered at a small midwestern grocer with a balance sheet like Meijer's trying to run department stores—discount or otherwise. ''The result,'' Fred recalled, ''was that Meijer Supermarkets, with a half-million dollar credit limit in foods, was good for only $500 in soft goods, which made it impossible for us to buy.'' Not until both Fred and the company's treasurer flew to New York to explain what they were doing did the credit bureaus relent and approve adequate credit for Al Meijer to begin to stock the new stores.

But the company's troubles did not end there. Sales continued to lag behind expectations. It would take time to build traffic for this radically different kind of store. And taking over the leased departments only plunged the company deeper into debt. Harvey Lemmen was sales manager then. As Fred recalled, ''I went into Harvey's office one day and he pointed out that we had lost $400,000 (in the separate Thrifty Acres operation). Now, we'd never made much over $100,000 a year at the peak of our earnings in our supermarkets. . . . We had trouble. We had to pay income tax on the $100,000 we'd made in the supermarkets and couldn't deduct the $400,000 in losses.''

Yet father and son were convinced that they were on the right track. "If the goal is right," Hendrik often said, "we'll find a way to get there." But he could not have imagined how hard finding that way would be. Nor could his son. Faced with all the red ink, Fred "turned white as a sheet," Harvey Lemmen recalled, and "Hendrik was too much of an optimist to believe we were as bad off as we were." Bad off indeed! As Fred put it, "We were losing our shirt and our pants and our underwear—everything."

During the last months of 1962 the squeeze was on. Across the country that year, nearly 150 discount stores closed their doors. The shakeout was underway, and Hendrik, Fred, and company had to act fast to save Thrifty Acres. Quickly they combined the two corporations, Thrifty Acres and Meijer Supermarkets. As Reges had suggested, Meijer had signed leases with its tenants that could be terminated on short notice. One after another, they dropped the original tenants, operating more and more of the departments themselves, while Al Meijer and a handful of new buyers learned their way around New York.

Scrambling in every direction, Fred, in Earl Holton's words, "wrenched this company loose and turned it around." It was the younger man's show now, and Hendrik recognized that. He had reconciled himself to that transition years before—a state of mind not always characteristic of entrepreneurs. And yet as Fred assumed the reins, Hendrik was there with him—still sharing the office, still touring the stores. Despite the flood of red ink, Hendrik approached his seventy-ninth birthday with his confidence unshaken. "Hendrik was a key factor in keeping Fred thinking we could make it," Lemmen noted. "It took a lot of guts. We were going deeper and deeper into debt. Everything looks very logical, but at crucial moments it could have failed. . . . It was at the point of the company going down or turning it around." Added Fred later, "Thrifty Acres was close to being a mistake, but it wasn't. It could have bankrupted us."

The threat of failure was almost a necessary ingredient in creating the sense of grand adventure with which they undertook the new enterprise. "They succeeded," said one salesman, not because they were cautious or expert but "because they reveled in what they were doing."

It was imperative that they have a good Christmas season in 1962, and they did. Sales climbed as the leased departments came under the umbrella of Meijer operations and merchan-

Thrifty Acres' exhaustive list of items and services in this grand opening ad from the Grand Rapids Press *included, in alphabetical order, ''luggage, meats, and men's furnishings.'' The name Meijer was nowhere to be found.*

dising. Advertising began to identify the stores as *Meijer* Thrifty Acres; no longer would the new stores comprise a separate entity. "In harmony," Hendrik loved to say, "is strength." Buoyed by his conviction that the path was right, the company embraced the concept of Thrifty Acres and made it work. The word "discount," in western Michigan, at least, was losing its negative connotations, and the Meijers' big stores in Grand Rapids, Muskegon, and Holland appeared to be gathering momentum. By the latter part of 1963, a year after the three openings had brought the company to the brink, its detractors had been disproven. Meijer was in the discount business to stay.

Not until years later, however, after Meijer bought the 28th Street store back from the Swiss, and the first three stores were successful enough for others to follow—after Hendrik had died, in fact—did someone discover that new stores were still being built with extra-thick, five-inch floors. It was time to stop that, Fred decided. Unnoticed was the irony that this most modern version of the supermarket (a "super-supermarket" as one writer described it) was still preparing itself for possible conversion to a car dealership—a reversal of the Depression-era practice of starting supermarkets in defunct garages.

II

As far as the circumstances of his life were concerned, he could have experienced much. And that he had really experienced much, that he had not gone through life without seizing the impressions it offered him so abundantly—for that, the nimbleness of his mind might go bail, and the receptiveness of his heart.

—Multatuli, Max Havelaar

Despite two heart attacks and against all actuarial odds, Hendrik assumed he would outlive his wife. Perhaps it was the memory of her frailty as a young woman and the goiter operation in 1911. When they returned to Europe again in 1963, he was seventy-nine years old, she was seventy-seven. He was more enthusiastic than she was about making the trip, and was relieved and delighted when she did not get seasick. "I had to give her a pill to keep things moving," he wrote to Fred. "I believe she is surprising herself." Reclining in his deck chair, Hendrik read *The Young Lions* by Irwin Shaw, and in the ship's theater he saw the new film *Peyton Place.*

Although he was probably the oldest delegate, Hendrik did not miss a meeting at an international grocers' conference in London. "I saw a lot of people from the states," he told Fred. "Syl Goldman [the inventor of the shopping cart and a grocer from Oklahoma], Jimmy Cook [president of the Penn Fruit supermarkets in Philadelphia], Sidney Rabb [chairman of the Stop & Shop supermarkets in Boston]." After one grocer's speech on the benefits of trading stamps to American supermarkets, the audience was invited to comment. "I was the only one that raised a hand," Hendrik wrote. "I told them that my friends from the states give a very nice presentation, but there are two sides to the question and I would like to give our story."

His own company had been skeptical about the benefits of trading stamps at first, he noted, before being inundated with testimonials from converts to stamps. One operator claimed his sales had doubled. "So we took a second look and got on the bandwagon," Hendrik told the Europeans. "We got the best catalog we could produce and copied the best companies in the United States. Our business had only a slight increase and we had to lay thousands of dollars on the line for the stamps. [So] we threw the stamps out and are happy with the result. The stamp-giving merchant thinks he has a captive customer. . . . The fact is that he himself is the captive. . . . The stamp company takes the money. . . ."

In October 1963, little more than a year after fire destroyed the store at Michigan and Fuller, the Quonset hut Greenville supermarket burned down. Hendrik, then nearly eighty years old, immediately drove to Greenville to survey the destruction. The $300,000 fire collapsed the Quonset and gutted the store's interior. So hot were the walls, the fire chief said later, that "the blocks started going like popcorn from the high heat." Hendrik's response to queries from employees and customers was automatic. "Of course we shall rebuild," he told the *Greenville Daily News;* "Greenville is where we started in business. . . . After our fire in 1946 we got back in business in fourteen weeks. We'll try to be ready in record time." That afternoon he ran an ad that included a "fire coupon" good at the stores in Cedar Springs and Ionia "to help compensate for driving the extra distance."

Hendrik Meijer was "young of mind," as more than one friend remarked. Never did he stop thinking about better ways to run a store. In a notepad in 1963 he scribbled a slogan he was always fond of: "Every day is bargain day at Meijer."

The office staff threw a surprise party for Hendrik's eightieth birthday on December 28, 1963. On the cake stood eight candles, one for each decade of his life. He was quite satisfied with himself when, in a single breath, he blew out all eight candles. He was looking around for a knife to cut the cake when someone said, "Mr. Meijer, the candles . . ." One had flickered back to life. Hendrik bent down again and drew a long breath; again he blew, and again the flame died—but just momentarily. "Mr. Meijer straightened up," recalled John Veldman, "looked at all of us around him, picked out Chuck Westra [the chain's advertising and personnel director], and a big smirk came over Chuck's face." "I knew it," Hendrik said. "It had to be Chuck." As Veldman, a recent Dutch immigrant working as a buyer, later observed, "It showed me the relationship of management and employees [at Meijer]—it was a complete surprise to me, unthinkable in the Old Country."

There was a paternal aspect to Hendrik Meijer's employee relations, but "paternalistic" would be a gross simplification. He approached the creation of work, of gainful employment, with an almost missionary enthusiasm. Early in 1964, as ground was broken for two stores in Kalamazoo, he remarked to the construction supervisor on one site, "We've got jobs for three hundred people here." It was a preoccupation—to provide people with a good place to work. His memories of physical labor were still fresh, and when he watched the men who were building his new stores, he relived the strenuous occupations of his youth. "I hated to see him on a construction job," said Fred Welling, then the company's engineer. "He always wanted to talk to a guy digging a ditch, and he always talked to him at his level. Employees held the old man in awe."

*   *   *   *   *

Recognition of what Hendrik Meijer's company had achieved was never widespread. Even with the launching of the Thrifty Acres stores, retailers elsewhere paid little attention to what was happening in western Michigan. Because none of its stores was located in a major metropolitan area, and because its stock was privately held, Meijer could expand dramatically while keeping a low profile in the industry. Thrifty Acres was an anomaly to conventional grocers, as it was to conventional discounters. That did not displease its founder, who did nothing to invite attention.

Indeed, the company sometimes appeared to outsiders to have succeeded almost in spite of itself. To listen to Hendrik's explanations was to hear an optimism nearly as naive as it was unshakable. As *Grocer's Spotlight* observed on the occasion of his eightieth birthday: "Traditionally, he should be saluted as a 'grand old man of the food business,' although many younger men—including his own son—have been in the business that long (almost thirty years). He should also be regarded as a wise old man, especially in view of his accomplishments. But in truth, many in the trade prefer to consider him a blind old man, a lucky old man, and particularly a funny old man. People have been laughing at Hendrik ever since he entered the business."

He had to laugh at himself sometimes. One morning he misread his clock and arrived at the Michigan and Fuller store an hour ahead of opening, then scolded employees because the front door was still locked. On another occasion, at the Muskegon Thrifty Acres, he forgot about a shoplifting prevention program then in progress and noticed from a balcony window that people were putting things in their pockets. He thought the thieves were real and stalked downstairs in a fury before Fred caught up with him to explain that these suspicious-looking people were not shoplifters at all, but his own co-workers.

He was not so naive, however, as to approve expansion of the Thrifty Acres idea before it had proven itself in the first three stores. The company needed time to catch its breath, and the new concept was far from a complete success. The next two stores opened as conventional supermarkets. Simultaneous with the opening of a new store in Greenville—on a site that adjoined the farm where Hendrik and Zien had lived for most of thirty-five years—came a new supermarket on Alpine Avenue in Grand Rapids. Both stores were situated on enough property to accommodate their expansion into Thrifty Acres units. Until the three big existing stores ceased to be a drain on the company, however, Thrifty Acres expansion was halted. Yet Hendrik sensed their success. He felt comfortable with the idea—"the path was right"—and he had faith in the people responsible for the execution. Soon plans were made for a pair of "Thriftys" in Kalamazoo, stores whose completion he would not live to see.

After his eightieth birthday, Hendrik continued to go to the office in the remodeled basement of the Fuller Avenue store nearly every day. He customarily wore a starched white shirt. "To me he was 'Mr. Meijer,' " recalled Pam Kleibusch, who became Hendrik's secretary—and Fred's, because they shared the same office—not long after her high school graduation. Yet "Mr. Meijer" presided over a company otherwise remarkable for its informality. He was fastidious without being fussy. "He liked to play jokes on people," Mrs. Kleibusch added. "He was always trying to get something over on somebody else."

A salesman for Armour & Company recalled a presentation on meat buying that Hendrik attended. The salesman, George Zain, was listening to others make a long report when Hendrik said to the small group, "Let's go get coffee." Fred, who was conducting the meeting, said gently but firmly, "We're not through yet, Dad." At that Hendrik stood up and replied, "Well then, George and I will go." In the snack bar that adjoined the basement offices, a salesman or employee who shared a coffee break with Hendrik was as apt to receive a lesson in nineteenth-century European history as in the finer points of supermarket operations.

As alert as he was to the possibilities of expanding on the Thrifty Acres idea, Hendrik showed a founder's distaste for the complexities of organization. As the company grew, lines of authority became extended. If he noticed a problem, he could not always take the simple, direct actions that had been appropriate when his company was smaller. He respected the young men who shared the reins with Fred; but there were so many layers of management to work through, with vice-presidents and district managers and store managers and department managers, that it was sometimes hard for the old man to know where he stood.

Frustrated by some little thing one day, he complained to Fred, "I don't know who's responsible for what anymore." And sometimes, when action was not forthcoming, he pouted. "Nobody listens to me," he told Fred once, his voice turning bitter. "I ask for things to get done, and they just don't get done." The outburst surprised his son, who hardly knew what to say. In a sudden rage, the old man stalked into their private bathroom and slammed the door. "I'm going home and I'm going to stay home," he shouted. "Nobody pays any attention to me anymore." Fred was worried. He had seldom seen his father so upset. But then, just as though he had been arguing with Van Maldegan, the vinegar man, twenty-five years earlier, and needed a moment of quiet to collect his thoughts,

Hendrik emerged from the bathroom with a smile on his face. "Aw, come on, Fred," he said quietly. "Let's go to the stores. I wouldn't be happy staying home either."

In fact, there were few things either man preferred to "going to the stores." (Hendrik, naturally, would insist that they stop along the way for coffee, while Fred's inclination was to get to their destination as quickly as possible. Hendrik "never seemed to be in a hurry," observed Jack Koetje, then a young store manager, now a senior vice-president with the company.) Inside a store, few men were more observant than Hendrik. He would notice dirt under a meat case or a cashier who was having trouble. "He seemed to have that awareness," said another executive, "and he retained it." His son took for granted Hendrik's participation in every significant decision. Said Mrs. Kleibusch, "Maybe it was harder on Fred when [Hendrik] was slowing down." Slowing down was a gradual process, however. Even after Hendrik turned eighty (when, as Mrs. Kleibusch observed, "I didn't consider him to be *that* old"), he mowed his own lawn. On a bright spring day he might touch up the paint on the miniature windmill in his backyard or walk through the cemetery down the street while his grandchildren careened around its curving drives on their bicycles.

For more than fifty years Hendrik maintained his barber's license. He called the trade his safety valve—as he said with a smile of his retail business, "This won't last forever." Visiting a retired salesman or an old friend, he would bring the barber tools he kept in a worn leather case. Sunday mornings were reserved for Fred and the grandsons. Hendrik spread newspapers under a stool in the middle of the kitchen floor, unfolded a faded cloth, and pinned it on his "customer" at the back of the neck.

His gestures with scissors and clipper were meticulous. He stood over the stool in a plaid flannel shirt, pleated trousers and leather slippers. As he cut the boys' hair, Fred watched and talked, leaning back against the wall with his hands cushioning the small of his back while the sun streamed through the kitchen window. The barber was careful to consult his customers on questions of style. The Princeton—short around the ears and neck, a little longer in front—was the standard choice. The boys always wanted it a little longer in front, and Hendrik at least pretended to oblige. At intervals he turned off the electric clipper to brush a few hairs from a little boy's brow. When he was finished, the results were examined in a hand mirror. Then, loosening the cloth, he carefully gathered it up, carried it to the door, and shook the tufts of hair into the breeze.

He cut the boys' hair on Sunday, May 31, 1964. It was a warm, sunny day, and that afternoon he took Zien for a drive in the Buick. When they came home, Zien started dinner while he walked to the cemetery. After dinner he read for a while, then told his wife, "I guess I'll go to bed. I'm kind of tired." That night, in his sleep, his heart failed for the last time.

The attitudes Hendrik and Zien had brought to America in a different age still showed in many of their beliefs, but they no longer bristled as they once had at social convention and religious ritual. The funeral was held in a Congregational church—albeit one Hendrik had rarely stepped inside. A young minister from Greenville delivered the eulogy, incorporating notes Fred had made the day after his father died. "During the last two days of his life," his son wrote, "he painted on his windmill, cut hair, talked business, talked politics, told jokes, watched TV, visited stores, went to a golden wedding anniversary, took his naps, joked with the children." Down to its final days it was a curiously rounded life, with a momentum not always apparent in the unexpected turns it had taken.

In Greenville, Mrs. Emmett Green, an elderly friend, was expecting his visit to celebrate her birthday. Hendrik placed a priority on spending time with friends, especially the frail or the sick. "Mr. Meijer will come. He always comes," the old woman declared. She was still expecting him when she was informed that he had died the night before.

*   *   *   *   *

So gradual and complete had been the shift of authority from father to son that the business suffered few strains, organizationally or with his estate, when Hendrik Meijer died. The biggest change belonged to Fred, who shouldered full responsibility for decisions he had always made with the help of the white-haired man who rode with him to the stores. It was his show now, although Zien came to the office more frequently. She toured the stores with the same devotion that she had displayed that day in 1935 when Johanna left for the university and she had come down to the store and put on an apron for the first time.

Zien outlived her husband by fourteen years. For employees and customers of Meijer, she became the link between present and past. Her life spanned the decades between the frustrated dreams of the Old Country and the novel enterprise her husband had inspired, now shooting off in a dozen different directions.

In the hands of a younger generation, the ideas of Hendrik Meijer would seem less eccentric, would seem utterly logical, as Harvey Lemmen observed of Thrifty Acres. But to Zien those ideas had grown out of a lifetime of change, experiment, and upheaval. In her last years, details of that lifetime were not always easy to remember. But she had *been there* and had seen what succeeding generations could only imagine.

Sometimes it almost seemed as though her husband were still alive. She saw him in snapshots from the early days in Greenville, and the memories came flooding back. "Here's me and Johanna," she said, studying photographs through a magnifying glass at her kitchen table when she was ninety years old. "And here is Johanna kissing the doll. And here is Henry with Johanna and me of course, and here again. And here's Henry with the baby, and that's me giving her a bath. Here I'm nursing the baby. And that's me in the coat again, and Henry and the baby and me again. Oh my goodness what pictures! And here is Henry with the baby, and here he is asleep. . . ."

Afterword

After Hendrik Meijer died in 1964, Gezina became president and later chairman of the board. Although the roles were largely ceremonial, her interest in the company and its people never waned. After a broken hip confined her to a wheelchair, she continued to visit with associates and tour stores much as her husband had. She was appointed chairman emerita in 1975 when Fred became chairman. The change made possible the promotion of Harvey Lemmen, and five years later Earl Holton, to president. She attended board meetings until her death in 1978 at the age of 91.

Hendrik Meijer lived long enough to see great possibilities for the stores called Thrifty Acres. Had he lived longer, he would have seen those possibilities take shape in brick and mortar. He would have seen his company transformed. And he would have seen it alter the shopping habits of millions of people.

In 1994, more than thirty years after Hendrik and Fred opened the first Thrifty Acres store on 28th Street in Grand Rapids, their company opened its first locations in Indiana — in Fort Wayne, South Bend and Indianapolis.

In the team member breakrooms of these new stores hang copies of a picture of Hendrik astride a mechanical pony at the opening of that original big store in Grand Rapids. At the front of each new store will be the 1994 version of the same pony. Children, including Hendrik's great-grandchildren, buck and sway in the saddle just as they did in Hendrik's day. And the ride still costs a penny — just as it did more than thirty years ago.

At the time of Hendrik's death, Meijer operated fifteen supermarkets and three of the Thrifty Acres stores. (Two more were under construction in Kalamazoo.) In the decades since 1964 the path of expansion has proceeded east and south out of western Michigan.

Other retailers have grown more rapidly. Wal-Mart stores,

moving north out of the sunbelt, have spread through much of the country as their parent company has grown into the largest retailer in the world. K-Marts have long been a ubiquitous feature of our suburban landscape. And both of these mass-merchandising giants are pushing ahead with combination stores based on the Meijer format — suggesting that the company will face its stiffest competitive tests in years to come.

Unlike such publicly-owned companies, however, Meijer has remained private, without benefit of great capital resources. Sometimes the company seemed to grow in fits and starts. In 1967, after opening two big stores in Lansing, expansion was halted. The company had become overextended. Bankers were nervous. There would be other delays, as Fred and his colleagues carved the path that would take them to Ohio and Indiana.

In the early 1970s came stores in Ypsilanti, Flint, Jackson, Battle Creek and finally Canton Township, Michigan, west of Detroit. As though mirroring the inflationary momentum of the age, the buildings grew larger and larger. New departments were added, and existing categories of merchandise expanded. The Canton Township "hypermarket" — a term the company adapted from the French "hypermarche" — occupied 247,000 square feet. It dwarfed by two and one-half times the original Thrifty Acres store in Grand Rapids.

Fred Meijer predicted the imminent opening of half a dozen more such behemoths in metropolitan Detroit, but his optimism proved premature. Although similar stores were opened three years later in Royal Oak and Taylor, neither they nor the Canton store held the promise of near-time profits. Instead, they were a drain on scarce resources. Sales soared, but years passed before any of the stores showed a profit, and when they did, it was not uncommon for Detroit's notorious grocery price wars to plunge them back into the loss column.

The gargantuan dimensions of the Detroit stores allowed space for selling products that soon proved impractical in a self-service environment. Just as in earlier years Meijer had tried and failed selling men's suits, and had been unsuccessful with auto service centers and fast food ("Thrifty's Kitchen"), now attempts to sell floor coverings and furniture had to be scaled back.

As a result, the generation of stores the company was opening by 1980 was downsized to a format little larger than the original Thrifty Acres. (It would be almost a decade before

K-Mart, Wal-Mart and expansionist French retailers would try to breathe life back into the grandiose "hypermarket.") And rising fuel costs and gasoline shortages suggested that Americans might someday lack the means to drive several miles, often past competing supermarkets, to shop for their groceries. Some Meijer executives feared that the giant stores could become dinosaurs, dependent as they were on sales volume that could be achieved only by drawing customers from a wide area. Perhaps the solution was to build smaller stores, closer together.

Finally, the combination of recession and high interest rates prompted a decision that would redirect the company's expansion plans. In 1975, W. T. Grant, then the country's second largest discounter, declared bankruptcy. Grant's failure was a bonanza of sorts for some of its competitors. K-Mart, for example, acquired scores of locations, often with favorable leases from landlords grateful for a strong tenant.

Meijer took over two Grant locations, in Traverse City and Sterling Heights, Michigan, because they could be expanded into Thrifty Acres units. Otherwise, Meijer found few new opportunities — and contemplated a future in which it would be unable to capitalize on similar situations. With its combination food and general merchandise format, it was a prisoner of its own uniqueness. The stores required far more space than those of typical discounters, which tended to be located in shopping centers where a supermarket tenant had the exclusive right to sell food. There was a sense in some quarters of the company that Meijer was — or should be — sufficiently versatile to operate a straight-forward discount-store format that might open up other expansion opportunities. A continuing shakeout in discount retailing appeared to make such opportunities inevitable.

In 1981 Meijer decided to test the waters by opening conventional discount stores, called "Meijer Square." The response was encouraging — so much so that when an acquisition opportunity presented itself, the company no longer felt obliged to sit on the sidelines.

At this point, too, the Michigan economy had become synonymous with rustbelt recession. Meijer executives, anxious about further expansion in a state whose population was actually shrinking, began to look further afield. Some even suggested the answer lay in creating a second nucleus of stores in another part of the country. Such was the thinking when the company was approached by a floundering, Buffalo-based discount chain called Twin Fair. Although there was nothing like a consensus among Meijer managers, the company agreed to acquire fourteen stores — one a combination unit of the Meijer type, the rest conventional discount stores — in Cincinnati and western Ohio.

The experience of the Michigan "Meijer Square" operations proved to be an unreliable indicator of how such stores would perform in cities where there was not only more discount competition, but where shoppers had not heard of — indeed could hardly be expected to pronounce — Meijer.

For a company accustomed to occupying a unique niche, the Twin Fair acquisition proved a costly and humbling experience. The chain was an undistinguished collection of outlets which faced major competitors with bigger, better-located stores. And Meijer managers quickly realized how much they preferred operating the biggest, best stores of their kind in town.

The experience left the company with capable associates in several Ohio cities, but also with stores that showed little prospect of profit. Within five years, as leases began to expire, most of the stores were closed or sold off. The balance were replaced by full-line Meijer stores.

Just before the Meijer Square adventure, the company embarked on another short-lived bid for diversity. It combined two of its old supermarket locations in Grand Rapids with two leased storefronts to open a four-unit discount drugstore chain called "Spaar," from the Dutch verb "to save." Although the stores achieved respectable sales, their financial statements were smothered by the operating costs of the big corporation. Economies of scale called for dozens of stores instead of four, but the company saw little reason to divert time and money from its core business. Within two years, the Spaar stores were also sold.

Other diversification efforts met similar fates. An unsuccessful effort to persuade Levi Strauss to sell blue jeans to Meijer in the early 1970s prompted the opening of a string of men's shops called "Copper Rivet." The name was suggested by a Levi executive and the shops featured brand-name apparel. But Levi, then at the height of its popularity, insisted that only a shop selling Levi's exclusively would do. Thus Sagebrush, a Levi's shop, was born. Sagebrush evolved into a chain of nearly forty young men's and women's fashion stores before Meijer sold it in 1988.

Lessons had been learned, but the complexities of retailing

are often at odds with the urge to streamline. By the 1990s, the fastest-growing format in mass distribution was the membership wholesale club. Wal-Mart, with its Sam's Clubs, and K-Mart, with its Pace division, were among those plowing new ground in low-cost distribution. Their buildings derived their sales from a limited base of fee-paying "members" — many of them small businesses and institutions — and relied on the high turnover of a limited variety of goods. They were distinctly different from the Meijer one-stop shopping concept, yet their emphasis on low prices threatened a competitive overlap.

In 1992 Meijer opened its first SourceClub membership warehouses near Lansing and Detroit. With these buildings came none of the one-stop shopping format advantages Meijer stores still enjoyed. SourceClub managers anticipated a challenge. They were attempting the untried — a start-up in the face of entrenched competitors. While their "partners," as employes were known, created inviting shopping destinations, the membership club niche did not grow as expected. Indeed, the club industry was changing rapidly in ways no one had anticipated even as the first SourceClubs opened.

Consolidation within the industry left the upstart Source-Clubs in a duel with the industry giant, Sam's Club — a match-up in which the newcomer was outgunned. Sales were growing, but any hope of operating profitably was remote. Less than a year after launching the first clubs, Meijer announced that it was leaving the business. Six of the seven clubs were put up for sale, with the unit in Fraser, Michigan to be expanded into a Meijer store. Once again, the emphasis was to be on one-stop shopping.

In 1974 much of Meijer's grocery warehousing was shifted from Grand Rapids to a new distribution center in Lansing. As new stores in eastern Michigan accounted for an increasing share of sales, the Lansing warehouse became the cornerstore of a two-million-square-foot complex. Grand Rapids and Lansing were joined in 1989 by a facility in the tiny hamlet of Newport, Michigan, between Detroit and Toledo. In 1993 came the first distribution facility outside Michigan — a produce warehouse in Tipp City, Ohio, north of Dayton. A second building in that complex opened in 1994.

The corporate offices have remained in Grand Rapids, and are housed in buildings named for Hendrik, Gezina and Fred Meijer. Ironically enough for a man with little expertise in running a cash register, the building named for Hendrik is devoted in large part to data processing and the increasingly sophisticated information systems demanded by large-scale retailing. The application of new technology has become indispensable. The Gezina Meijer Building, home of the company's planning and design efforts, was originally the store of a defunct competitor.

In 1984 a Meijer store was opened in Cascade Township, southeast of Grand Rapids and just five miles down the road from the original "Thrifty Acres." Although it shared its predecessor's format, it was the first unit of a newer generation, with an updated interior and a new Meijer logo that dropped the "Thrifty Acres" name. Newer stores featured one-hour photo processing, delicatessens, bulk food departments, bulk produce, fresh pizza, service meat and seafood departments, shoe repair shops, expanded cafes and video shops, along with pharmacies, floral shops, pizza and other amenities.

As the list of ingredients in a one-stop shopping environment has grown, so has the pressure for larger stores. The company has never developed the sort of prototype that its national competitors build over and over again. There is always significant tinkering going on. In this case, the downsizing trend has been reversed, and stores opened recently have grown well over 200,000 square feet.

When the Twin Fair acquisition drew the company south of the Michigan border for the first time, a pyschological border disappeared as well. After southeastern Michigan, Meijer chose Columbus, Ohio for its next metropolitan commitment, followed by Dayton and Toledo. In 1994 the company entered its third state with expansion to Indianapolis, Fort Wayne and South Bend, Indiana. This new generation of stores includes a food court complete with Chinese restaurant, and a facade which seeks to bring a human scale warmth to suburban shopping. Near-term growth will be concentrated on smaller cities in Indiana, Ohio and Michigan, to be followed by Cincinnati, Cleveland, Akron and Canton. Also on the horizon are stores in Louisville and Lexington, Kentucky.

The thirty years since Hendrik's death have changed the scale of the organization dramatically. Annual sales in the $40 million range in 1964 had climbed one-hundred fold by 1994. Meijer ranks among the nation's hundred leading retailers. Yet its stockholders, all of whom are involved in the company, have chosen to reinvest profits in the company's future — its ability to grow and compete — rather than to receive substantial dividends.

And innovation continues. In 1988 the company began opening its stores twenty-four hours a day — a supermarket-industry commonplace that had never been attempted with stores so large. In 1989 Meijer committed itself to promoting "earth-friendly" products and increasing public awareness of environmental issues. Hendrik most likely would have approved. And his desire to provide people with a good place to work would have been gratified by the current payroll of more than 50,000 associates.

The great challenge to Hendrik's descendants and to all Meijer managers will be to communicate the values he held dear to the young bagger in Lima or the cashier in Fort Wayne who were born years after he died — and to enable them to feel a part of an adventure that has more to do with a smile than with shopping carts and checkouts. In recent years those values have expressed themselves in the notion that customers are "guests" in Meijer stores, and deserving of the hospitality that term implies.

Succeeding generations have taken a hand in shaping the company's future, but in ways that frequently reflect its past. When residents of a conservative suburb of Grand Rapids blamed Fred Meijer a few years after Hendrik's death for the decision to open their Meijer store on Sundays, they did not realize that the seeds of such a move had been sown long before. A willingness to court controversy for customer convenience always went hand in hand with a commitment to low prices and a clean, well-lighted place to shop. All flow naturally, if far from inevitably, from the sober virtues of the Dutch and the unsinkable optimism of a middle-aged barber.

March 15, 1994
Grand Rapids, Michigan

Index